Arachne's Tapestry

The Transformation of Myth in Seventeenth-Century Spain

MARCIA L. WELLES

TRINITY UNIVERSITY PRESS

Trinity University Press gratefully acknowledges the assistance of the *Program for Cultural Cooperation Between Spain's Ministry of Culture and North American Universities* in making this publication possible.

Grateful acknowledgment is extended to the following for allowing us to reproduce the works of art used in the text: Rare Books and Manuscript Library, Columbia University; The Hispanic Society of America; The London National Gallery; the Prado Museum; and to Ampliaciones y Reproducciones Mas for permission to use photographs of Velázquez's works.

Library of Congress Cataloging-in-Publication Data

Welles, Marcia L.
  Arachne's Tapestry.

  Bibliography: p. 171
  Includes index.
    1. Spanish poetry – Classical period, 1500-1700 –
History and criticism. 2. Spanish poetry – Classical
influences. 3. Ovid, 43 B.C.-17 or 18. Metamorphoses.
4. Mythology in literature. I. Title.
  PQ6064.W44 1985   861'.3'0915   85-20862
  ISBN 0-939980-11-8

Printed in the United States of America
Trinity University Press, 715 Stadium Drive, San Antonio, Texas
78284

For David,
Dede, Michael, and Margaret

Acknowledgments

My first acknowledgment is to Professor Gonzalo Sobejano, who taught me to understand and appreciate, and then to love, the literature of the Golden Age. His excellence as a scholar, his generosity as a teacher, and his dignity as a person have been a constant source of inspiration to me.

Many people have helped me in the completion of this study; I can mention but a few. I thank Jonathan Brown, Carol and Milton Petrie Professor of Fine Arts, Institute of Fine Arts, New York University, and Theodore Beardsley, Jr., Director of The Hispanic Society of America, for making available to me materials about which I otherwise would not have known. My colleague, Lydia Lenaghan, and my friend, Rosaria Vignolo Munson (both Classicists) have given willingly of their time when I sought their help with translations from Latin. I owe a special debt of gratitude to my colleagues in the Spanish Department, in particular to Helene Farber, for their support. Although Margarita Ucelay has now retired, her indomitable and cheerful spirit remains among us as her legacy. My sincere thanks go also to the Grants Committee of Barnard College for its help in defraying the costs of the typing and preparation of the manuscript. At publication stage, the *Program for Cultural Cooperation Between Spain's Ministry of Culture and North American Universities* awarded Trinity University Press a matching funds grant. I thank the Program and its General Coordinator, Mr. Antonio Ramos Gascón, for this generous subsidy.

I consider myself fortunate to have been able to avail myself of the resources of the Columbia University Libraries, the New York Public Library, and the library of The Hispanic Society of America. I wish to thank in particular Martha M. de Narváez, curator of Manuscripts and Rare Books at The Hispanic Society, for her kindness.

I thank Lois A. Boyd of Trinity University Press for her patience and scrupulous attention; I thank the readers of the manuscript for their corrections and many helpful and thoughtful suggestions. Nora Weinerth's skill and patience as a proofreader have been exemplary. I alone bear the responsibility for any errors and omissions.

Contents

List of Illustrations

List of Abbreviations

AEA	*Archivo Español de Arte*
BAE	*Biblioteca de Autores Españoles*
BH	*Bulletin Hispanique*
BHS	*Bulletin of Hispanic Studies*
BSS	*Bulletin of Spanish Studies*
CL	*Comparative Literature*
ELH	*English Literary History*
HR	*Hispanic Review*
JAAC	*Journal of Aesthetics and Art Criticism*
MLN	*Modern Language Notes*
MLR	*Modern Language Review*
NBAE	*Nueva Biblioteca de Autores Españoles*
NRFH	*Nueva Revista de Filología Hispánica*
PMLA	*Publications of the Modern Language Association of America*
PQ	*Philological Quarterly*
RenQ	*Renaissance Quarterly*
RFE	*Revista de Filología Española*
RHM	*Revista Hispánica Moderna*
RL	*Revista de Literatura*
RomN	*Romance Notes*
TAPA	*Transactions and Proceedings of the American Philological Association*

Dictionaries Cited

Corominas, Juan. *Diccionario crítico etimológico de la lengua castellana.* 4 vols. Berna: Francke, 1954-57.

Covarrubias Horozco, Sebastián de. *Tesoro de la lengua castellana, o española* (1611). 2 vols. (in one). Madrid: Melchor Sánchez, 1674.

Diccionario de autoridades (1726-37). Facsimile edition. Real Academia Española. 3 vols. Madrid: Gredos, 1969.

Diccionario de la lengua castellana. 6 vols. Madrid: Real Academia
Española, 1726-39.

Diccionario de la lengua española. Real Academia Española. 16th ed.
Madrid: Espasa Calpe, 1936.

The Oxford Classical Dictionary. Ed. N. G. L. Hammond and H. H.
Scullard, 2d ed., 1970; rpt. Oxford: Clarendon Press, 1978.

A Note to the Reader

The original spelling and punctuation have been maintained except for
the modernization of the long "s" of old Spanish.

Arachne's Tapestry

Introduction

Centuries later we react with puzzlement, even with irritation toward the too moral Emperor Augustus for having banished Ovid from his beloved Rome, exiling him to Tomis, the wild and barren outpost on the shores of the Black Sea. The charge against him, *maiestas*, "degradation of the national dignity or insult to the imperial family,"[1] was at least partly due to the alleged immorality of the *Ars amatoria*.[2] One wonders whether a close reading of the *Metamorphoses* would not have elicited the same response from the Emperor, had he fully recognized the frank sexuality and lack of proper marital fidelity among the gods. Ovid, in his attempted refutation of the charges in *Tristia*, reminds the Emperor of the ubiquitousness of the gods' adulteries, both in art and in literature, arguing that if a woman is susceptible to suggestion, even the temples of worship become suspect, for "Standing in Jupiter's, she will recall/The women Jupiter made mothers all" (*cum steterit Iovis aede, Iovis succurret in aede,/quam multas matres fecerit ille deus*).[3] The Emperor was apparently unmoved by this argument, for Ovid died still in exile, but the church fathers were quick to concur with Ovid on this point, however light-hearted or satirical this portion of his rebuttal may have been. Thus Isidore, bishop of Seville (ca. 560-636), sternly inveighs against pagan authors: "Ideo prohibetur Christianus figmenta legere poetarum, *quia per oblectamenta inanium fabularum mentem excitant ad incentiva libidinum*" (Therefore the Christian is forbidden to read the fictions of the poets, because through the enjoyment of vain tales they excite the mind to the stimuli of pleasures).[4]

Successfully eclipsed by the great prestige of Virgil, understandable during the early centuries of intensive Christianization, it was not until the late eleventh and early twelfth centuries that Ovid once again attained eminence in the world of letters. A vital ingredient of the evaluation was the transformation of Ovid himself into an "Ovidius Ethicus," or, more significantly, into an "Ovidius Theologus."[5] The tendency towards allegorization appeared as early as the beginning of the sixth century in the *Mythologiae* of Fulgentius, which included the *Metamorphoses* as one of its sources. The seminal reading was given in the eighth-century poem of Theodulph, bishop of Orléans, which posited an explicit contrast between exterior "appearance" as opposed to the interior "reality,"[6] a distinction that laid the foundation for future interpretations, the most famous and influential being the late medieval *Ovide moralisé*.[7] Such interpretations managed to obviate the charges of moral laxitude as well as the suggestion of frivolity, appearing early in Quintilian's use of the term *lascivia* to characterize Ovid's verse (*Institutio oratoria*, 4.1.77, 10.1.88 and 93), and echoed well into the fifteenth century in Spain by the poets of the *Cancionero de Baena*, who, primarily familiar with the early love elegies, considered Ovid's works "obras baldías," the writing of which was an "oficio infructuoso."[8]

This tradition of interpretation was tenacious in Spain, as the sixteenth-century translations and commentaries of the *Metamorphoses* attest to. Thus the popular prose translation of Jorge de Bustamante (1543?) openly commits the "intentional fallacy" of stating that the purpose of the tales "no fue otro sino solo mostrar a los hõbres muchos auisos y astucias, para mas sabia y prudentemente viuir,"[9] and Pérez de Moya's manual, *Philosophia secreta* (1585) includes as part of the title "donde debajo de historias fabulosas se contiene mucha doctrina provechosa a todos estudios, con el origen de los Idolos o dioses de la Gentilidad."[10]

These interpretations correspond to the traditional concept of allegory as an essentially didactic device, a rhetorical instrument whereby the primary, literal level of narration serves to clarify and therefore make more accessible to the average reader the secondary, abstract, moral level of meaning, a tradition well represented in the literary theory and practice of Gracián and Calderón. Implicit in this interpretation is the absolute need for clarity and straightforwardness in the imaginative fiction; ambiguity and obscurity only obstruct the process of moral instruction. Whether the intent of the allegory be to provide the proverbial "sugar coating" for the bitter pills of truthful disillusion as it is for Gracián, or whether its intent be to provide the appeal to the imagination necessary to make theological doctrine apprehensible as it is for Calderón, in none of these formulations are difficulty or inaccessibility positive attributes of the technique.

In contrast to this current of thought, another understanding of allegorical intent is promulgated. Pedro Sánchez de Viana, in his commentaries to his excellent verse translation of the *Metamorphoses* (1589), stresses a reading that echoes the long tradition of Christian apologetics in its search for religious messages in pagan writings, according to which sacred truths must be kept hidden from the profane and unworthy.[11] Pérez de Moya had mentioned this facet as a justification for the use of fables in his explanation that:

Y también el no querer que sus secretos fuesen comunes a todos, porque de la suerte que el vino pierde algo de su ser o suavidad puesto en malos vasos, así las cosas divinas de Filosofía, puestas en modo que sean vulgares a rústicos, se corrompen y pierden mucho de su estima.[12]

It was, however, Sánchez de Viana who fully developed such an interpretation. He subscribed to the belief that before the time of Plato and Aristotle the ancients disguised their philosophy and theology in fables principally to prevent their desecration by the less worthy:

Lo primero, porque justamente juzgaron ser cosa odiosa, y aborrecible a naturaleza y diuinidad manifestar sus exceletes secretos a qualquier hombre. Pues dezir claramente verdades apuradas a los que no lo estan para oyrlas, es dar occassion que en el entendimieto de los tales se corropa la sciecia como suele el precioso vino en mal lauada vasija: de donde se sigue la destruycion vniuersal de las doctrinas, y cada hora se va haziendo mas prejudicial este daño, andado ellas de vn ingenio rudo en otro mas. Y ansi dize santo Thomas que las cosas diuinas no se deuen reuelar a los hombres, sino coforme a su capacidad, porque no menosprecien lo que no entienden.[13]

He is of the opinion that the philosophical significance has not been thoroughly commented on before in Spain, for "nadie o pocos creo que hasta agora han tomado la pluma en nuestra España que sean tolerables"[14] and avails himself impressively of the authorities for his exegesis, including, among others, Cicero, Lactantius, Fulgentius, Poliziano, translator and commentator of Homer, Natale Conti, author of the very popular *Mythology*, Horologgi, author of the moralizations appended to dell'Anguillara's Italian translation of the *Metamorphoses*.[15]

This is not merely a feat of erudition, a dry, exhaustive compendium of sources, but reflects a definite concept of poetry as inspiration rather than as mere imitation. The care Sánchez de Viana dedicates to the allegorical readings, the depth he finds therein, is symptomatic of his almost religious awe of poets. Making reference to Plato's *Ion*, which bore the subtitle *De furore poetico* in Ficino's translation, Sánchez de Viana compares poets to prophets, both being privy to divine inspiration and esoteric knowledge, and verifies his argument by means of the etymology of the name "poet," which, he writes, is derived from the verb meaning "vn medio entre criar obra propia de Dios."[16] The intention of the poet in writing is polysemous, and the occult mysteries will be difficult to decipher, but the effort will be more worthwhile when the acute reader experiences the thrill of discovery and recognition, in the manner of a treasure hunter:

De donde el oyente reconosciedo su error, no solamete viene en conoscimieto de secretos altissimos, q poco antes (por venir disfraçados) no echaua de ver: Pero aū recibe marauilloso plazer, y gusto de tal fruzimieto.[17]

This current of interpretation involves a dramatic change in emphasis. Its novelty lies not in the dualistic literal-figurative distinction, for medieval tradition had long established the meanings of allegory as multiple (literal, moral, allegorical, anagogical). The novelty lies in the unusual emphasis on the aesthetic qualities of the primary, literal level of narration, as opposed to the usual stress on the didactic properties of the secondary level. Such a shift in attention leads to the estimation of obscurity, ambiguity, and complexity as positive values, in contradistinction to the accepted standards of clarity and ready intelligibility as the necessary attributes of the literal meaning. The traditional Horatian dictum of *utile dulci* became less and less viable as inspired *ingenium* gained recognition, for, as Clark Hulse points out in his discussion of Marlowe:

The purpose of such poetry is hardly to teach, at least not to teach anything socially constructive; nor does it bring that moderate delight that Horace admired. Its goal is to astonish, to enthrall, and to puzzle.[18]

It is not surprising that this concept of "necessary difficulty," which values the skill and ingenuity of the creative artist, is used to further the cause of the *culterano* position in the literary battle being waged in Spain in the late sixteenth and early seventeenth centuries. Góngora's defense of his *Soledades* alludes to precisely this concept. Recalling parenthetically that "vates se llama el profeta como el poeta," he specifies that the obscurity and stylistic complications of Ovid's *Metamorphoses* require more than a superficial reading to be understood, and concludes:

luego hase de confesar que tiene utilidad avivar el ingenio, y eso nació de la obscuridad del poeta. Eso mismo hallará V.m. en mis *Soledades*, si tiene capacidad para quitar la corteza y descubrir lo misterioso que encubren.[19]

This prevailing tradition of the translators and mythographers of an Ovid "mysteriously meant," read at various levels of symbolic meaning, was slowly eroded by the impact of successive waves of Renaissance poets who eschewed the didactic intent and instead took advantage of the possibilities of the literal level of narration in these erotic tales. Thus Garcilaso, who with Boscán ushered in the new Italianate meters, and with them the new spirit of the Renaissance, concentrates on the plastic, pictorial qualities in his use of mythological material, the delicate beauty of which is best summarized by Fernando de Herrera's comment on Sonnet XIII (the metamorphosis of Daphne) that "El estilo es perspicuo, blando y suave."[20] Another development is the use of these tales as pretexts for the subtle analysis of love, typically by poets of the traditionalist school who echo the *cancionero* tradition.[21] Following the translation of the Pyramus and Thisbe tale by Cristóbal de Castillejo (1528), the sixteenth-century poets who develop this tragic tale of love–Gregorio Silvestre, Jorge de Montemayor, and Antonio de Villegas–focus their attention on the internal drama of the lovers.[22] By the seventeenth century the suggestive subtlety of Garcilaso's use of the Ovidian tale will have blossomed into luxuriant and lengthy descriptive digressions in which the actual events of the tale form but a flimsy skeletal base for an ornamental wealth of sensuous appeal, as exemplified by such poems as Carrillo de Sotomayor's *Fábula de Acis y Galatea* (1611), Góngora's own notorious *Fábula de Polifemo y Galatea* (1613), or Juan de Jáuregui's *Orfeo* (1624), lengthy and melodramatic, in a style so *culto* that it earned Jáuregui the reputation of being a traitor to the cause of the *llanistas* in the raging literary battle and provoked the publication of yet another *Orpheus*, allegedly by Juan de Montalván, bearing the reproachful title of *Orfeo en lengua castellana.*[23]

It was within the theatre that the tradition of an allegorical reading of pagan texts survived, the mythological *autos* of Calderón being particularly noteworthy in this respect. At least one of Calderón's sources is considered to be Pérez de Moya's immensely popular *Philosophia secreta*, as well as Baltasar de Vitoria's *Teatro de los dioses de la gentilidad* (I, 1620; II, 1623).[24] In the *loa* to *El verdadero Dios Pan* it is explained that the ancients had dimly perceived, though misinterpreted, theological verities which they then expressed in their myths:

> que tuvieron los gentiles
> noticias, visos y lejos,
> de nuestras puras verdades,
> y como las oigan ciegos,
> sin lumbre de fe, a sus falsos
> dioses las atribuyeron.[25]

Undoubtedly the sumptuous staging and rich musical effects of these *autos*, which were presented in the *fiestas reales* of the Palacio de Buen Retiro, facilitated the audience's understanding and appreciation of the Christian truths "hidden" within the pagan garb.

But where can we find a sense of "the sweete wittie soule of Ovid"?[26] Author of the sophisticated and erotic *Amores* and *Ars amatoria*, Ovid's irreverent wit leads him to dismiss conventional, sanctimonious morality with the concise opinion that *casta est, quam nemo rogavit* ("chaste is she whom no one has asked" [*Amores*, I.viii.43]).[27] This same playful spirit permeates his amatory epic. He was writing of the gods, but recent critics agree that it was no longer a question of belief, and no religious reverence was necessary.[28] He spun tales of men and women, of their loves and, more commonly, of their lusts, and the result necessarily had to be comic, even ludicrous at times, but not dignified and serious, for *non bene conveniunt nec in una sede morantur/maiestas et amor* ("Majesty and love do not go well together, nor tarry long in the same dwelling-place" [*Metamorphoses*, II. 846-47]).[29]

We remember with delight the version of Pyramus and Thisbe offered by Peter Quince and his company in *A Midsummer Night's Dream*, or Rosalind's cynical comment in *As You Like It* that Leander died not of love, but because "he went but forth to wash him in the Hellespont, and being taken with the cramp, was drown'd" (IV.1.101-03).[30] In England the subtle ambivalence and irony present in the early epyllia, Shakespeare's *Venus and Adonis* and Marlowe's *Hero and Leander* (both written ca. 1593), developed into full-fledged satire by the end of the seventeenth century, when the proliferation of travesties of classical myth hastened their collapse into triviality.[31] In seventeenth-century France the epic burlesque of Scarron's *Virgile travesti* was soon directed towards Ovid, as exemplified in Richer's *L'Ovide bouffon* and D'Assoucy's *L'Ovide en belle humeur*.[32]

In Spain the first glimpses of an erosion in the serious high treatment of classical myth appear in the poems of the *castellanistas*.[33] This in no way reflects a new subversive understanding of Ovidian poetry; it is merely a superficial manifestation of the underlying literary polemic. The favored mythological themes of the Italianate school, the metres of their composition, their verbal extravagance, were suitable targets against which to direct their poisoned arrows. Cristóbal de Castillejo (ca. 1490-ca. 1550), leader of the traditionalist school and noted author of "Represión contra los poetas españoles que escriben en verso italiano," includes among his realistic, familiar renditions of tales from the *Metamorphoses* a poem on Pyramus and Thisbe (1528). The poem is preceded by a detached and ironic statement by the author, who comments that "Simples fueron, a mi parecer, en matarse así con el calor del amor y de la edad; porque pudieran esperar a resfriarse y envejecerse, especialmente si vinieran a palacio y a Alemaña, como yo; pero quisieron perder la vida a trueco de la fama."[34] The Andalusian wit, Diego Hurtado de Mendoza (1503-75), in his "Poesías satíricas y burlescas" vituperates various mythological figures, including Venus, the "alcahueta y hechicera," and Cupid, the "Rapaz tiñoso."[35] His compatriot, the Sevillian Baltasar del Alcázar (1530-1606), joins him in witty frivolities directed against mythological figures, Cupid once more being favored with such imprecations as "Suelta la venda, sucio y asqueroso;/Lava los ojos llenos de lagañas;/Cubre las nalgas y el lugar opuesto,/Hijo de Venus." His epigram on Hero and Leander – "Tiempo fué en que se dudó/Si tuvo ó no doña Hero/La vela en su candelero/ Cuando Leandro se anegó" – cannot be accused of being overly subtle.[36] Venus, Cupid, Mars, Apollo, Syrinx and Pan – among others, will become stock figures for jocose treatment.[37]

There is, of course, a difference between a casual allusion and a fully developed treatment of a narrative tale, or substantial portion thereof, which as critical parody posits the existence of a literary text against which it plays, and is more than just an occasional witticism. Maintaining the original etymology of the Greek term for parody as "singing in imitation, singing with a slight change," the *OED* adds to this neutral definition the element of humorous intent: "[a text] in which the characteristic turns of thought and phrase in an author or class of authors are imitated in such a way as to make them appear ridiculous."[38] This is certainly a fair assumption in view of the connection between parody and humor in its incipient form, the mock-epic, and is reflected in the usual description of parodic poems in Spain during this period as "a lo burlesco."

This very association with humor was to condemn parody to a critical blight. The etymological relationship specified by Corominas between *burla* and the late Latin *burra* meaning "necedad, bagatela" is maintained in later definitions, which include, in addition to the sense of "ridiculization," that of "trivialization": "Se llama tambien una cosa que es de poca entidád y valór"; its adjectival form "Equivále à jocóso, lleno de chanzas, chistes y graciosidades. Comunmente se dice, y aprópria à los escritos que tratan las cosas en estílo jocóso y gracioso" (*Dic. de autoridades*). In fact, as R. Jammes notes, the terms "burlesco" and "de burlas" generally acquire the connotations of "obscene" or "licentious" as evidenced in the *Cancionero de obras de burlas* of 1519.[39]

The literary theoreticians of the day certainly hold the genre in low esteem. As humorous, derivative exercises, these so-called *poemas contrahechos*, lacking mimetic truthfulness or didactic intent, are relegated disdainfully to the minor genres. López Pinciano in his *Philosophia antigua poética* (1596) classifies parody as a minor genre precisely because it does not imitate an "acción graue" and defines it as "La Parodia no es otra cosa que vn poema que a otro contrahaze, especialmente aplicando las cosas de veras y graues a las de burlas."[40] Luis Alfonso de Carvalho in his *Cisne de Apolo* (1602), while praising the *contrafactum* "a lo divino," denounces those who "bueluen y contrahazen la compostura graue en ridiculosa, y torpe, a la qual llaman parodia."[41] They no doubt would have been particularly offended by parodies of myth, which they continue to interpret allegorically according to sanctified medieval tradition. This is true of López Pinciano,[42] and Juan Díaz Rengifo in his

Arte poética española (1592) carefully prefaces his "Fábula de Apolo, y Dafne" with the earnest counsel to the reader that "debaxo de la qual hay una doctrina moral, en la qual se nos advierte lo que devemos hacer, y de lo que devemos nos guardar."[43]

Yet, in spite of this theoretical denigration, major poets of this period write notable parodies. Lope de Vega creates his mock-epic *La Gatomaquia*; Quevedo, in addition to shorter pieces, produces his lengthy "Poema heroico de las necedades y locuras de Orlando el enamorado," a parody primarily of Boiardo's *Orlando innamorato*; Góngora writes numerous parodies of the various *romancero* traditions as well as his stunning and lengthy mythological parodies. The negative conversion of their model, the chivalric novel, is inherent in the intent and meaning of the major and most original literary creations of sixteenth- and seventeenth-century Spain, the *Lazarillo* and the *Quijote*.[44] Such creations defy the theoreticians' understanding of parody as trivial, pejorative mimicry, a merely "parasitic" genre, living on "serious," standard literature and contributing little or nothing on its own account.

The pervasiveness of parody in modern times in literature, as well as in art and music, has redeemed it from this critical deprecation, and from its secondary position as mere supplement it has moved to a position of centrality.[45] The word "parody" must now contend with the overlapping and confusing uses to which it is subjected as a critical term, careening from the strict classical definition of "singing after the style of an original but with a difference" to the all-encompassing meaning it acquires in the criticism of the Russian formalists.

Victor Shklovsky, proponent of what an opponent has labelled the formalist *law* of "automatization-perceptibility,"[46] defines the perception of a work of art as an awareness of difference which interferes with the usual automatic response. To promote a reader's "defamiliarization" or "making-it-strange" (*ostraneniye*), standard parodic devices of "laying-bare" or "mechanization" of any conventional devices become crucial in the perception of artistic quality: "Art is a way of experiencing the artfulness of an object; the object is not important."[47] As used by Tynyanov, this deliberate divergence from the norm is erected into a scheme for literary evolution:

There is no continuing direct line; there is rather a departure, a pushing away from the known point—a struggle. . . .Any literary succession is first of all a struggle, a destruction of old values and a reconstruction of old elements.[48]

Parody thus becomes not merely a discrete literary device, but the prime element of literary evolution, with the positive function of destroying in order to create.

As developed within the Bakhtin school, the concept of "art as device," the product of one subjective consciousness, develops into a broader sociological approach, with an emphasis on social intercourse and the ideological context of art. In his seminal study of Dostoevsky's "polyphonic" novel (1929), Bakhtin uses the term dialogism (characteristic of the carnivalesque genre, which includes parody) in contradistinction to monologism (the epic, the realistic novel, all that purports to an impersonal, unconditional, somewhat "official" truth). The status of the word in dialogical texts is always "double-directed" or "double-voiced," for "it is directed both toward the object of speech, like an ordinary word, and toward *another word*, toward *another person's speech*"; it thus becomes ambivalent, relative, at times polemical.[49] Bakhtin's notion of a text being "the absorption and transformation of another"[50] is named *intertextuality* by Julia Kristeva.[51]

However broadly or narrowly explained, all these definitions have in common the essentially literary nature of parody, which does not purport to establish a relationship between text and world, but rather between text and word—the previous text or texts to which it is responding. As in the simple instance of word puns, and jokes in general, in Saussure's terms parody is a paradigmatic phenomenon, "it is a relationship *in absentia* within a virtual and mnemonic series," as opposed to a syntagmatic chain, which functions actively and explicitly, *in praesentia*.[52] More demanding than word puns and jokes, which posit linguistic competence for comprehension, parody (which employs many of the humorous techniques of jokes) also requires literary competence. The counter-text can only be appreciated in terms of the text that it re-creates, not in imitation, but in deviation; in other words, the standard text "made strange." Parodistic tendencies in music and art also require of their audience knowledge of the preceding norms with which they are engaged in polemical discourse. The seeming paradox of "serious" parody is therefore both an act of criticism as well as one of transgression, as the official, sanctified art is deconstructed.

Painters and poets share a common body of humanist knowledge in the classical texts (and translations) and mythological handbooks. As they read the poems anew, they perceive previously submerged elements of ambiguity, wit, and eroticism which cause them to change their perspective. Velázquez avoids the unidimensional moral-allegorical interpretations of the painters of his day, uncovering depths of humor—as well as of pathos—in Ovid; with derision and scorn the poets repudiate certainly any vestiges of didacticism, but particularly the facile Renaissance rhetorical elegance and pictorial ornateness that had drained these pagan tales of their vitality, reducing their characters to stereotypes, their style to Petrarchan clichés. The brittle remains were found to be mere form without content, having neither moral meaning nor artistic significance. As the artists struggle towards a new aesthetic, their awareness of the bankruptcy of the previous stylistic and ideological norms reveals itself in a highly self-conscious and self-reflexive stance: "Art" is exposed as "artifact," not "imitation of" but a "product of" the artist, whose importance as creator is immortalized in Velázquez's *Las Meninas*.

In the following pages we shall unravel the threads in this tapestry of textual polemics. Each work is necessarily studied separately because of its distinct etiology and specificity of counter-text or texts.

The polemical engagement with previous conventions can be brilliantly aggressive, as occurs in Góngora (whose 1589 *romance* on the theme of Hero and Leander, "Arrojóse el mancebito," is credited with being the first full-length mythological parody),[53] or it can be brutally witty, as seen in Quevedo; its tone can be sharp and ingenious, as manifested in the minor poets, or ironic, as occurs in the deliberate rupture of comic illusion in the parodic play, *Céfalo y Pocris*. This "dialogue" with preceding works receives its most gentle, yet most profound, expression in Velázquez's subtle displacements of accent.

The transformations of received practice can take many forms, but at all times their essential "playfulness" contains the same "deadly" serious implications of a joke, which, according to anthropologist Mary Douglas (and Freud before her), constitutes a form of attack:

A joke is a play upon form. It brings into relation disparate elements in such a way that one accepted pattern is challenged by the appearance of another which in some way was hidden by the first.[54]

The fable of Arachne in Ovid's *Metamorphoses* (VI. 1-145) well demonstrates the grave consequences of such "a play upon form."

In her contest with Pallas Athena, Arachne plays a "joke" on the goddess. In her tapestry Arachne represents a story that defies the narrative of Pallas Athena; to the goddess's representation of the majesty and power of the Olympians, she responds with a recollection of the gods' lust and rapes (beginning with Jupiter's amatory escapades), thereby emphasizing the brutality rather than the divinity of the gods. Arachne's "joke," it turns out, merits the most severe punishment. Her tapestry is destroyed, and she is transformed into a spider, sentenced to spin rather than to weave; to reproduce rather than to produce; to re-create rather than to create. She is condemned to sterility; the "voice of the shuttle" is effectively silenced.[55] Arachne's woven parody, as is true of all serious parody, constitutes a significant transgression of the accepted (and acceptable) cultural texts.

These "transformations" of myth reflect a time of transition during which an old order is giving way to the new, and different ways of experiencing and perceiving begin to emerge. As we read the poems, the play, and yes, as we "read" the paintings, we discover subversive explorations of these much-read and well-loved tales of divine love and divine wrath that challenge both the established literary conventions and the social hierarchy of the period.

Notes

1 L. P. Wilkinson, *Ovid Recalled* (Cambridge: Cambridge University Press, 1955), p. 301.

2 Wilkinson, pp. 297-300 and Hermann Fränkel, *Ovid: A Poet Between Two Worlds* (1945; rpt. Berkeley and Los Angeles: University of California Press, 1969), pp. 111-17.

3 As quoted and translated by Wilkinson, pp. 305-06.

4 Rudolph Schevill, *Ovid and the Renascence in Spain*, University of California Publications in Modern Philology, vol. 4, no. 1 (Berkeley: University of California Press, 1913), p. 9 from *Sententiarum libri tres (de summo bono)*, III, cap. xiii, *de libris gentilium*. Italics in Schevill; translation mine.

5 Edward K. Rand, *Ovid and His Influence* (New York: Cooper Square Publishers, 1963), pp. 131-37. See also Jean Seznec, *The Survival of the Pagan Gods*, trans. Barbara F. Sessions, Bollingen Series, no. 38 (1953; rpt. Princeton: Princeton University Press, 1972), bk. I, chap. III, "The Moral Tradition," pp. 84-121.

6 Lester K. Born, "Ovid and Allegory," *Speculum*, 9 (1934), p. 363, n.2: "*In quorum dictis quamquam sint frivola multa, Plurima sub falso tegmine vera latent*" [Migne, *Patr. Lat.* CV, col. 331]. (In whose words, although there are many silly things, there are also many true things hidden under a false exterior.)

7 The date of the *Ovide moralisé* is considered to be between 1291-1328, probably 1316-1328, according to C. De Boer in his edition of the *Ovide Moralisé en prose (Texte du quinzième siècle) (Amsterdam: North Holland Publishing Co., 1954), p. 3, n.1. Antonio G. Solalinde, "La fecha del Ovide Moralisé," RFE, 8 (1921), 285-88, argues for an earlier date (ca. 1275), considering it one of the sources used by Alfonso X in his *General estoria*.

8 José María de Cossío, *Fábulas mitológicas en España* (Madrid: Espasa-Calpe, 1952), p. 19.

9 "Prologo y argvmento general sobre toda la obra," *Las transformaciones de Ovidio en lengua española* (Anvers, Pedro Bellero, 1595). Courtesy of The Hispanic Society of America.

10 In the edition of Eduardo Gómez de Baquero (Madrid: Blass, 1928), I, p. XVI.

11 For example, Don Cameron Allen, *Mysteriously Meant* (Baltimore and London: Johns Hopkins University Press, 1970), p. 10, writes of Clement of Alexandria, citing from the *Stromateis*, V. 9, 56-59, that "Nonetheless, truth should not be commonly bestowed on all or communicated 'to those . . . who are not purified in soul,' nor are 'the mysteries of the Word to be explained to the profane.'" The Italian humanist, Pico della Mirandola, planned to write a book called *Poetica Theologia*, believing, as he explained elsewhere, that the ancients concealed their revelations in myths: "showing only the crust of the mysteries to the vulgar, while reserving the marrow of the true sense for higher and more perfected spirits" (*Commento sopra una canzona de amore composta da Girolamo Benivieni*, III, xi, 9 [ed. Garin, p. 580]). See Edgar Wind, *Pagan Mysteries in the Renaissance* (New Haven: Yale University Press, 1958), p. 24, and in general chap. I, "Poetic Theology," pp. 24-30.

12 *Philosophia secreta*, I, p. 10.

13 In the *Anotaciones sobre los qvinze libros de las Trasformaciones de Ouidio* (Valladolid, Diego Fernandez de Cordoua, 1589), p. A3r. Bound with *Las transformaciones de Ouidio*. Courtesy of The Hispanic Society of America.

14 Ibid., p. A3v.

15 These various translators, interpreters, and mythographers are studied by Allen, *Mysteriously Meant* and by Seznec, *The Survival of the Pagan Gods*, in particular bk. II, chap. I, "The Science of Mythology in the Sixteenth Century," which stresses the importance of Giraldi's *The History of the Gods* (1548), Conti's *Mythology* (1551), and Cartari's *The Images of the Gods* (1556). The Italian translations of dell'Anguillara, as well as of Lodovico Dolce, were popular in Spain (Cossío, *Fábulas mitológicas*, p. 47).

16 In the prologue to the translation, *Las transformaciones*, **3r.

17 Ibid., **2v.

18 *Metamorphic Verse: The Elizabethan Minor Epic* (Princeton: Princeton University Press, 1981), p. 94.

19 "Carta de Don Luis de Góngora, en respuesta de la que le escribieron" (¿Septiembre de 1613 o de 1614?), *Obras completas*, ed. Juan e Isabel Millé y Giménez, 6th ed. (Madrid: Aguilar, 1972), p. 896. John R. Beverley, *Aspects of Góngora's "Soledades"* (Amsterdam: John Benjamins B.V., 1980), analyzes the aesthetics and ideology of the *Soledades* in terms of the "hidden sense" alluded to in this passage from Góngora's letter (see in particular part I, chap. 1, pp. 11-25, "Góngora's 'Carta en respuesta.'") B. W. Ife, *Dos versiones de "Píramo y Tisbe": Jorge de Montemayor y Pedro Sánchez de Viana (Fuentes para el estudio del romance "La ciudad de Babilonia" de Góngora)* (Exeter: University of Exeter, 1974), mentions the relationship between the concept of allegory as a "darke conceit" (as it were) and the poetics of *culteranismo*, pp. VI-X.

20 Antonio Gallego Morell, *Garcilaso de la Vega y sus comentaristas* (Granada: Urania, 1966), p. 326 (H-91). In addition to that of Daphne and Apollo, the following erotic narrative tales are utilized by Garcilaso: Hero and Leander, based on Martial's epigram (Sonnet XXIX); Anaxarete and Iphis (Canción V); Orpheus and Eurydice, Venus and Adonis, Apollo and Daphne (Egloga III). On Garcilaso's use of mythology see Rafael Lapesa, *La trayectoria poética de Garcilaso*, 2d ed. (Madrid: Revista de Occidente, 1968), especially pp. 162-73, and Cossío, *Fábulas mitológicas*, pp. 75-80.

21 Discussed in Cossío, *Fábulas mitológicas*, pp. 98-121, ch. 4, "La reacción castellanista." For *cancionero* tradition see Schevill, "The Art Lyric in the Fif-

teenth Century," *Ovid and the Renascense in Spain*, pp. 55-86 and Otis H. Green, "Courtly Love in the Spanish *Cancioneros*," *The Literary Mind of Medieval and Renaissance Spain* (Lexington: The University Press of Kentucky, 1970), pp. 40-92, rpt. from *PMLA*, no. 1 (1949), 247-301.

22 These, as well as later versions of the tale, are analyzed by Daniel P. Testa, "The Pyramus and Thisbe Theme in Sixteenth and Seventeenth Century Spanish Poetry" (Ph.D. diss., University of Michigan, 1963).

23 It is generally considered that this was written by Lope de Vega. D. José Jordan de Urríes y Azara, *Biografía y estudio crítico de Jáuregui* (Madrid: Sucesores de Rivadeneyra, 1899), p. 38, n.1 suggests that Lope used the pseudonym of Montalván in order to maintain his friendship with Jáuregui, and includes the scathing anonymous verses, as well as Góngora's, pp. 105-07, n.4a. Pablo Cabañas in his edition of Montalván's *Orfeo en lengua castellana* (Madrid: C.S.I.C., 1948), p. vii, n.2 expresses his belief that it is Lope's poem, although Victor Dixon, "Juan Pérez de Montalbán's *Segundo Tomo de las Comedias*," *HR*, 29 (April 1961), 109 does not find the evidence at all convincing. Jack H. Parker in his monograph *Juan Pérez de Montalván* (Boston: Twayne Publishers, 1975) outlines the arguments (pp. 77-79). He tends to agree that the work is Lope's, but admits that documentary proof is lacking.

24 These sources are identified by W. G. Chapman, "Las comedias mitológicas de Calderón," *RL*, 5 (1954), 49; A. Valbuena Briones, *Perspectiva crítica de los dramas de Calderón* (Madrid: Rialp, 1965), pp. 325, 361; F. Schalk, "Zur Rolle der Mythologie in der Literatur des Siglo de Oro," in *Classical Influences on European Culture, A.D. 1500-1700*, ed. R. R. Bolgar (Cambridge: Cambridge University Press, 1976), p. 263; Sebastian Neumeister, *Mythos und Repräsentation: Die mythologischen Festspiele Calderóns* (Munich: Fink, 1978), pp. 94-100. For a general discussion of Calderón's *autos* see A. A. Parker, *The Allegorical Drama of Calderón* (Oxford: Dolphin Book Co., 1968).

25 Quotes are from the edition of José M. de Osma, University of Kansas Humanistic Studies, no. 28 (Lawrence: University of Kansas Press, 1949), p. 66.

26 Francis Meres, *Palladis Tamia* (1598), quoted in William Keach, *Elizabethan Erotic Narratives* (New Brunswick: Rutgers University Press, 1977), p. 3.

27 Quoted from the Loeb Classical Library edition of the *Heroides* and *Amores*, trans. Grant Showerman (1914; rpt. Cambridge: Harvard University Press and London: William Heinemann Ltd., 1963).

28 This sense of Ovid's *Metamorphoses* is stressed in the interpretation of Brooks Otis, *Ovid as an Epic Poet*, 2d ed. (Cambridge: Cambridge University Press, 1970) who sees this amatory "epic" as a "deliberate antithesis" of the *Aeneid* (p. 2). In contrast to Virgil "the poet's attitude toward characters and events is no longer serious and intense but relaxed and comic, or at any rate human in the broadest sense. The epic style does not so much disguise as provocatively distort the author's essential levity" (p. 59). L. P. Wilkinson's *Ovid Recalled* had stressed Ovid's comic anthropomorphism of the gods: "The sophisticated no longer believed in their literal existence, and we cannot doubt that they were amused at the aroma of burlesque which anthropomorphism produced when pushed to extremes" (pp. 194-95).

29 All references to the *Metamorphoses* refer to the Loeb Classical Library edition, trans. Frank Justus Miller, 3d ed. (1916; rpt. Cambridge: Harvard University Press and London: William Heinemann Ltd., 1977).

30 Cited from the edition of S. C. Burchell, The Yale Shakespeare, rev. ed., vol. 10 (1954; rpt. New Haven and London: Yale University Press, 1965).

31 These specific epyllia are studied by William Keach, *Elizabethan Erotic Narratives*, pp. 52-116. Douglas Bush, *Mythology and the Renaissance Tradition in English Poetry* (Minneapolis: The University of Minnesota Press, 1932) comments on these later burlesque poems that "They may be roughly classified as dull and obscene, and merely dull" (p. 287).

32 In his edition of the *Virgile travesti* (Paris: Garnier Frères, 1875), Victor Fournel notes with perceptiveness that "Ovide, par exemple, avait un côté par lequel on se prêtait mieux au travestissement, et avec de moindres dangers aux yeux des gens de goût: c'est un ancien par la date, mais par la nature de ses ouvrages, un bel esprit moderne, presque un Français du dix-huitième siècle" (p. xv). The Italians, undisputed masters of burlesque genre, dedicated their wit to the classical or chivalric epic, as opposed to Ovid. It was the Italian Luigi Pulci who had "created" the mock-epic of the heroic romance with his *Morgante Maggiore* in the fifteenth century, followed in the sixteenth century by Francesco Berni's burlesque rewriting of Boiardo's *Orlando innamorato*, *Rifacimento dell'Orlando innamorato*. This national tradition of burlesque continued to be cultivated in the seventeenth century by such authors as Tassoni (*Secchia rapita*), Bracciolini (*Scherno degli Dei*), Lalli (*Eneide travestita*), a *contraffazioni* of the *Aeneid*. See Carmelo Previtera, *La poesia giocosa e l'umorismo*, Storia dei generi letterari italiani, vol. 16, 2 vols. (Milan: Francesco Vallardi, 1939 [vol. I]; 1942, 2d ed., 1953 [vol. II]).

33 Cossío, *Fábulas mitológicas*, notes Castillejo's spirit of realism, p. 116, as does Andrée Collard, *Nueva poesía* (Madrid: Castalia, 1967), pp. 15, 74-75, 77.

34 "Obras de amores," in *Obras*, ed. J. Domínguez Bordona (Madrid: Ediciones de "La Lectura," 1927), II, p. 183. This first version of the tale will be followed by the subsequent renditions of Gregorio Silvestre, Jorge de Montemayor(?), Antonio de Villegas, Miguel Botello de Carvallo, and Tirso de Molina. These, as well as Góngora's parody, are studied by Daniel P. Testa, "The Pyramus and Thisbe Theme in Sixteenth and Seventeenth Century Spanish Poetry." B. W. Ife, *Dos versiones de Píramo y Tisbe*, seriously doubts Montemayor's authorship.

35 *Obras poéticas*, ed. William I. Knapp, Libros españoles raros ó curiosos, vol. 11 (Madrid: Miguel Ginesta, 1877), pp. 439 (X) and 434 (II) respectively. Michael Ruggerio, *The Evolution of the Go-Between in Spanish Literature Through the Sixteenth Century*, University of California Publications in Modern Philology, vol. 78 (Berkeley and Los Angeles: University of California Press, 1966) studies the gradual "degradation" of the classical deities of love (Venus, Amor, Eros) into their contemporary version, the go-between or *alcahueta*, the Celestina (procuress and witch figure) being the culmination of this process. Hurtado's "Soneto a Venus" is discussed on p. 31.

36 In "A Cupido," p. 135 and "Duda si Hero gozó á Leandro," LXXV, p. 68 in *Poesías*, ed. Francisco Rodríguez Marín (Madrid: Librería de los Sucesores de Hernando, 1910).

37 See, for example, T. W. Keeble, "Some Mythological Figures in Golden Age Satire and Burlesque, *BSS*, 25 (October 1948), 238-46 and Raymond R. MacCurdy, "Parodies of the Judgement of Paris in Spanish Poetry and Drama of the Golden Age," *PQ*, 51 (January 1972), 135-44.

38 For a definition and discussion of parody see F. J. Lelièvre, "The Basis of

Ancient Parody," *Greece and Rome*, 1 (June 1954), 66-81 and Fred W. House-holder, Jr., "ΠΑΡΩΙΔΙΑ," *Classical Philology*, 39 (January 1944), 1-9.

39 Robert Jammes, *Etudes sur l'oeuvre poétique de Don Luis de Góngora y Argote*, Bibliothèque de l'Ecole des hautes études hispaniques, fasc. 40 (Bordeaux: Féret et Fils, 1967), p. 43.

40 In the edition of A. Carballo Picazo (Madrid: C.S.I.C., 1953), vol. III, p. 177 and vol. I, p. 289 respectively.

41 In the edition of Alberto Porqueras Mayo (Madrid: C.S.I.C., 1958), II, Diálogo quarto, VIII, p. 175.

42 *Philosophia antigua poética*, vol. III, p. 176.

43 "De la fábula," cap. CVI, p. 162 (Barcelona: Imprenta de María Martí, viuda, ded. 1703).

44 Alberto del Monte, *Itinerario de la novela picaresca española*, trans. Enrique Sordo (Barcelona: Editorial Lumen, 1971) includes a succinct contrast between the *Lazarillo* and the *Amadís*, pp. 41-43. For other parodistic aspects see R. W. Truman, "Parody and Irony in the Self-Portrayal of Lázaro de Tormes," *MLR*, 63 (July 1968), 600-05 and his "Lázaro de Tormes and the 'Homo Novus' Tradition," *MLR*, 64 (January 1969), 62-67. On the parodistic humor of *Don Quijote* see P. E. Russell, "*Don Quixote* as a Funny Book," *MLR*, 64 (April 1969), 312-26 and Anthony Close, *The Romantic Approach to "Don Quixote"* (Cambridge: Cambridge University Press, 1978).

45 G. D. Kiremidjian, "The Aesthetics of Parody," *JAAC*, 28 (1969), 231-42.

46 P. N. Medvedev/M. M. Bakhtin, *The Formal Method in Literary Scholarship. A Critical Introduction to Sociological Poetics*, trans. Albert J. Wehrle (Baltimore and London: Johns Hopkins University Press, 1978), p. 161.

47 "Art as Technique," in *Russian Formalist Criticism: Four Essays*, ed. Lee T. Lemon and Marion J. Reis (Lincoln and London: University of Nebraska Press, 1965), p. 12.

48 Quoted in Boris Eichenbaum, "The Theory of the 'Formal Method,'" in *Russian Formalist Criticism*, p. 134 from *Dostoevsky i Gogol* (Petrograd, 1923).

49 *Problems of Dostoevsky's Poetics*, trans. R. Rotsel (Ann Arbor: Ardis, 1973), p. 153. (Italics in original.)

50 Julia Kristeva, "Word, Dialogue, and Novel," in *Desire in Language*, ed. Leon S. Roudiez, trans. Thomas Gora, Alice Jardine, Leon S. Roudiez (New York: Columbia University Press, 1980), pp. 64-91. Quotation on p. 66.

51 Ibid., p. 66.

52 G. B. Milner, "Homo Ridens: Towards a Semiotic Theory of Humour and Laughter," *Semiotica*, 5 (1972), 15 as quoted from Saussure's *Cours de linguistique générale*, ed. Charles Bally, Albert Sechehaye, and Albert Riedlinger (Paris: Payot, 1931), p. 171.

53 Cossío, *Fábulas mitológicas*, p. 517.

54 Ragnar Johnson, "Two Realms and a Joke: Bisociation Theories of Joking," *Semiotica*, 16, no. 3 (1976), 215, as quoted from Mary Douglas, "The Social Control of Cognition: Some Factors in Joke Perception," *Man* (n.s.) 3 (1968), 356. Freud, in *Wit and Its Relation to the Unconscious*, trans. A. A. Brill (1916; rpt. London: Kegan Paul, Trench, Trubner and Co., [1922]) analyzes the sexual and aggressive components of "tendency" wit and describes how they function to evade societal restrictions: "*wit affords us the means of surmounting restrictions and of opening up otherwise inaccessible pleasure sources*" (p. 150) [italics in

original]; one can rebel against authority through wit–"Wit then serves as a resistance against such authority and as an escape from its pressure" (p. 153).

55 See Patricia Klindienst Joplin, "The Voice of the Shuttle is Ours," *Stanford Literature Review*, 1 (Spring 1984), 25-53, for a penetrating commentary on this quote (from Aristotle's *Poetics* [16.4]), from a play by Sophocles, now lost, on the tale of Tereus and Philomela. I am grateful to my colleague Nancy K. Miller for directing me to Joplin's article and for sharing with me her own study, "Arachnologies: The Text, the Woman, and the Critic," in *Poetics of Gender* (forthcoming), in which she interprets Arachne's tapestry as a "feminocentric" protest against the "theocentric" version of the goddess.

Góngora: *Hero and Leander*

This wondrous and woeful tale of love is not, properly speaking, a "myth," for there are no gods nor supernatural interventions, nor does it involve a metamorphosis. It is, however, a short narrative poem, or epyllion, of sentimental and tragic interest, whose star-crossed lovers acquired legendary stature. Although the origin of the legend is unknown, it has a decidedly local character by virtue of its specific setting at Sestos and Abydos, cities on opposite sides of the narrowest point of the Hellespont. Hero's tower may well have been a beacon tower, which, once abandoned and reduced to fragments, gave rise to poetic conjecture.[1] Although erosion has changed the coastal configuration, and the tower was in ruins centuries ago, these topographical features remain firmly intact as literary signs that any competent reader recognizes as indicators of the tale.

The allusions to the tale in various early Roman writers as well as geographers indicate general familiarity with the legend, but its first full development occurs in Ovid's *Heroides* (Epistles 18 and 19).[2] The letters between Hero and Leander are exchanged after the consummation of their love, before the final and fateful crossing. Passionately tragic in tone, bathed in the irony of the known and certain death of the lovers, these soliloquies are emotional outpourings with little emphasis on any sequence of external events.

These lovers from the *Heroides* do not seem to have exactly captivated the medieval Spanish imagination. Hero and Leander are mentioned in the *General estoria* of Alfonso X and some of the epistles, though not the exchange between Hero and Leander, are included in *La Crónica troyana* (1490), which utilized the *General estoria* as its source.[3] The only fifteenth-century translation into Spanish that includes these epistles is found in the *Bursario*, generally attributed to Juan Rodríguez de la Cámara (or del Padrón), where moral intention is ascribed to each "case." The translator's interpretation of Leander's letter is that "su entinçion del actor es de reprehenderlo de loco amor, porque ponia su vida a peligro de muerte cada vez que yva a ver su enamorada."[4] Aside from these examples, Hero and Leander are relegated to the familiar heap of lovers catalogued by the *cancionero* poets, as seen in the following verses from the Marqués de Santillana's *Infierno de amor*:

> e mas en el dolorido
> tormento vimos a Ero,
> con el su buen compañero
> en el lago perescido.[5]

One wonders whether this absence was due to lack of interest or precaution. These openly desirous "love-sick" women of the *Epistles* would surely have been considered models to be avoided, rather than examples to be followed. Later translations of the *Heroides* display great caution: Diego Mexía in his 1608 version freely admits to omitting "lo que . . . podía ofender a las piadosas i castas orejas,"[6] and the impressive title chosen by Sebastián de Alvarado y Alvear, *Heroyda Ovidiana con parafrasis Española y morales Reparos* (1628) is deceptively inclusive, for there is only one epistle (VII) and many, many "morales reparos."[7]

During the sixteenth century the tale of Hero and Leander was certainly familiar enough–Garcilaso himself had cultivated the theme in his Sonnet XXIX, "Pasando el mar Leandro el animoso,/en amoroso fuego todo ardiendo," itself a rich paraphrase of Martial's epigram.[8] Renewed interest in the tale was caused by the Italian publication in the late 1490s of the highly esteemed Greek epyllion of the fifth-century Musaeus. The addition by the Aldine Press of a Latin translation in a later copy assured its rapid divulgation, as well as immense popularity throughout Europe.[9] Spain was not an exception, and one of the earliest editions after the *editiones principes* was that of Demetrius Dukas, at Alcalá in 1514.

Musaeus's epyllion might have remained within the privileged realm of the *cognoscenti* of Greek and Latin had not Boscán chosen to "translate" it, as his "Historia de Leandro y Hero" (published posthumously in 1543).[10] His poem is in effect a moralized adaptation of the epyllion, so notoriously amplified (from 343 Greek hexameters to 2,793 *endecasílabos sueltos*) that even the indefatigable Menéndez Pelayo was driven to comment that "En vez de una traducción hizo una paráfrasis verbosa, lánguida y descolorida."[11] It nevertheless managed to capture the public's imagination and elicited a plethora of *romances* on the subject (Alatorre's monograph lists nine before 1589).[12] During his early Córdoba period (1582-1596) Góngora had already brandished the sword of parody at various *romance* traditions (carolingian, pastoral, *morisco*), and once again, although there is evident cognizance of Boscán's text, it is the *romances* of Hero and Leander that are the principal target of Góngora's first parody, "Arrojóse el mancebito" (1589, no. 27).[13] We will therefore turn our attention to these before braving Boscán's "Historia." In Musaeus's poem the final, most tragic elements of the plot sequence (Leander's last swim across the Hellespont, his death by drowning, Hero's suicide) are treated with disproportionate brevity (vv. 309-43); in Boscán's poem these incidents merit only the final sixty-six verses. The static elements of character and atmosphere are preferred, and the meeting of the beautiful youths, the awakening of their love, are clearly the most significant elements in these narrative structures. The *romances*, on the other hand, in typical *romance* fashion, concentrate exclusively on the last, most dramatic moment of Boscán's prodigious elaboration, Leander's final swim across the stormy Hellespont. The standard components of the plot sequence (the night, the storm, Hero's tower and her lamp, Leander's drowning, Hero's suicidal fall to her death) appear in various and sundry combinations, but the tone of the compositions is uniformly exclamatory and sentimental. Because these *romances* are not easily accessible, an example of one published in 1551 (the first one listed by Alatorre) is given here:

Romance de Leandro y Ero, y cómo murió

El cielo estaba ñublado, – la luna su luz perdía,
los vientos eran tan recios – que el mar espanto ponía,
cuando la hermosa Ero – muy penada se sentía;
aguardando está Leandro – a quien mas que a sí quería,
asomóse a la ventana – de la torre do vivía.
Los ojos levanta al cielo – por ver qué tiempo hacía,
nocturna y muy tenebrosa – la noche le parecía,
los truenos con sus dislates – mucho miedo le ponían,
su corazón se desmaya – con el temor que sentía,
la seña que era la lumbre – l'ayre no la consintía,
púsola dos o tres veces, – tantas en tierra caía,
viendo tan triste señal – por agurio [*sic*] la tenía,
con una voz delicada – desta manera decía:
«¡Oh dioses! ¿y qué es aquesto? – ¿Por qué robais mi alegría?»
«¡Oh mis hados, y en tal punto – mostrais vuestra tiranía!»
Con estas lamentaciones – la media noche venía;
cansada se siente Ero, – mas por eso no dormía,
con temor está aguardando – hasta que viniesse el día,
mirando al pié de la torre – por ver si algo vería.
Un bulto vido en la arena – pero no lo conocía,

el corazón se lo dice–mas ella no lo creía,
mirando de hito en él–muy claro lo conocía:
conoció que era Leandro–por quien pena padecía;
el corazón se le aprieta,–el alma se le salía,
la color del fresco gesto–pura tierra parecía,
sus manos muy delicadas–de rato en rato torcía,
con este tormento fuerte–mil veces se amortescía:
desque ya en sí tornada,–¡oh qué llanto que hacía!
Maldice su desventura–y la vida en que vivía;
hablando está con el cuerpo–como si tuviera vida:
«Díme, cuerpo, ¿qué es del alma–do partiste compañía?
¿Qué es de la fé que me diste?–¿Cómo dejaste la mía?
O mi leal amador,–do la lealtad vivía,
no quiero vivir sin tí,–que el vivir muerte sería,
recíbeme allá contigo,–y ansina descansaría.»
Estas palabras diciendo–de la torre se caía.[14]

(Tercera parte de la *Silva*, fol. 122v)

Góngora's poem duplicates their compositional structure in his exclusion of any narrative sequences other than the final moments, and in addition he incorporates lexical features of the *romances*. Thus, for instance, the opening "Arrojóse el mancebito" recalls the *romance* verses "en el ancho mar se arroja/como mancebo atrevido,"[15] and the verse "ya más veces se zambulle" (v.54) harks back to the lines "zabullóle el agua al hondo,/murió el triste sospirando."[16] In some instances, compositional details in these extant *romances* are included but have undergone a negative transformation. Góngora includes the potentially comic feature of contemporarization by means of dress details, but the *romance* verses "tiende el manto en el arena,/el sombrero, espada y daga,/rompe apriesa los botones,/un pie con otro descalza ..."[17] are reduced to the mention of "pedorreras azules" ("Ya se va dejando atrás/ las pedorreras azules" [vv.5-6]), humorously ambiguous in its two possible meanings—one neutral, "calzones ajustados," and one scatological, "frecuencia o muchedumbre de ventosidades expelidas del vientre" (*Dic. de la lengua española*). The same is true of the imploration to Venus and the inclusion of a final epitaph, both of which had appeared in the *romances*, with, of course, serious sentimental intent. Boscán's final rewarding of the lovers, "Y así se fueron juntas las dos almas/A los campos Elisios para siempre," a detail captured by the *romancistas*, becomes a punishment.[18] Góngora transforms this pagan paradise into a Christian Hell by condemning the lovers' souls to "adonde se queman/ pastillas de piedra azufre" (vv.71-72).

The saturation of "literariness" in this poem, the constant presence of other texts, determines semantic connotation. Seemingly positive markers, such as the epithet in the phrase "el animoso joven" (v.25), are voided of their positive connotations, neutralized by the fact of their literary provenance, this being but a reproduction of Garcilaso's opening verse of Sonnet XXIX, "Pasando el mar Leandro el animoso." In the same way, the weighty seriousness of the learned mythological allusions (the periphrasis "el Griego de los embustes" [v.20], or the esoteric reference to Xerxes' crossing of the Hellespont [v.23]) is lightened into comicality as the competent reader recognizes the textual corpus against which Góngora posits his own—the gratuitous pedantry and intrusive classical circumlocutions of Boscán's "Historia."[19]

The treatment of Hero in the poem is a masterful example of ironic annihilation by means of semantic conversion from one text to another. Góngora successfully exploits the sexual ambiguities inherent in the tale. In Musaeus Hero is a "maiden" (v.20), a "priestess of Aphrodite" (v.31);[20] in Boscán she is referred to as "la vírgen" (p. 293), "sierva de Vénus" (p. 307). A virgin dedicated to the cult of Aphrodite/Venus is a paradox, for "Primarily, she is a goddess of generation and fertility, and in poetry often seems little more than a personification of the sexual instinct and the power of love," and she was even considered the patron "saint," as it were, of prostitutes.[21] This peculiar contradiction is utilized by the persuading lover—Musaeus's Leander notes that "It is not fitting a virgin attend on Aphrodite" (v.143); Boscán's hero, as usual more verbose, states that "Las vírgenes irán tras su Diana/En soledad de vida por los yermos;/Tú y las que estais á Vénus consagradas,/En lecho conjugal habeis de veros" (p. 309). The suggestiveness of Hero's situation, who according to the subtle Musaeus "Was maiden by day, by night a wife" (v.287), was assiduously avoided by Boscán in his efforts to convert her into the quintessential "Renaissance *dama*."[22] Góngora's first comparison of Hero to "ninfa de Vesta" (v.29) is ambiguously suggestive. No longer the expected "virgen de Vesta," she assumes all the dubious connotations of the designation of "ninfa" ("Joven hermosa. Tómase a veces en mala parte," *Dic. de la lengua española*).[23] In his next reference Hero is alluded to, again periphrastically, as the "dama de Sesto" (v.31), a description pointedly anachronistic, ridiculing Boscán's attempts at "Hispanification."[24] It is also markedly ironic, for the alternate meaning of "dama" is "mancéba ò concubína con quien se tiene comunicacion ilícita" (*Dic. de la lengua castellana*), and Góngora himself associates this term with the corruption of the court.[25] The sexual connotations continue throughout the poem as Hero's burning lamp, the traditional token of her devotion, is seen not as the instrument of her love, but of her lust ("porque ve lo que le cumple" [v.34]), and the final plea not to mourn, but to celebrate because unity has been achieved at last (« . . .pues un fin tuvimos,/que una tierra nos sepulte» [vv.95-96]) suggests sexual consummation rather than the eternal love of the medieval epitaph tradition. This anachronism of an epitaph had been incorporated in the tale in one of the *romances*, supposedly written by the father of Leander:

> "Sabed, amantes,
> que el que aquí está sepultado
> con corona muy preciosa
> del amor fue coronado,
> la más rica y sumptuosa
> que nunca a amador ha dado".[26]

Instead of transcribing this message of undying, spiritual love, Góngora transcribes a message of undying, physical union, a sentiment uttered *viva voce* by Hero before her death in a later *romance*:

> "Y pues fui suya en la vida,
> no es bien en muerte negallo:
> los cuerpos vivieron juntos,
> y ansí me he determinado
> que queden juntos agora
> adonde sean enterrados . . . ,
> para que juntos estén
> en tormento o en descanso".[27]

Góngora exposes the ambiguity inherent in the repetitive insistence of the *romances* on dying "juntos" ("Hero y Leandro en compañía/ sepultaron juntamente"; "y así fenecieron juntos"),[28] a word used by Boscán, but applied to the lovers' souls, not bodies—"Y así se fueron juntas las dos almas/A los campos Elisios para siempre" (p. 376).[29] By means of ironic reversal, the *pudor* of Boscán's heroes is converted to *lascivia*, a subversive triumph of desire rather than of discretion.

Throughout the poem there is a general comic confusion between animate and inanimate, as the personification of the natural elements ("el enemigo cielo/disparó sus arcabuces" [vv.13-14], "se orinaron las nubes" [v.16], "cuatro palanquines vientos" [v.59]) contrasts with the consistent reductionism of the human elements—tears are rigidified into such mechanical measurements as "dos almudes" (v.80) or "dos mil perlas" (v.42),[30] and Leander's drowning and Hero's suicide are voided of any emotional impact by their transformation into the notorious, dazzling pun of the eggs, Leander is "pasado por agua" (v.91), Hero is "estrellada" (v.92).[31] In keeping with this tendency, a metonymic assimilation occurs that will reappear in Góngora's later poem. Hero's tower is, of course, an inevitable feature of the *romances* and is characterized by its physical appearance, be it as "alta" or "gran," for instance.[32] By means of a hyperbolic metonymic feat, Hero and the tower, container and contained, become one, and the tower itself becomes the object of Leander's love, his "amada torre" (v.61).

Góngora's authorial stance in this early parody is impersonal and noninstrusive, in imitation of the impersonal "epic" pose of the anonymous *romancero* tradition. He is not explicit with the reader; there is no title and the action begins abruptly *in medias res*. It is the early mention of location, "Abido" (v.7), that dictates the appropriate reading, which will be double rather than single, bilinear rather than linear. Thereafter the various parodistic techniques of negativization (belittling diminutivization; reification of the human; comic anthropomorphism of the inanimate; inappropriate juxtaposition, such as the scatological "se orinaron las nubes" [v.16] posed near the learned references to Odysseus or Xerxes, as well as irony) will be recognized as different from the known and the expected, and will produce the requisite humorous reaction.

Góngora's second parody of the theme, "Aunque entiendo poco griego," although written later (1610, no. 64), deals with the earlier narrative elements of this tale that had received such extensive treatment in the poems of Musaeus and Boscán. Its independence from the earlier poem is externally marked by a change in rhyme scheme (an *á-o* assonance replaces the previous *ú-e* assonance), but the most significant difference is the conspicuous presence of an external narrator, who, as he transcribes a found text, asserts his own creative and critical power. The emergence of a "speaking" first-person in the very first verse – "Aunque entiendo poco griego" – signals a poem characterized by an aggressive manifestation of subjectivity. This establishment of a controlling subject, the ever-intrusive "I" throughout the poem ("he hallado" [v.2], "no sé" [v.50], "yo a pie quiero ver" [v.57], "no sé dónde" [v.61], "Sé al menos" [v.65], "Esto solo de Museo/entendí" [vv.69-70]) acts as a metalinguistic enunciation making the previously implicit intertext thoroughly explicit.[33] From the first moment the reader is aware that this is an elaborate literary game, and that his reading is being controlled and manipulated by the author. It is indeed possible, as Ball suggests, that this new, highly sophisticated narrative stance reflects Góngora's own awareness in 1610 of his recently increased stature and prestige in the world of letters.[34] Confident now in his ability, he can

attack not only his predecessor, Boscán, but also his contemporary enemies, Quevedo, which will be discussed below, and Lope de Vega,
whose famous *romance* verses "Sale la estrella de Venus" are closely
imitated in the later verses "«¡Oh de la estrella de Venus,/le dice, ilustre
traslado!»" (vv.207-08)[35] and included as yet another dull and worn-out
cliché among many others, such as the metaphor of the lover as boat,
"Norte eres ya de un bajel/de cuatro remos por banco" (vv.209-10),
repeated *ad nauseum* in the Hero and Leander *romances*.[36]

The opening verses of "Aunque entiendo poco griego" refer to the
finding of Musaeus's poem ("en mis gregüescos he hallado/ciertos versos de Museo,/ni muy duros ni muy blandos" [vv.2-4]), but this is problematical because the explicit model is obviously Boscán's translation,
later identified as "el carro largo/de las obras de Boscán" (vv.54-55). His
next allusion to Musaeus, "Esto solo de Museo/entendí" (vv.69-70), is
equally enigmatic, and once again functions to undercut his "authority"
as translator or transcriber because it emphasizes his dubious knowledge of Greek. To those closely familiar with Musaeus's text this would
be especially amusing. The verses immediately preceding ("Sé al
menos que concurrieron/cuantos baña comarcanos/el sepulcro de la que
iba/a las ancas de su hermano" [vv.65-68]) are an oblique periphrastic
allusion to Helle, who drowned in these waters and after whom the
straits are named – an etymological detail included in the *Heroides* letters but not mentioned by Musaeus. The verses immediately following
refer to the festival day, vulgarized to an Hispanic "vela o romería"
(v.71). While the festival of Aphrodite is mentioned by Musaeus as the
occasion for the meeting of the two youths, his account certainly does
not feature the lackluster and mundane details of dress and transportation that characterize Góngora's description. It is not surprising that, in
his comparison between the Greek text and Góngora's, G. Cirot concludes that, while it is indeed possible that Góngora read the work in
Greek, there is no evidence in his text of dependence on Musaeus.[37]
Ball considers that this oblique allusion to Helle, and its pointedly
incorrect attribution to Musaeus, are a means whereby "by calling the
reader's attention to his remote classical source, Góngora momentarily
measures his superior ability at poetic innovation against a model of the
highest prestige."[38]

Before coming to any conclusion concerning Góngora's stance
towards Musaeus's text, another disconcerting feature of the opening
verses of this poem should be taken into account. They read as follows:

> Aunque entiendo poco griego,
> en mis gregüescos he hallado

ciertos versos de Museo,
ni muy duros ni muy blandos.

(vv.1-4)

The salient point is that the pun on the common derivational core of "griego" and "gregüesco" (wide Greek-style pants) receives subsequent scatological development ("ni muy duros ni muy blandos" [v.4]), for which Ball offers the following elegant interpretation: " 'Musaios' does not appear in the text as such, but only as 'consumed' (read) and 'digested' (rewritten) by Góngora, who finds his thematic target already 'processed' by the literary version of Boscán."[39] However, neither Boscán, and certainly not Musaeus, are subjected to this kind of vituperation elsewhere. Obscenity is, however, typical of Góngora's continuous, and continuously vulgar, diatribe against Quevedo. Furthermore, following the publication of Quevedo's *Anacreón castellano* (1609), translations of the Greek lyric poet, Góngora directed a vitriolic sonnet against him, "Anacreonte español, no hay quien os tope," negating his pretensions to Greek scholarship in verses that bear obvious resemblance to no. 64:

Con cuidado especial vuestros antojos
dicen que quieren traducir al griego,
no habiéndolo mirado vuestros ojos.

Prestádselos un rato a mi ojo ciego,
porque a luz saque ciertos versos flojos,
y entenderéis cualquier gregüesco luego.

(MG LXII, 1609-1617)[40]

The mocking self-doubt of the references to the Greek text might well be construed as derision of Quevedo, not only for his translations of Anacreon, but also for his learned pretensions in the final verse of his own Hero and Leander poem, which is "aunque más jarifa/Museo la canta." This is, admittedly, mere speculation, as the dating of Quevedo's poems is notoriously difficult. For reasons of "artistic logic," Alatorre corrects Astrana Marín's assignation of the early date of 1604 to Quevedo's burlesque *romancillo*, and dates it after 1610, after *both* of Góngora's poems on this theme, an opinion to which Blecua refers in his edition. Alatorre's assignation of a late date to Quevedo's poem on the basis of "tone," however, is problematical. The bitterness and destructiveness that characterize this *romancillo* are typical of all his mythological burlesque and are not *necessarily* motivated by the subtle irony of Góngora as suggested by Alatorre: "el cruel esperpento de la desventurada Hero tiene que venir después del retrato irónico."[41] One might also conjecture that this brilliant, multilayered second parody of Góngora was motivated by his competitive desire to improve upon Quevedo's own version "a lo burlesco," pointedly and maliciously "foregrounding" Quevedo's probable source – not the prestigious Greek Musaeus, but the tedious Spanish Boscán.

The structure of this 1610 poem is markedly dialogical. Following Bakhtin's definition, it is clear that Góngora's word is ever "double-directed" or "double-voiced" throughout the poem, for "it is directed both toward the object of speech, like an ordinary word, and toward *another word*, toward *another person's speech*."[42]

"Aunque entiendo poco griego" incorporates a level of historical narration – a mock duplication of Boscán's so-called "historia," related in the preterit or imperfect, marked off by such phrases as "Dice, pues" (v.9) or "También dice" (v.21), as well as a level of discourse, in which the speaker relates and comments in the present tense.[43] This speaker, as he recounts Boscán's tale through the medium of reported speech, repudiates Boscán's static authorial stance of certainty, emphasizing instead his own more dynamic stance of uncertainty ("no sé si a pie o a caballo" [v.50]; "Y así, no sé dónde fueron/ni cómo se convocaron" [v.61-62]). His parenthetical comments – the word "asno" is followed by "(con perdón de los cofrades)" (v.75) and the enumeration of Hero's pulchritudinous physical attributes is curtailed by the Church Latin phrase "*sed libera nos a malo*" (v.144) – are a mock-deference to Boscán's notorious prudery and subvert the entire ethical stance of the older poet. In this polemic, Góngora's word is ever directed toward Boscán's, whose declarative, unambiguous certainties he devastates with his own interrogative, playful uncertainties.

Góngora reveals a merciless understanding of Boscán's distortions of the Greek text. As has been mentioned previously, Musaeus's delicate eroticism is assiduously minimized in both its visual and psychological aspects. Musaeus describes not only Hero's face, but her limbs, "a meadow of roses" (v.60), glimpses of which incite even old men to lust; in Boscán this is reduced to the bland, neo-Platonic cliché, "En su cuerpo su alma se mostraba,/Y víase tambien claro en su alma,/Que á tal alma tal cuerpo se debia" (p. 294). Musaeus's Hero is an actively desirous as well as desirable woman – "And the maiden Hero glowed in her heart with sweet fire,/And trembled at the beauty of Leander, quickener of desire" (vv.167-68); in Boscán Hero submits not to the heat of desire, but to its domesticated version, the "yugo del amor" (p. 311), and looks not at the whole of Leander (his body), but only at his face –

"Pero poniendo en fin todos sus ojos/De una parte en el rostro de Leandro,/El qual era notable en hermosura" (p. 311), whereupon she is moved by his suffering. Neither does Boscán mention the rite of consummation or the nuptial bed, which Musaeus so suggestively had sketched:

> Thus she spoke these words, and forthwith he loosed
>   her girdle,
> And they entered into the rites of most wise
>   Cythereia.
> Wedding it was, but without a dance; bedding, but
>   hymnless.
>
> (vv.272-74)

Boscán's lovers speak about love, described as "hablar estas blanduras" (p. 358), but they do not "on stage," as it were, perform the act of love; faithful to Spanish Catholicism, Boscán replaces the sexual act with a tedious and prolonged discourse.

This ethical distortion in favor of what Reichenberger succinctly characterizes as "sentimentalism and Christian struggle against love,"[44] is accompanied by what Góngora perceived as a crucial flaw in presentation: Boscán's distortion of Musaeus's suggestive vagueness by means of his own "realistic, bourgeois Hispanification of the classical story."[45] In Musaeus's text the young lovers are shrouded in mystery. Of Hero we know that she is beautiful, of distinguished descent, destined by her parents to be a priestess. Of Leander, whose family is not mentioned, it is said that he is "a vagabond,/A stranger and not to be trusted" (vv.177-78), "a roaming alien" (v.181). He is also beautiful and has a seductive tongue. This is all that we know. The lovers, freed from the bonds of psychological causation, without a past (or future), float in an undefined time and space and exist only in and for the present moment of their love. In keeping with his general tendency towards amplification, Boscán includes contemporary forms of address, details of clothing, and comportment; he suggests pseudological motives for action (Leander *swims* across the Hellespont because "Que ir en barco sería perder tiempo"! [p. 316]), he intrudes cozy geographical specifications (Sestos and Abydos are so close that "Oíanse los gallos y los perros/De entrambos, y los humos se topaban" (p. 290). By saturating his own poem with such "anchoring" devices as pejorative details of family lineage, financial status, and dress styles, Góngora exposes, through systematic exaggeration and negativization, the manifest inappropriateness of Boscán's "grounding" the tale in realistic detail, creating an artificial "cultural vraisemblance" in order to make it more intelligible to the average reader.[46] If, as stated by Arnold Reichenberger, Boscán can indeed be credited with having founded two new genres in Spain—the short classical epic, and, with Diego Hurtado de Mendoza, the *epístola de cosas familiares*[47]—it is also clear that his "Historia de Leandro y Hero" is a bizarre conflation of these two genres. Such a hybrid was obviously unacceptable to Góngora; its sentimentalization and trivialization betrayed the spirit of the classical text.

Once again, the treatment of Hero involves masterful ironic playfulness. The first extended description of the heroine develops the metonymic substitution already apparent in the phrase "amada torre" (v.61) of the earlier *romance*. Hero is now described in terms of a tower; her white veil is the wall and its eye openings narrow gratings ("que el muro del velo blanco/tenía dos saeteras/para los ojos rasgados" [vv.86-88]), and upon this edifice birds may land, including Leander of Abydos, the so-called "Abideno" (v.92), distinctly avian in its comic phonetic associations. The subsequent description of Hero creates a tonal dissonance because of its florid *culterano* diction, generously sprinkled with flowers and precious stones. These descriptive passages of Hero cannot be considered serious affective statements.[48] Góngora's legacy from Boscán includes the bland, familiar synthetic simile,

> Con su color las rosas imitando
> Y el oro figurando en sus cabellos,
> . . . .
> Así salió la virgen, . . .
>
> (p. 293)

which Góngora subjects to a pitiless analysis until he reduces Hero to a mere word heap. Her portrait is created by subtle ironic understatement, whereby the initial, seemingly positive epithets are subjected to a process of meiosis and quickly reduced to their negative connotations: the "crepúsculo" (v.113) of Hero's hair is redefined as pitch black; the ebony eyebrows become jagged or bushy ("aserrado" [v.120]); the nose, at first merely "algo aguileña" (v. 129), becomes a full-fledged "alfanje" (v. 132). The jasmine, roses, and carnations, the pearls and alabaster, are mere code-statements, emblematic rather than metaphoric, equally ironic in their hyperbolic overstatement. Góngora's Hero is the negative reversal of the expected Renaissance Botticellian beauty; her description an anti-Petrarchan mockery, an exercise already cultivated by his predecessor, Baltasar del Alcázar, who was not averse to erotic intimations:

Cabellos crespos, breves, cristalinos,
Frente que de miralla turba y mata,
Cejas cuyo valor vence á la plata
Y el alabastro y nieve hace indignos,
    Ojos de perlas, blandos y benignos,
Nariz que á cualquier otra desbarata,
Boca, sin fin alegre al que la trata,
Dientes donosos, raros, peregrinos,
    Trepado cuello digno de respeto,
Manos conformes al trepado cuello,
Pecho profundo y tierno sin defeto,
    Melindroso ademán, dulce y discreto...
Si lo que vemos público es tan bello,
¡Contemplad, amadores, lo secreto![49]

Góngora's description terminates in a flourish of sexual innuendo, as the verses "que se contaron sus vidas,/y sus muertes concertaron" (vv.155-56) exploit the double meaning of "morir" as literal death as well as sexual consummation.

If, by means of his parodies, Góngora himself had hoped to "concertar la muerte" of the tale, he failed. Both burlesque poems (by minor poets such as Medrano y Barrionuevo and Manuel de Melo, for example) as well as serious versions, follow thereafter.[50] But surely this was not his intent, for if myths have no beginning, neither do they have an end.

What, then, is the target, as well as the intent, of Góngora's polemic? Is his an ideological message against the very notion of idealized love, first presented fully by Musaeus and imitated thereafter? This is the opinion of R. Jammes, who considers that Góngora's object of attack is

une certaine conception idéalisante de l'amour, qui s'exprime aussi bien dans le poème de Musée que dans la poésie courtoise ou dans les romans de chevalerie.[51]

R. O. Jones specifies Góngora's probable target as "the folly of useless ideals";[52] R. Ball emphasizes that Góngora's deconstructive efforts were aimed against the potent "illusionary power" that the idealizing poetry and message combined to create in these love myths, so strong as to be able to falsely and dangerously condition thought and behavior.[53] In terms of specific poetic targets, the repetitious "automatized" *romance* versions and Boscán's Italianate poem are decidedly implicated, but can it be said that the target is *necessarily* also "the classic Musaios himself," as Ball suggests,[54] especially when the allusions to Musaeus are, pointedly and ironically, *not* to Musaeus?

Without doubt, Góngora subverts the *romance* texts and Boscán's poem and with great independence recombines them in a new negative code. Their flaws, however, are not Musaeus's flaws, but rather result from *misreadings* of Musaeus, distorted and endlessly amplified in Boscán, incomplete and hackneyed in the *romances*, mere parasites of Boscán's poem.

Góngora's devastation of Boscán reveals a deep understanding of the Greek text. Appreciative of the succinctness, mysterious vagueness, and delicate eroticism of Musaeus, Góngora develops and stresses these gaps in his own version. Profoundly versed in the Classics, Góngora reacts against the sentimentalization, trivialization, and misinterpretation of the epyllion. Neither the poetic medium nor the ideological message of Musaeus is attacked by Góngora; it is his Spanish predecessor's miserable failure of understanding that he ridicules. Boscán's classicism was pedantic and pompous; he captured the letter, but not the spirit, of the bittersweet Musaeus.

Notes

1 Suggested by Thomas Gelzer in the "Introduction" to his Loeb Classical Library edition of Musaeus's *Hero and Leander*, trans. Cedric H. Whitman, which also includes "Fragments" of Callimachus (Cambridge: Harvard University Press; London: William Heinemann Ltd., 1975), p. 303. He notes that Strabo (64 B.C.-A.D. 19) mentions Hero's tower in his *Geography* and that it is already in ruins.

2 Allusions are found, among others, in Virgil (*Georgics*, III. 258-63); Horace (*Epistles* I.3.4); Statius (*Thebaid*, VI. 542-47). In addition to Strabo, the geographer Pomponius Mela (*De situ orbis*) recalls the lovers. A possible Hellenistic antecedent has been suggested on the basis of the fragments of ten hexameters, probably of the first century A.D., preserved in the Rylands Papyrus (p. 305, n.*b*). See Gelzer, pp. 302-07.

3 Theodore S. Beardsley, Jr., *Hispano-Classical Translations Printed Between 1482 and 1699*, Duquesne Studies Philological Series, no. 12 (Pittsburgh: Duquesne University Press, 1970), pp. 22-23, n.5.

4 In *Obras de Juan Rodríguez de la Cámara (o del Padrón)*, ed. Antonio Paz y Melia, La sociedad de bibliófilos españoles, no. 22 (Madrid: M. Ginesta, 1884), p. 273.

5 Quoted in Cossío, *Fábulas mitológicas*, p. 23. Schevill, *Ovid and the Renascence in Spain*, p. 71, notes that at the beginning of his seventh sonnet, Santillana refers to the *Libro de las Epístolas*.

6 Beardsley, *Hispano-Classical Translations*, p. 68, n.131.

7 Ibid., p. 80, n.166.

8 In *Poesías castellanas completas*, ed. Elias L. Rivers (Madrid: Castalia, 1969), p. 65. Martial's epigrams are found in *De speculis*, I, XXV and XXV (bis). The commentators of Garcilaso, El Brocense (1574) and Herrera (1580) refer to Ariosto's canto 19, "Tutto infiammato d'amoroso fuoco" (st. 26). See *Garcilaso de la Vega y sus comentaristas*, ed. Antonio Gallego Morell, pp. 245 and 361 respectively. The theme of Hero and Leander in Spain is outlined in M. Menéndez Pelayo's "Bibliografía española de Leandro y Hero," *Antología de poetas líricos castellanos*, X (Santander: Aldus, 1945), pp. 314-32, and is studied by F. Moya del Baño, *El tema de Hero y Leandro en la literatura española* (Murcia: Universidad de Murcia, 1966).

9 Two *editiones principes* of the Musaeus poem appeared, one in Venice printed by Aldus Manutius (before the 1st of November, 1495), one in Florence (between 1494 and 1496) with the text by Janus Lascaris. Which of the two was earlier has not been ascertained. See Gelzer's "Introduction" to *Hero and Leander*, p. 342. Gelzer also notes that the Latin translation added to the Aldine edition (not before 1497) is by the printer himself (Aldus Manutius) rather than by Marcus Musurus, as has been assumed traditionally (p. 323, n.*e*).

10 The inversion of Boscán's title probably reflects the influence of Bernardo Tasso's 1537 poem "Favola de Leandro ed Ero." See Menéndez Pelayo's discussion, *Antología de poetas líricos castellanos*, X, pp. 303-07, and David H. Darst, *Juan Boscán* (Boston: Twayne Publishers, 1978), pp. 81-93, who stresses the novelty of the "lack of a moral ending" (p. 93). Beardsley does not include Boscán's poem in his *Hispano-Classical Translations*, considering it an "original work" within the classical tradition (p. 130).

11 *Antología de poetas líricos castellanos*, X, p. 301.

12 The fundamental study of these *romances* is that of Antonio Alatorre, "Los romances de Hero y Leandro," in *Libro jubilar de Alfonso Reyes* (México: Dirección General de Difusión Cultural, 1956), pp. 1-41.

13 Robert Ball, "Góngora's Parodies of Literary Convention," (Ph.D. diss., Yale University, 1976), p. 403. He further notes that this *romance* is externally marked by its peculiar *-ú-e* assonance (p. 415). Erich Segal, "Hero and Leander: Góngora and Marlowe," *CL*, 15 (1963), 338-56, does not take into account the *romance* tradition in his discussion of Góngora's poem, restricting his comparison to Boscán.

Góngora's parodies of the *romance carolingio* from the *romancero viejo* are "Diez años vivió Belerma" (1582, no. 8) and "Desde Sansueña a París" (1588, no. 25); parodies of the *romancero nuevo* include that of the *romance pastoril* "En la pedregosa orilla" (1582, no. 9) and those of the *romance morisco* "Ensíllenme el asno rucio" (1585, no. 18) and "Triste pisa y afligido" (1586, no. 21). These are thoroughly studied in Ball, chaps. I-III. All references to Góngora's *romances* refer to the Antonio Carreño edition of the *Romances* (Madrid: Cátedra, 1982). References to the Millé Giménez edition of the *Obras completas* are indicated as MG.

14 Published in the Apéndice I to the *Primavera y flor de romances* of Wolf and Hoffmann by M. Menéndez Pelayo, *Antología de poetas líricos castellanos*, IX (Santander: Aldus, 1945), pp. 45-46.

15 Alatorre #8, p. 13, MS. 3294 in the Biblioteca Nacional de Madrid (fols. 69v-70v), *Obras de diuersos recopiladas* (1582). Included in *Jardín de amadores*, 1611.

16 Alatorre #2, pp. 3-4, "Romance de Leandro," in *Silva de varios romances* (Barcelona, 1561).

17 Alatorre #9, pp. 14-15, MS. 3294 in the Biblioteca Nacional de Madrid (fols. 17v-18r), *Obras de diuersos recopiladas* (1582).

18 In the "Libro Tercero," *Las obras de Juan Boscán*, ed. William I. Knapp (Madrid: M. Murillo, 1875), p. 376. All further quotations from the "Historia de Leandro y Hero" refer to this same edition and will be incorporated in the text.

19 These classical amplifications are studied by Arnold Reichenberger in "Boscán and the Classics," *CL*, 3 (Spring 1951), 97-118; "An Emendation of the Text of Boscán's *Historia de Leandro y Hero*," *MLN*, 65 (November 1950), 493; "Boscán and Ovid," *MLN*, 65 (June 1950), 379-83.

20 All quotes from Musaeus refer to the Loeb Classical Library edition.

21 See the *Oxford Classical Dictionary*, ed. N. C. L. Hammond and H. H. Scullard, 2d ed. (1970; rpt. Oxford: Clarendon Press, 1978), p. 80, "Aphrodite."

22 O. H. Green, "Boscán and *Il Cortegiano*: The *Historia de Leandro y Hero*," in *The Literary Mind of Medieval and Renaissance Spain*, p. 133, rpt. from *Boletín del Instituto Caro y Cuervo*, 4 (1948), 3-14. This interpretation is reiterated by Reichenberger, "Boscán and the Classics": "Instead of pagan sensualism we find sentimentalism and Christian struggle against love" (pp. 104-05).

23 The example that immediately comes to mind is Cervantes's ironic euphemism for the prostitute in the *Coloquio de Cipión y Berganza*, who is named "la ninfa Colindres," p. 267 in the edition of the Clásicos Castellanos, ed. Francisco Rodríguez Marín, II (Madrid: Espasa-Calpe, 1943). W. Keach, *Elizabethan Erotic Narratives*, pp. 247-48, n.18, mentions that the Aldine translation was "Veneris erat sacerdos," and that Marot's was "Estoit nonnain, a Venus dediée." For his comments on Christopher Marlowe's phrase "Venus' nun," see pp. 88-94.

24 Erich Segal, "Hero and Leander: Góngora and Marlowe," p. 343, points to the "realistic bourgeois Hispanification of the classical story." Ball also mentions Góngora's intent to ridicule Boscán by means of these anachronistic terms (pp. 433-34).

25 To quote but a few examples from Góngora's poetry: In MG 252 (1588) the "damas de haz y envés" are included in a poem that ends "esto es la Corte. ¡Buena pro les haga!" (p. 459); in MG 278 (1603) appear the verses "Serenísimas damas de buen talle,/no os andéis cocheando todo el día,/que en dos mulas mejores que la mía/se pasea el estiércol por la calle" (p. 473); MG 99 (1585) commences with "Si las damas de la Corte/quieren por dar una mano" (p. 293); MG IV (ca. 1588) includes "Y también manda a las damas/que en su amor hagan concierto,/y que tengan sus medidas/conformes a cada precio" (p. 255).

26 Alatorre #5, p. 9, "Romance de Leandro compuesto por Juan de Boraualias Mayayo," MS ca. 1570.

27 Alatorre #6, p. 11, by Pedro de Padilla, *Thesoro de varias poesías* (Madrid, 1580).

28 Alatorre #3, p. 6, "Romance de Hero," in *Cancionero llamado Flor de enamorados* (Barcelona, 1562) and Alatorre #5, p. 8, "Romance de Leandro compuesto por Juan de Boraualias Mayayo," respectively.

29 The *romance* of Juan de Boraualias Mayayo (Alatorre #5) contains the verses "Allá en el Monte Eliseo/están ambos sepultados/dentro de una sepultura/do su nombre es celebrado" (p. 8). Ball, p. 452, also notes Rodríguez del Padrón's epitaph to himself (" 'una tierra los crió,/una muerte los leuó,/una

gloria los possea' ") and corrects Cossío's impression that Góngora's allusion is "serious" (*Las fábulas mitológicas,* p. 522). An example of a burlesque epitaph can be found in the "Poesías festivas" of Baltasar del Alcázar, the "Epitafio á los mismos" (LXXVI):

> A Hero y Leandro encierra,
> Esposos de mala data,
> Esta poca arena ingrata;
> Que aun no alcanzan buena tierra.
> Consumaron, para dar
> De loco amor testimonio,
> En el templo, el matrimonio;
> El disparate, en el mar.

(pp. 68-69)

30 Segal refers to the "comic exactitude" of these measured expressions of grief (p. 347). Ball's comments (pp. 435 and 444) further specify hyperbole and mechanization of clichés as causes of humor.

31 See A. Alatorre, "Fortuna varia de un chiste gongorino," *NRFH*, 15 (1961), 483-504.

32 Lucas Rodríguez, *Romancero historiado,* "al pie de su alta torre" (Alatorre #7, p. 12); Pedro de Padilla, *Thesoro de varias poesías,* "En la gran torre de Sexto" (Alatorre #6, p. 9).

33 M. Riffaterre, *Semiotics of Poetry* (Bloomington and London: Indiana University Press, 1978) uses the term "implicit intertext" and discusses the difficulties that can be experienced by readers until recognition occurs (pp. 134-38).

34 "Góngora's Parodies of Literary Convention," pp. 457-58. According to Jammes, *Etudes,* eleven of his ballads appeared in the "Dozena Parte" of the *Romancero general* of 1604 and thirty-seven of his sonnets and *canciones* in Pedro de Espinosa's *Flores de poetas ilustres* (Valladolid, 1605), pp. 272-75, n.66.

35 Alatorre, "Los romances de Hero y Leandro," p. 26, comments on this burlesque allusion to Lope, and Ball, pp. 505-06, establishes its "corrosive effect."

36 The *topos* of lover as boat is found in Musaeus, "His own oarsman, his own escort, himself his ship" (v.255), repeated by Boscán, "Eran allí sus brazos los sus remos;/Servíanle los piés de gobernalle" (p. 355). Some examples from the *romances* include:

> su lindo cuerpo es navío,
> el amor le va animando;
> sus brazos sirven de remos
> qu'el agua van apartando,
> y los pies por gobernalle
> a su trabajo ayudando,
> por aguja su cabeza...
> > (Alatorre, #2, p. 4, "Romance de Leandro,"
> > *Silva de varios romances* [Barcelona, 1561])

> de su cuerpo hace navío,
> él solo va navegando;

> sus brazos sirven de remos
> que el agua van desviando;
> > (Alatorre #5, p. 7, "Romance de Leandro compuesto por Juan de Boraualias Mayayo," ca. 1570)
>
> Sus brazos sirven de remos
> y su cuerpo de navío,
> sus pensamientos de velas
> y el cielo por enemigo.
> > (Alatorre #8, p. 13, *Obras de diuersos recopilados*, MS. 3294, Biblioteca Nacional de Madrid, fols. 69v-70v. Included in *Jardín de amadores*, 1611)

37 "Góngora et Musée," *BH*, 33 (1931), 328-31.

38 "Góngora's Parodies of Literary Convention," p. 482.

39 Ibid., p. 466.

40 Ball points out the allusions to Quevedo's translations (pp. 467-69) and adds that, although the date listed for MG LXII is 1609-17, the poem must have been written immediately after Quevedo's publication (p. 522, n. 215). He discounts the possibility of a direct allusion to Quevedo's Hero and Leander poem, based on Alatorre's statement (p. 469). It is interesting to note that in his response to Góngora's poem, Quevedo includes a sexual innuendo (III, #828):

> No entendemos los greguescos
> por acá, aunque los usamos;
> dánoslos a entender tú,
> que andas siempre en esos barrios.
>
> > (vv.89-92)

All quotes from Quevedo refer to the edition of José Manuel Blecua of the *Obra poética*, 4 vols. (Madrid: Castalia, 1969-81). "Hero y Leandro en paños menores" (#771) is found on pp. 82-90 of vol. III.

41 Astrana Marín, *Obras completas en verso* (Madrid: Aguilar, 1943) suggests the early date (p. 243), which is rejected by Alatorre, "Los romances de Hero y Leandro," p. 30, n.28. Blecua refers to Alatorre's opinion concerning a probable dating after 1610 (III, p. 82). Neither Menéndez Pelayo nor Cossío mentions Quevedo's burlesque poem, restricting themselves to the *romance* "Esforzóse pobre luz" (I, #210) and the sonnet "Describe a Leandro fluctuante en el mar (I, #311). Alatorre (p. 23) rejects the supposition of Astrana Marín (p. 36, no. 1), repeated by Cossío (pp. 255, 523) that Góngora's "Aunque entiendo poco griego" was written in reaction to Quevedo's rather "culterano" *romance*.

42 *Problems of Dostoevsky's Poetics*, p. 153 (italics in original).

43 This distinction is established in Emile Benveniste's "The Correlations of Tense in the French Verb," in *Problems of General Linguistics*, trans. Mary Elizabeth Meek (Coral Gables: University of Miami Press, 1971), pp. 205-15.

44 "Boscán and the Classics," pp. 104-05.

45 Segal, "Hero and Leander: Góngora and Marlowe," p. 343.

46 See Jonathan Culler, *Structuralist Poetics* (Ithaca: Cornell University Press, 1975), in particular pp. 141-45 in his discussion of "Convention and Naturalization."

47 "Boscán and the Classics," p. 117.

48 The "mixed" tone of the poem led Cossío to consider it an "híbrido trata-miento" (p. 520). Ball (pp. 491-98) takes strong exception to Jammes's interpretation of Góngora's feminine burlesque portraits which is that "non seulement elles ne sont pas ridicules, mais leur beauté est magnifiquement décrite, en termes qui laissent transparaître, à travers la vulgarité affectée du burlesque, une véritable émotion esthétique" (p. 66).

49 This sonnet, XIV (pp. 34-35), is included among the "Poesías amatorias" in the edition of Francisco Rodríguez Marín, who admits, however, that it should be placed among the "Poesías festivas" (p. LXXXIX, n.2).

50 See Menéndez Pelayo, "Bibliografía española de Leandro y Hero," pp. 325 ff.

51 *Etudes*, p. 161, n.30.

52 In his edition of *Poems of Góngora* (Cambridge: Cambridge University Press, 1966), p. 21.

53 "Góngora's Parodies of Literary Convention," p. 406.

54 Ibid, p. 456.

Góngora: *Pyramus and Thisbe*

In contrast to Hero and Leander, this tale is properly Ovidian (*Metamorphoses*, IV.55-166) and does terminate in a transformation, though far less dramatic and suggestive than most. In response to Thisbe's mournful prayers, the gods change the color of the ripe mulberry fruit from white to a deep red. Introduced tantalizingly as a tale "not commonly known as yet" (*quoniam vulgaris fabula non est* [v. 53]), it is the first and most chaste in a series told by Minyas's daughters, which includes Mars and Venus, Leucothoë and Clytie, Salmacis and Hermaphroditus. Their common theme is the overwhelming power of love: "Even the Sun, who with his central light guides all the stars, has felt the power of love" (*hunc quoque, siderea qui temperat omnia luce,/cepit amor Solem* [vv.169-70]). Because the metamorphosis is a natural rather than an anthropomorphic one, the direct relationship between the lovers' tragedy and the phenomenon of the color change is less than obvious, beyond the superficial metamorphic link between the ripe fruits' yearly color change and the blood shed for love. The very ambiguity of this blood mystery provided rich soil for the fanciful imaginations of the Christian allegorists, as seen in Douglas Bush's summary of the account in a fourteenth-century Latin prose work:

Pyramus, the son of God, loves Thisbe, the human soul, but the wall (sin) stands between them. Through the blessed incarnation they are to come together under the cross (the mulberry tree), at the baptismal font (the fountain). But the soul cannot approach the font because of the devil (the lion), and awaits the coming of Christ in silence. The son of God endures death for the human soul (Pyramus commits suicide). The soul should imitate his death, as Thisbe kills herself, and suffer the same anguish mentally.[1]

We shall see that later poets apprehend connotations in this blood mystery quite unsuspected by the Christian allegorists! By the sixteenth century, a less exalted justification for the tale is offered by such Spanish mythographers as Sánchez de Viana, who explains that the ancient writers created such fictions "para darnos a entender, que a semejantes despeñaderos, y desastrados fines, podran ser traydos los desenfrenados amantes, si no toman escarmie̅to en estas fictiones, pues de casos mas raros estan llenas las verdaderas historias."[2] This sole emphasis on the moral meaning reduces the tale to a mundane level, to merely another example of *loco amor* receiving its due castigation.

This *exemplum* tradition is not altogether absent from the verse translations, the first of which is Cristóbal de Castillejo's "La historia de Píramo y Tisbe" (1528). Though preceded by the author's ironic remark that "Simples fueron, a mi parecer, en matarse así con el calor del amor y de la edad," a serious moralizing residue remains.[3] While in the Ovidian text the generalization concerning the power of love is restricted to the framework encompassing the tale, in Castillejo's version the author's intrusive generalizations appear within the body of the tale itself:

> Guárdeos Dios que amor atice
> El fuego qu'el mesmo hace;
> Que aunque temor amenace,
> El hace en fin lo que dice,
> Y dice lo que os place.[4]

Without doubt such avuncular warnings contribute to the "manera realista" that Cossío stresses in his assessment of Castillejo's contribution to the treatment of myth in Spain,[5] but they also make the myth more pedestrian by imposing upon it a Catholic cultural relevance. A later translation by Gregorio Silvestre (between 1540 and 1560), in addition to adding similar generalizing intrusions, contains the traditional moral justification for the tale: "será ejemplo, que es mejor."[6]

Only with the "Historia de los muy constantes y infelices amores de Píramo y Tisbe," attributed to Jorge de Montemayor,[7] does translation free itself from the constraints of didacticism, a radical departure noted by Cossío:

Ningún comentario moral o aleccionador le inspira la desdichada historia, y en esto se aparta radicalmente de lo usado por poetas castellanistas; rasgo de espíritu renacentista.[8]

First appearing in the 1561 Valladolid edition of the *Diana*, it was included in most of the numerous subsequent editions of the book and received wide praise and recognition.[9] Although another version by Antonio de Villegas appeared shortly thereafter, included in the *Inventario* of 1565, the popularity of Montemayor's novel made it the definitive version, and therefore the inevitable victim of parody. A 1603 burlesque *romance* significantly does not refer to the many "serious" sixteenth-century *romances* on this theme, but rather pinpoints Montemayor as its target:

> Afirma Montemayor
> que era primero de enero,
> y no va descaminado
> por ser de gatos el tiempo.[10]

Góngora's first, unfinished *romance* on the subject "De Tisbe y Píramo quiero" (1604, no. 55) also implicitly specifies Montemayor as the parodic target, in the duplication of the opening verse "De Tisbe y Píramo quiero."[11] This is a curious inversion of the order of naming, which had traditionally repeated the Ovidian opening "*Pyramus et Thisbe*" (v.55) and, in the case of Montemayor reflects, intentionally or unintentionally, the greater role ascribed to Thisbe throughout this poem.[12] Góngora's opening quatrain includes the verb "cantar," a lexical item with which Montemayor's opening verses are saturated ("aunque yo cante" [v.8], "el triste canto" [v.12], "cantaré muerte y amores" [v.27]). He also uses the paired phrase "de firmeza y de desgracia" (v.4), in mock-duplication of a stylistic feature rampant in the "Historia"–an insistent bifurcation of terms ("muerte y amores" [v.2], "firme y constante" [v.7], "muerte y espanto" [v.13], "muerte y amores" [v.27]). In opposition to Montemayor's epic invocation to the Muse ("musa mía" [v.11], "Nimpha más que humana" [v.21]), Góngora pleads with his lowly instrument, his guitar, an obvious indication of the burlesque key.

In the following quatrain,

> No sé quién fueròn sus padres,
> mas bien sé cuál fue su patria;
> todos sabéis lo que yo,
> y para introducción basta,
>
> (vv.5-8)

the emergence of the speaker's subjectivity ("No sé," "mas bien sé") destroys the serious assertions and pretensions to "truth" of a Montemayor (or a Boscán in such matters) and openly reveals this as fictional discourse. The readers are so familiar with the narration ("todos sabéis lo que yo") that Góngora pointedly omits the key feature, the mention of "Babilonia," precisely the element with which Montemayor had begun: "En Babylonia nascieron" (v.31).

Hereafter the parody becomes autonomous, as Góngora constructs a mock-Petrarchan portrait of Thisbe that in its frenzied saturation of metallic and jewel clichés ("plata," "oro," "cristal," "rubí," "esmeraldas," "nácar," "perlas blancas" [vv.10-24]) – metaphors absurdly hardened into emblems through overuse – prefigures the descriptive passages of Hero in the 1610 poem "Aunque entiendo poco griego."[13] The irreverent familial descriptions, such as "Señor padre era un buen viejo,/señora madre una paila" (vv.33-34) indicate the "Hispanification" of this pagan tale, which will be a salient characteristic of the later "Hero and Leander" poem. Although there is a suggestion of an attempt at naturalization in Montemayor (he specifies the cause of parental disapproval: "Al padre de ella enfadó/la mucha conuersación" [vv.161-62]), he does not approach the artificial extremes of Boscán.

The *romance* remained unfinished.[14] In his manuscript Chacón added the laconic note that "No pasó adelante en este romance. Y pidiéndole después, el año de [1]618, algunos amigos suyos que le continuase, gustó más de hacer el que se sigue."[15] He then proceeds to copy the 1618 *romance*, without elaborating further either the cause of abandonment of the piece, or the cause of renewal of the project.

Whatever the reasons may be, in 1618 Góngora produced his longest (508 verses) and most complex *romance*, "La ciudad de Babilonia" (no. 74). According to his ardent defender and commentator, Salazar Mardones, this is the poem "que mas lima costo a su Autor, y de la que hazia mayores estimaciones,"[16] and Pellicer before him had written that "Entre las obras que más estimó en su vida don Luis de Góngora, según él me dixo muchas vezes, fué la principal el Romance de *Píramo y Tisbe*."[17] Because of this testimony concerning the effort ("lima") involved in its creation, one cannot suppose, as the critic Arthur Terry suggests, that "The writing of the *Píramo y Tisbe* must have compensated Góngora for the strain of the *Soledades* controversy and the difficulties of his life in Madrid."[18] Neither should one discount too hastily the evidence of Góngora's own positive evaluation, as does R. Jammes with the psychological truism that "le dernier-né est toujours l'enfant le plus beau."[19]

Robert Ball rectifies such notions by analyzing in depth the implications of an aspect of the poem mentioned by other critics, but not fully developed by them – that of self-parody.[20] Conspicuously marked by what Cossío terms an "invasión, o más bien inundación, de cultismo,"[21] and written after Góngora had completed his controversial *culterano* masterpieces, the *Polifemo* and the *Soledades*, as well as the *Panegírico al Duque de Lerma*, the poem coincides in time with Góngora's famous/notorious stature as an innovator. His contemporary Pedro Díaz de Rivas notes that "El estilo del señor Don Luis de Góngora en estas últimas obras...ha pareçido nuebo en nuestra hedad"[22]; Góngora himself professes pride in the attribution of novelty, as he retorts to a critic in his "carta en respuesta" that "me holgara de haber dado principio a algo; pues es mayor gloria en empezar una acción que consumarla."[23] But the same critic had warned him of the "vicio que se introduciría entre muchos, que procuran imitar el lenguaje destos versos, entendiendo que V. m. habla de veras en ellos."[24] The "commercialization" of his poetic innovations did indeed occur, and a plague of *gongorismo* affected Spain, touching some of the best poets, Lope and Quevedo (in spite of their hostility), seriously diseasing the mediocre.[25]

Ball suggests that Góngora became painfully aware of the mechanization and ensuing trivialization of his poetic procedure and suffered a literary *desengaño*, "a crisis of poetic language itself," which may account also for his abrupt termination of the *Soledades*, lest they too be doomed to the empty and meaningless insult of cheap imitation.[26] Góngora's malaise, then (or *desengaño*, in less modern terms), would be the one described by Baudelaire:

Un système est une espèce de damnation qui nous pousse à une abjuration perpetuelle; il en faut toujours inventer un autre, et cette fatigue est un cruel châtiment.[27]

This implies that not only others, but Góngora himself felt enslaved, tied by a chain, albeit a golden one, to a system no longer vital and innovative.

Since its publication the poem has elicited critical attention because of its seeming incongruities. In spite of its obvious malice, the anonymous verse lampoon that allegedly prompted Salazar Mardones's elaborate *Ilustración y defensa de la Fábula de Píramo y Tisbe* (1636) does pinpoint two essential features of the *romance*—its unusual length and *culterano* obscurity:

> Este romance compuso
> el poeta Soledad,
> en lo largo la cuidad
> Babilonia en lo confuso.[28]

Neither the length of the poem, nor the weight of its stylistic elaboration, seem consonant with its burlesque intent. This mixture of obvious burlesque intent and traditionally "serious" narrative procedures creates a definite tonal ambiguity, to which critics ascribe different causes. Some interpreters perceive the cause to be the discrepancy between the "substance" (an inherently tragic theme) and the form, the comic treatment, which led the admiring Salazar Mardones to consider Góngora "el primer inventor deste linage de poesia, Heroi-Comica, misto de Iocoso, y Serio, cosa tan estimable en la esfera ingeniosa" (64v).[29] Certain modern critics are still uncomfortable with the seeming disjunction between theme and treatment, notably R. Jammes who considers "la contradiction entre le style plaisant du poème et son contenu tragique" unresolved.[30] Other critics, in particular A. Terry, perceive the tension to be essentially between styles (the mixture of *cultismos* and *vulgarismos*) rather than between style and content. He believes that the crucial innovation of the poem is the conflation of serious and comic styles, which as a "calculated breach of decorum," such as that found in the English metaphysical school, leads to a more exciting and varied poetic form.[31]

In fact, a breach of poetic decorum, as traditionally conceived, had already been noticed and criticized by his contemporaries in his "epic" works, the *Polifemo* and the *Soledades*. Even the admiring Pedro de Valencia recommends a stricter separation of "burlas" and "veras," censuring the incursion of the comic into this lofty material, deploring the "alusiones burlescas y que no convienen a este estilo alto y materias graves, como convenían a las antiguas, *quae ludere solebas*," and adding that "no sufro que se afee en nada ni se abata con estas gracias o burlas, que pertenescían más a las otras poesías que V. m. solía *ludere* en otra edad."[32] He warns him against seeking quantity, rather than quality, in his audience: "no se desfigure por agradar al vulgo diciendo gracias y juegos del vocablo en poema grave y que va de veras," for later "los buenos escritores han de querer agradar antes a los buenos que a los muchos, como lo profesa Terencio."[33] Dámaso Alonso, commenting upon the *romance* "Angélica y Medoro," noted in Góngora the importance de "la veta humorística del gongorismo, y que en él el poeta serio y el humorístico no están separados, sino que son sólo dos apariencias externas nutridas de la misma sustancia, y entre las cuales hay profundas concomitancias e intercambios."[34]

Although a mixture of styles may be a characteristic of Góngora, the intrusion of the "burlas" upon the "veras" in the serious poems was relatively slight. In "Píramo y Tisbe" the intrusion of the "veras" upon the "burlas" was so intense that it was perceived as incongruous. As concluded by D. Alonso in his study of the *Polifemo* and the *Soledades*, it would seem that it was the intensification and concentration of previously existing elements that scandalized the poetic world.[35]

Aside from the lexical and syntactical eccentricities, the complexities of the text are due to the intricate bilevel construction, which requires it to be read both "horizontally" and "vertically." Using Benveniste's distinction, as *histoire* this "story" of a past event is related horizontally to a set of conventions determined by previous texts, which this poem, as parody, subverts and ridicules; as *discourse*, the poet, the speaking "I," relates vertically in the present to an extratextual world, a "you" which is implicitly addressed and here opposed.[36] We will first address this latter level of discourse before discussing the substance and intent of the textual parody.

The city of Babylonia mentioned in the first verse is related, of course, to the level of historical utterance, for this is the setting of the tale. It is significant, however, that although Spanish versions invoke the city by name, Ovid prefers the learned periphrasis "in the city which Semiramis is said to have surrounded with walls of brick" (*ubi dicitur altam/ coctilibus muris cinxisse Semiramis urbem* [vv.57-58]) and uses the place name only later in its adjectival form, *Babylonia Thisbe* (v.99). Góngora's aggressive foregrounding of the place name and concomitant negation of the Ovidian verses ("famosa, no por sus muros" [v.2]) has important implications at the level of discourse.[37] The homonymic proximity of Babylon and Babel, biblical city of the confusion of tongues, had caused semantic identification of the two. Covarrubias says of large, bustling cities that "dezimos por encarecer el trafago grande que ay, y la confusion, que es vna babilonia: especialmente si cō esto concurren vicios, y pecados que no se castigan," and refers to the prophet Jeremiah's curses on the iniquities of Babylon. Góngora had already had occasion to defend himself against the malicious critic's assertion about the "jerigonza" of the *Soledades* that "muchos se han persuadido que le alcanzó algún ramalazo de la desdicha de Babel,"[38] and the anonymous censor of the "Píramo y Tisbe" bears testimony to the conventionalization of this meaning in the verse "Babilonia en lo confuso." Because of the shared characteristic of confusion, Madrid was closely identified with Babylon, as indicated in various contemporary texts by Lope, Quevedo, and Góngora himself, among others.[39] By mid-century it had been codified into an example of *antonomasia*, as evidenced in Critilo's perception of Madrid in *El Criticón* as "una Babilonia de confusiones" (I, XI, 628).[40] The denotation (place name) and the connotation (evil confusion) of Babylon combine to make a felicitous nexus of the two levels of utterance in the poem.

The complex polysemous play on the meanings of Babylon is understandable only in reference to an implied intertext, the raging literary battle in Madrid occasioned by Góngora's *Polifemo* and *Soledades*. This particular intertextual play continues throughout the poem, although subsequent allusions, more clearly identified as metalinguistic enunciations, refer to the chief actors or antagonists in this drama, Quevedo and Lope. When Góngora, with ironic detachment, asks that "los críti-cos me perdonen/si dijere con ligustros" (vv.147-48) he may well be responding to Quevedo's verses in "Búrlase de todo estilo afectado" (II, #672)–"Si bien el palor ligustre/desfallece los candores" (vv.51-52).[41] The very inundation of *cultismo* in the poem mimics Quevedo's system of chaotic enumeration of such words in the "Receta para hacer Sole-dades en un día" (III, #825). The presence of typical stylistic formulas, such as in the verses

> Las pechugas, si hubo Fénix,
> suyas son; si no lo hubo,
> de los jardines de Venus
> pomos eran no maduros
>
> (vv.69-72)

had merited the vitriolic, exaggerated imitation of Quevedo (III, #833):

> Tantos años y tantos todo el día;
> menos hombre, más Dios, Góngora hermano.
> No altar, garito sí; poco cristiano,
> mucho tahúr; no clérigo, sí arpía.[42]
>
> (vv.1-4)

The pun on "rima" ("chink" in the Ovidian text, simply "verse" in Span-ish) in the verses

> halló en el desván acaso
> una rima que compuso
> la pared, sin ser poeta,
> más clara que las de alguno
>
> (vv.173-76)

is most generally considered to be an allusion to Lope.[43] His collections were entitled *Rimas* (1602 and 1604), *Rimas sacras* (1614), and later *Rimas humanas y divinas del licenciado Tomé de Burguillos* (1634). Lope's "claridad" and "naturalidad" were the hallmarks of his style, and Góngora will later label him the "Conde Claros," who is, among other things, "un idïota" (MG LXXVII, 1621). His contempt for Lope's "art-less" style is evidenced in his judgment that a non-poet ("sin ser poeta") could prove his successful rival.

The ancient Horatian *topos* of *ut pictura poesis* is tentatively suggested in the older Spanish versions of Pyramus and Thisbe–in Montemayor's verses "y si piensas esta muerte/muy al natural pintalla" (vv.16-17),[44] and in Villegas's speech of Pyramus:

> Yo sigo en mis palabras los pintores
> que hacen en su tabla imprimadura;
> tras esto perfeccionan las labores.[45]

It would seem that this tradition is continued in Góngora's verses, albeit "a lo burlesco":

> En el ínterin nos digan
> los mal formados rasguños
> de los pinceles de un ganso
> sus dos hermosos dibujos.

> (vv.41-44)

However, with commendable *conceptista* concision, pun, literary allusion, and ellision are all present in the word "ganso." Covarrubias explains its metaphoric meaning: "Por ser él clamoroso y de voz aspera, y desagradable a los oidos, es simbolo del mal Poeta, como el cisne del bueno." He adds a quote from Virgil's Ninth Eclogue, where the shepherd singer Lycidas, also a "poet," states that "Unworthy still of Varius and Cinna,/I'm a goose who cackles among tuneful swans" (*nam neque adhuc Vario videor nec dicere Cinna/digna, sed argutos inter strepere anser olores* [vv. 35-36]).[46] Significantly, the following fragment of the poem is a recollection of the Galatea theme, treated in earlier eclogues. Lázaro Carreter notes the irony of the self-reference, for "tan 'ganso' era Góngora como Virgilio."[47] Góngora is clearly a swan, not a goose; even Lope refers to him as the "cisne andaluz" in a sonnet written around 1614 ("Canta, cisne andaluz, que el verde coro") and appended to his insidious "Respuesta . . . en razón de la nueva Poesía" (written about 1617, published 1621 in the *Filomena*).[48] Another variation of the avian insult is found in Góngora's sonnet against the Lope de Vega contingent, which begins "Patos de la aguachirle castellana," and in which he recommends: "Los cisnes venerad cultos" (MG LXXVI-¿1621?). In Eclogue 9, the two herdsmen bemoan the loss of the poet Menalcas (identified with Virgil), evicted and dispossessed, leaving them impoverished and saddened without the beauty of his song. Thus, in the view of the learned *culteranos*, the Madrid geese, cackling their "clear" and "natural" tongue, apotheosized by the vulgar masses, drive out the divine and inspired swans.

If the subject of the "vertical" discourse is literature, this too is the

subject of the "horizontal" discourse. At the level of the "story,"
Góngora flaunts expectations of epic decorum, making explicit the "literariness" of the text by commencing with a flamboyant paradox. He
announces as his subject the illustrious pair "que muertos, y en un
estoque,/han peregrinado el mundo" (vv. 7-8), thus exposing the
mimetic fallacy of other poets' versions (Castillejo, Montemayor, Villegas, etc.) who have "sung" the pathetic events as though "real," and
have preferred the title of "Historia" for their poems. He furthermore
subverts his predecessors' efforts by reversing their ennobling epic pretensions. Montemayor had specified,

> óyanme sólo amadores,
> y el que no, como grossero,
> trate de cosas menores,
>
> (vv.3-5)

and Villegas had pleaded "Y salgan grandes cosas de mi boca" (p. 12).
Góngora states that his poem, on the other hand,

> digno sujeto será
> de las orejas del vulgo;
> popular aplauso quiero,
> perdónenme sus tribunos.
>
> (vv.13-16)

Later, the ironic authorial intrusion commenting Thisbe's weakened
will—"¡trágica resolución,/digna de mayor coturno!" (vv.279-80)—again
underscores the comic, as opposed to the tragic, key. The comic
detachment of this exclamation is made explicit by its juxtaposition
with the banal, decidedly inglorious *romance* verse that follows it,
"Medianoche era por filo" (v.281), also the beginning verse of the openly
vulgar parodic *romance* in the 1603 *cancionero*:

> Media noche era por filo,
> todo está puesto en silencio,
> quando el bochorno de Tisbe
> le erizó todo el cavello.[49]

The irony of this purported intention of seeking popular applause
was apparent even to Salazar Mardones, who observed that Góngora

no ignoro que contenia dificultad aun para los eruditos, pero que con esta iro-

nia, y cautela quiso engañar al vulgo, para que le aplaudiessen en lo dificultoso
como en lo facil....(11r)

Lope is again implicated, of course, in the mock-echo of his verses from
the *Arte nuevo de hacer comedias* (1609):

> y escribo por el arte que inventaron
> los que el vulgar aplauso pretendieron;
> porque, como las paga el vulgo, es justo
> hablarle en necio para darle gusto.[50]

With great self-consciousness and deliberate ambiguity, Góngora
"deceives" his readers "con esta ironia, y cautela" about his intention to
seek the approval of the "vulgo." Does he "deceive" also when he stipu-
lates his parodic target as Ovid? Can it be said, as does one critic, that
"El texto de Ovidio es seguido paso a paso en este romance" (barring
the addition of the go-between and the elaboration of the wall in
Góngora)?[51]

The notoriously elaborate and obscure description of the go-between
is itself a flagrant contradiction of the Ovidian text, which states that
"They had no go-between" (*conscius omnis abest* [v.63]), and there are
other significant intrusions, including the description of Thisbe, the
descriptions of nature, the epitaph, for example. The kernel events are
found in all versions of the tale, and the significant lexical borrowings
from Ovid are selected for their punning possibilities (*rima* = chink and
verse; *coctilibus muris* is decomposed to the alternative possibilities of
walls " de tierra cocidos" [brick] and "de tierra crudos" [adobe]). Salazar
Mardones notes that because Góngora

sigue la narracion de Ovidio, y algunas partes disienten della, me ha parecido
averiguar si es licita a los poetas la variacion, principalmente en las partes
menos considerables, y que mudadas no importan para la sustancia del caso,
como esta presente. (22v)

He later comments upon the amplification of details preceding Pyramus's death: "Notese como el texto finge este sucesso con mas color de
verdad que Ovidio" (139r).

The verses referring to Ovid are as follows:

> Píramo fueron y Tisbe
> los que en verso hizo culto
> el licenciado Nasón,

> bien romo o bien narigudo,
>   dejar el dulce candor
> lastimosamente oscuro,
> al que túmulo de seda
> fue de los dos casquilucios.
>
> (vv.17-24)

The passage is replete with word play on the word "nose": "Nasón" (both Publius Ovidius Naso and "large-nosed") is interwoven with "romo" (both "Roman" and "small-nosed"), which in turn is contrasted in its second meaning with "narigudo" ("pointed nose"). Ball is correct, I believe, in reading this as a self-reference to Góngora.[52] Góngora's nose is a topic of which Quevedo never tires as he spews forth his antisemitic tirades:

> En lo sucio que has cantado
> y en lo largo de narices,
> demás de que tú lo dices,
> que no eres limpio has mostrado.
>
> (III, #827, vv.1-4)

Other pleasantries include:

> ¿Por qué censuras tú la lengua griega
> siendo sólo rabí de la judía,
> cosa que tu nariz aun no lo niega?
>
> (III, #829, vv.9-11)

as well as "Tu nariz se ha juntado con el os" (meaning "mouth") (III, #837, v.9). The epithet "culto" had become synonymous with gongorism. In the tale the mulberry bush is transformed from white ("dulce candor") to red ("lastimosamente oscuro"); Góngora had been condemned for having "metamorphized" poetry from its pristine clarity to its contemporary mystification. The overlapping of readings here is indeed a masterful aesthetic achievement of Góngora.

It is he, Góngora, who creates a tale that is "lastimosamente oscuro," directed not against Ovid, whose difficulty he himself had praised on another occasion,[53] but against his enemies' misreadings and malice, as well as against the tradition of sentimental and saccharine "Hispanified" versions of Ovid's beautiful tale. Two distinct systems are interwoven in the poem—as language the poem is a parody of the myth of Pyramus and Thisbe, used and abused over the centuries; as metalanguage, infused with historical relevance, the poem questions the very concept of poetry. Góngora created a monster, whose hybrid nature makes Góngora once again an innovator. Its statement is aggressive and defiant, as is any very good joke.

This romantic tale of young love, infused with sentimental idealism, is not without its "gaps" of erotic suggestiveness and complications, which previous Spanish versions had perceived and skirted. In the eyes of the Spaniards, Thisbe, like Hero, lacks properly maidenly *pudicitia*. She succumbs too readily to Pyramus's demands, she arrives first at the "scene of the crime," and is in general too aggressive. Pyramus, on the other hand, arrives late, seems less resolute, and therefore is not properly virile. All Ovid says of Thisbe as she waits alone is that "Love made her bold" (*audacem faciebat amor* [v.96]); he presents no conjecture about the late arrival of Pyramus, who simply came out "a little later" (*serius egressus* [v.105]). Montemayor, as did Boscán, seeks to explain the suggestive silences of the text. He excuses her promptness:

> Tisbe fue más diligente,
> no por ser más la pasión,
> mas por sexo y condición
> do cabe naturalmente
> menos consideración.
>
> (vv.691-95)

Pyramus's situation is reported through indirect speech in multiple versions, without authorial certainty, but decidedly with authorial skepticism:

> Píramo diz que salió
> quando ella huyó del llano,
> y por creer que era temprano
> dizen que antes no partió,
> & otros que no fue en su mano.
>
> (vv.901-05)

Villegas also makes mention of the role reversal:

> Los dos de sus dos casas se salieron;
> y Tisbe, o porque pudo fue primera,
> o porque sus deseos la encendieron.
>
> (p. 40)

Her desire is such that even death does not cause it to cease:

> Y luego a todas partes le rodea;
> miraba aquellos miembros que, aunque estaban
> dañados de la muerte, los desea.
>
> (p. 45)

Such moralistic concerns regarding the characters are superimposed on the Ovidian text. There is, however, a suggestiveness inherent in the original text, for the end of the tale is fraught with sexual connotations within the symbolic framework of the loss of innocence through violence, caused by the appearance of the lion. As Charles Segal suggests:

> The symbolism of this landscape is in turn deepened by the more overt sexual symbolism of the torn and bloodied veil, the sword which wounds both lovers, the blood which shoots out from Pyramus' wound and changes the color of the berries. The simile in 121-24 which compares the spurting forth of Pyramus' blood to water from a burst pipe is perhaps the least subtle *double-entendre* in the poem. Ovid, here surely guilty of being *nimium amator ingeni sui*, cannot resist the temptation to exaggerate.[54]

Furthermore, the choice of the verbs *eiaculatur* (v.124) and *erexit* (v.146) cannot be overlooked [see *Fig. 1*].

These "gaps" in the Ovidian text (particularly the role reversal and double suicide) are insidiously exploited by Góngora. Appreciative of the erotic ambiguity of the tale, he intensifies these aspects instead of evading them, as did his predecessors, Montemayor and Villegas, for example. To the Ovid of the *Metamorphoses* he adds the urbane, unabashed sexual wit of the Ovid of the *Amores* and the *Ars amatoria*. Salazar Mardones notes that the periphrasis for Thisbe's body "El *etcaetera* es de mármol" (v.73) proceeds from Ovid (*Amores*, I.v.) who employed the word "por causa de la honestidad, y escusar la repeticion de palabras torpes" (35v). After describing Corinna's nude body, from which the tunic has been torn, Ovid asks *Cetera quis nescit? lassi requievimus ambo* (v.25) ("The rest, who does not know? Outwearied, we both lay quiet in repose"). The word is saturated with sexual meaning. Though grammatically different in Góngora, the spirit is the same, and the ironic evasion deliberately foregrounds the sexuality. Other details converge to strengthen the concept of Thisbe's sexuality. In the verses

> Luciente cristal lascivo,
> la tez, digo, de su vulto,
>
> (vv.53-54)

in spite of Salazar Mardones's protest that "lascivo" "aqui no vale lo que ordinariamente entre los Autores, torpe, deshonesto" (29r), the word does acquire precisely this meaning, and is used similarly in later verses referring to the "lascivos nudos" (v.304) of the elm tree. The seeming seriousness of the ideology implied in the clichés of "vergonzoso capullo" and "virgen rosa" (vv.274-75) is exploded by the authorial intervention ("¡trágica resolución,/digna de mayor coturno!" [vv.279-80]).

By tradition the lovers are young, but Góngora's groaning, lovesick Thisbe ("tórtola doncella/gemidora a lo viüdo" [vv.127-28]) seems more "mature"; she is even equipped, by intent or in error, with thirty-two teeth ("entre veinte perlas netas/doce aljófares menudos" [vv.63-64]), an excess sum reserved only for men (much to the distress of Salazar Mardones, whose erudite soul sought a source even for this!).[55] Pyramus, in contrast, is presented as very young, a Cupid without wings (vv.103-04), compared hesitatingly to the self-loving Narcissus (v.105) and then the beautiful Adonis (v.109), disparaged with diminutives ("joveneto" [v.102]), and later insulted with *portmanteau* creations ("protonecio" [v.339]), "Piramiburro" [v.340]). The net effect of his youthfulness and his Hispanified fashionable coiffure ("que traía las orejas/en las jaulas

Fig. 1. "Pyramus and Thisbe." *Las transformaciones,* trans. Jorge de Bustamante (Anvers, Pedro Bellero, 1595). *The Hispanic Society of America.*

de dos tufos" [vv.111-12]) is an ambiguous effeminacy ("sus mejillas mucho raso,/su bozo poco velludo" [vv.115-16]). As noted by Alicia Galaz Vivar in her edition, "Según Covarrubias, el uso del copete constituía un signo de afeminamiento; lo mismo el uso de guedejas, tufos, bufos, etc."[56] It is a fashion adopted by men, Covarrubias regrets, "Por nuestros pecados." This does not, however, impede his potency.

Salacious punning references to the male organ and sexual intercourse prepare the way for the final transformation of the sentimental "union in death" motif to an ironic one of sexual consummation ("« . . . a pesar del Amor, dos,/a pesar del número, uno»" [vv.507-08]). Salazar Mardones did not need Freud to comprehend the symbolism of Pyramus's "weapon," for he comments that "Con bien poco cuidado se alcançara lo lascivo desta copla en aquel verso, *con su herramienta al uso*" [in v. 124] (50v), to which may be added a similar allusion in the following verses:

> ¡Cuántas veces impaciente
> metió el brazo, que no cupo,
> el garzón, y lo atentado
> lo revocaron por nulo!
>
> (vv.261-64)

It is only at the end, when Thisbe joins him in death on the same literal sword, that consummation occurs ("se caló en la espada/aquella vez que le cupo" [vv.463-64]). Montemayor too, unlike Ovid, had the lovers die impaled together on the same sword:

> En la punta de la espada
> que a su Píramo sobró,
> luego al punto se arrojó,
> y su sangre misturada
> con la dél también salió,
>
> (vv.1231-35)

which the anonymous *romance* develops in its description of Thisbe:

> Puso a el coraçón la punta
> y echóse sobre él de pechos:
> lo que no estuvieron vivos
> estuvieron quando muertos,
>
> donde parecía la fuente
> puesto de bodegonero,

en un asador de carne
macho y hembra por lo menos.[57]

Góngora adopts not only the culinary metaphor of the roasting meat, but also the erotic connotations of the impalement.

In another potentially tender moment of the final death scene, when Thisbe offers her lap to her bleeding lover, another covert obscenity is presented in the guise of a learned allusion. The verses are as follows:

Ofrecióle su regazo,
y yo le ofrezco en su muslo
desplumadas las delicias
del pájaro de Catulo.

(vv.449-52)

The reference is to Catullus's poem "Passer, deliciae meae puellae" (I.2), a playful, lascivious description of Lesbia playing with her nipping sparrow, which Salazar Mardones explains by means of a Latin quotation to mitigate the impact of the obscenity:

El pajaro de Catulo es el gorrion, que en Latin llaman *Passer*, por la salacidad de este avecilla. Y assi dixo Festo. *Strutheum in Mimis praecipue vocant obscenam partem virilem, a salacitate videlicet passeris.* . . . (Especially in mimes they call the obscene male member sparrow-like, no doubt from the sexual aggressiveness of the sparrow.)

He adds that "que passarla en silencio fuera mayor acierto, lo qual he dexado de hazer, porque algunos no piensen que no entendi la mente de Don Luis," including another quote from Martial (II.7) (164v).

The subtext of obscenity is introduced in the framing verses of the poem, in the seemingly bland repetition of the cliché metaphor of the poet and his musical instrument:

si al brazo de mi instrumento
le solicitas el pulso,
    digno sujeto será
de las orejas del vulgo.

(vv.11-14)

As Ball has observed, the term "instrumento" is used with an explicitly sexual meaning in a poem about a mulatto poet, "A un poeta llamado Roa . . . ":

> Y al moreno de cara, y de instrumento,
> si rabiare, de lejos le saluda,
> si ya no quieres que tus huesos Roa.
>
> (LXIX ¿a. 1617?)[58]

Once again, Catullus is Góngora's master in salacious wit, in the verses in which he chides the lascivious Aurelius for not being a "chaste" guardian to Catullus's young man:

> *frustra: nam insidias mihi instruentem*
> *tangam te prior irrumatione.*
>
> (21.7-8)

("No use: I'll gag you with my tool/before you make me play the fool" or "But they won't work: for all your treachery,/I'll screw you first.")[59]

It is this *double entendre* that Góngora insidiously exploits throughout the *Fábula*, so unabashedly vulgar at times, indeed quite suited to the "vulgo" whom he pretends to be addressing. Aggressively sexual, its meaning is masked in the *culterano* language. Ironically, then, the "vulgo" could not understand the vulgarity, only the learned! Góngora, the "swan," addresses his pretentious "learned" censors as vile "geese," and the laugh is finally on them. Salazar Mardones, inadvertently perhaps, notes this stylistic disguise: "tal vez se dexo llevar de alguna deshonestidad, si bien paliada, y abscondida con palabras que no parecen torpes" (50v).

The disconcerting stylistic disharmony is, therefore, more apparent than real, for Góngora's self-conscious manipulation of exaggerated, indeed strained *culterano* excesses is ironic. In a poem of comic detachment and literary playfulness, Góngora, supreme master of his craft, uses his own creation, his *gongorismo*, as his weapon of annihilation. The poet, as parodist, has torn away from the tale its obfuscating veils of sentimental excess with which his predecessors had adorned it. The irony requires of the readers a "subtractive" reading, in order to bring about the "powerful shock of negative recognition" that enables them to realize that the preciosity conceals a much baser metal (appropriate, however, for these baser "heroes").[60] Jáuregui would easily encounter here the "materia pícara i disoluta" for which he criticized Góngora in his "light" poems—so inappropriate, he added, for an ecclesiastic![61]

Góngora is not suffering from literary *desengaño*; he is relishing his own genius. His delight in developing Ovid's innuendos is manifest; equally manifest is the creative stylistic exuberance, so intricately deceptive, with which he responds to the critics of his craft.

Notes

1 In *Mythology and the Renaissance Tradition in English Poetry*, p. 18, from the *Metamorphosis Ovidiana moraliter explanata* (Paris, 1509), fol. xxxvi by Petrus Berchorius. The *Ovide Moralisé en prose* also relates the tale to the Passion of Christ (pp. 137-38).

2 "Anotaciones" in *Las transformaciones*, p. 80r.

3 *Obras*, p. 183.

4 Ibid., p. 192 (stanza 24).

5 *Fábulas mitológicas*, p. 116.

6 Quoted in Testa, "The Pyramus and Thisbe Theme in 16th and 17th Century Spanish Poetry," p. 30 from the text in *Poesías*, ed. Antonio Marín Ocete (Granada, 1939), pp. 204-37.

7 Ife, *Dos versiones de Píramo y Tisbe*, pp. VI and VII, seriously doubts this attribution to Montemayor.

8 *Fábulas mitológicas*, p. 226.

9 See "Bibliografía de la *Diana*," in Jorge de Montemayor, *Los siete libros de la Diana*, ed. Francisco López Estrada, 3d ed. (Madrid: Espasa-Calpe, 1962), pp. LXXXVII-XCVII.

10 Robert Jammes, "Notes sur *La fábula de Píramo y Tisbe* de Góngora," *Les Langues Néo-Latines*, no. 156 (1961), p. 43. This *romance* (MS. 4117, fol. 118v of the B.N.M.) is included as an appendix, pp. 43-46. The *romances* on the subject are mentioned by Ball, pp. 533-36, and include Lorenzo de Sepúlveda's *romance historial*, "En la grande Babilonia" (publ. 1550) and a very popular ballad, "Tisbe y Píramo que fueron/leales enamorados," which appeared in the *Silva recopilada* of 1561, the *Flor de enamorados* of 1562, and in Timoneda's *Rosa de amores* of 1573. These appear reprinted in Agustín Durán, *Romancero general, o colección de romances castellanos anteriores al Siglo XVIII*, in the *BAE*, vol. 10 (rpt. Madrid: Atlas, 1945), nos. 465 and 464 respectively. In addition, Moncayo's first *Flor* (1589) includes another short *romance*. No *romances* on this theme appear in the *Romancero general* of 1600, though topical allusions continue.

11 Noted by Ball, pp. 542-44.

12 Testa, "The Pyramus and Thisbe Theme," writes of Thisbe's leading role that "It is perhaps in this area where Montemayor shows greatest innovation," (p. 67). Ife, "Dos versiones de Píramo y Tisbe," also points out "la inversión de lo masculino y lo femenino que hemos encontrado en el papel dominante de Tisbe y el dominado de Píramo" (p. XLI).

13 For a discussion of "anti-Petrarchism" see Leonard Forster, *The Icy Fire. Five Studies in European Petrarchism* (Cambridge: Cambridge University Press, 1969), pp. 56-58. Examples include Shakespeare's sonnet "My mistress' eyes are nothing like the sun," as well as the pictorial parody, "La belle Charite" in Charles Sorel's *Le berger extravagant* (1627). Forster does not consider this current a serious rejection of Petrarchism, which will not occur until the eighteenth century with its firm espousal of rationalism.

14 Fernando Lázaro Carreter, "Situación de la *Fábula de Píramo y Tisbe*," *NRFH*, 15 (1961) dismisses this first attempt: "Lo que va obteniendo resulta poco intenso: una docena de coplas transparentes, ni cómicas ni graves, sólo pálidamente ingeniosas. Góngora alzó la pluma, y dejó su intento para mejor

ocasión" (pp. 471-72). This opinion is probably due to his having read Thisbe's portrait "seriously," rather than ironically.

15 As quoted in the *OC*, p. 1110, n.55.

16 From the preface to his *Ilustración y defensa de la Fábula de Píramo y Tisbe* (1636) in the ed. of A. Rumeau, *"Píramo y Tisbe," con los comentarios de Salazar Mardones* (Paris: Ediciones Hispano-Americanas, 1961).

17 Quoted from *Lecciones Solemnes*, col. 775 in Dámaso Alonso, *La lengua poética de Góngora*, parte primera *RFE*, Anejo XX, 3d ed. (Madrid: C.S.I.C., 1961), p. 18, n.1.

18 "An Interpretation of Góngora's *Fábula de Píramo y Tisbe*," *BHS*, 33 (1956), 207.

19 "Notes sur *La fábula de Píramo y Tisbe* de Góngora," p. 41.

20 Elements of self-parody have been observed by other critics: Alonso, *La lengua poética de Góngora*, p. 143 and *Góngora y el "Polifemo,"* I, 6th ed. (Madrid: Gredos, 1974), pp. 110, 163. Arthur Terry, "An Interpretation of Góngora's *Fábula de Píramo y Tisbe*," 207-08; Pamela Waley, "Enfoque y medios humorísticos de la *Fábula de Píramo y Tisbe*," *RFE*, 44 (1961), 386, 395, 397; Guillermo Araya, "Shakespeare y Góngora parodian la *Fábula de Píramo y Tisbe*," *Estudios Filológicos*, no. 1: *En homenaje a Eleazar Huerta* (Valdivia: Facultad de Filosofía y Letras de la Universidad Austral de Chile, 1965), 32-33.

21 *Fábulas mitológicas*, p. 527.

22 "Discursos apologéticos," in *Documentos gongorinos*, ed. Eunice Joiner Gates (México: Colegio de México, 1960), p. 35.

23 In the "Epistolario" of the *OC*, "Carta de Don Luis de Góngora, en respuesta de la que le escribieron" (¿Septiembre de 1613 o de 1614?), p. 895.

24 Ibid., "Carta de un amigo de Don Luis de Góngora que le escribió acerca de sus 'Soledades' " (¿Septiembre de 1613 o de 1614?), p. 1093. Emilio Orozco Díaz, *Lope y Góngora frente a frente* (Madrid: Gredos, 1973), attributes the letter without a doubt to Lope, and dates it the 13th of September, 1615 (pp. 172-77). He corrects the date of Góngora's "Carta en respuesta" to the 30th of September, 1615 (p. 179).

25 Alonso, *Góngora y el "Polifemo,"* I, chap. XI, especially pp. 231-43.

26 "Góngora's Parodies of Literary Convention," pp. 582-86, quote on p. 570. Beverley, *Aspects of Góngora's "Soledades,"* considers this "suspended ending" an intended effect on the part of the poet (p. 105), the result of which is to emphasize the figure of the pilgrim as "a form of homelessness" (p. 106).

27 "Exposition universelle de 1855," I, in *Curiosités esthétiques*, ed. M. Jacques Crépet (Paris: Louis Conard, 1923), p. 223.

28 Quoted in A. Rumeau's edition of the *Ilustración y defensa . . .* from *Poetas líricos de los Siglos XVI y XVII*, ed. Adolfo de Castro, *BAE*, vol. 32 (Madrid: Rivadenyera, 1884), p. 524. In the *OC*, p. 1112, the third verse "en lo largo la ciudad" is omitted.

29 Ibid., (64v).

30 "Notes sur la *Fábula de Píramo y Tisbe*," p. 42. His opinion is determined by his "serious" reading of key passages, which leads him to believe that "Góngora, au fond, n'enlaidit rien, ou presque rien: Thisbé est belle, indéniablement, et Pyrame aussi, et le récit de leurs amours est finalement très attachant, de sorte que leur mort ne nous fait pas rire" (p. 40 n.*d*). Even P. Waley, "Enfoque y medios humorísticos de la *Fábula de Píramo y Tisbe*," who disagrees with Jammes's interpretation, considers Góngora's attitude towards these "heroes"

ambiguous: "En sí mismos los amantes no son cómicos, no son necesariamente risibles, sino que son seres con emociones, anhelos, recelos humanos. Pero se comportan de una manera que el poeta condena como tonta" (p. 388).

31 In "An Interpretation of Góngora's *Fábula de Píramo y Tisbe*," p. 216. Terry applies to Góngora the phrase used by C. S. Lewis to describe English metaphysical poetry, in *English Literature in the Sixteenth Century, Excluding Drama* (Oxford, 1954), p. 543. Lázaro Carreter, "Situación de la *Fábula de Píramo y Tisbe*," also makes this point: "Lo conceptista 'llano' se mezcla con su hallazgo de lo conceptista 'culto', y lo vulgar − voces triviales y rudas − se alía con quintaesencias léxicas, en turbadora y cómica confusión" (p. 482).

32 In the "Epistolario" of the *OC*, "Carta de Pedro de Valencia escrita a Don Luis de Góngora en censura de sus poesías," (30 junio 1613), pp. 1086 and 1087 respectively. Juan de Jáuregui in his *Antídoto contra la pestilente poesía de las "Soledades*," designates the mixture of styles as "desigualdad perruna," p. 99 in Gates's *Documentos gongorinos*.

33 Ibid., pp. 1086 and 1087 respectively.

34 *La lengua poética de Góngora*, I, p. 30, n.3 (cont.).

35 Ibid. See for example, "Resumen general," pp. 218-20.

36 "The Correlations of Tense in the French Verb," in *Problems in General Linguistics*, pp. 205-15.

37 See Ball's discussion, pp. 572-79 in "Góngora's Parodies of Literary Convention." Lázaro Carreter, "Situación de la *Fábula de Píramo y Tisbe*," notes that Salazar Mardones "No ha entendido el sarcasmo de eregir Babilonia − símbolo de todo lo vituperable y confuso − en tema digno del vulgo, y de solicitar disculpa a cuantos se amparan en él para combatirle" (p. 480).

38 "Carta de un amigo de Don Luis de Góngora que le escribió acerca de sus 'Soledades', " p. 1092 in the "Epistolario" of the *OC*.

39 For example, Góngora refers to Valladolid in the final stanza as "Todo se halla en esta Babilonia" (MG 275). Ball, pp. 576-77, lists references in Lope: "Hermosa Babilonia, en que he nacido/para fábula tuya tantos años"; "Cantar no puedo en Babilonia bella"; "Dejé, señor, la Babilonia ciega/de aquesa confusión confusa y varia" (Quoted from Américo Castro and Hugo A. Rennert, *Vida de Lope de Vega (1562-1635)* (Salamanca: Anaya, 1969), pp. 45, 46, 47, respectively. Also "¡Oh Babilonia, formada/de lenguajes tan diversos" (Quoted from José F. Montesinos "Notas sobre algunas poesías de Lope de Vega" (1926) in *Estudios sobre Lope*, rev. ed. (Salamanca: Anaya, 1969), p. 225, n.24. Quevedo's "Receta para hacer Soledades en un día" terminates: "Que ya toda Castilla,/con sola esta cartilla,/se abrasa de poetas babilones,/escribiendo sonetos confusiones" (III, #825).

40 In the *Obras completas*, ed. Arturo del Hoyo, 3d ed. (Madrid: Aguilar, 1967). These moral-allegorical implications are also apparent in the statement that the evil Falimundo presides over "la Babilonia, que no corte" (I, *crisi*, VIII, 592).

41 "Ligustre" appears in Alonso's list of "Censuras anticultistas," *La lengua poética de Góngora*, p. 103.

42 Alonso, *Góngora y el "Polifemo*," I, discussing the "A, si no B" formula and its variations, states that "Una de las características del estilo de Góngora, que es al mismo tiempo uno de sus defectos principales, es la tendencia a la repetición de las mismas fórmulas sintácticas" (p. 156). Jáuregui was also quick to criticize this in his *Antídoto*: "El *si* i el *no* de que estamos ya todos tan cansados i

ahitos, no es tan malo quanto mal usado de Vm.," p. 111, sec. 24 in Gates's *Documentos gongorinos.* Quevedo parodies the "si/no" in his *Aguja de navegar cultos,* pp. 764-65 in the *Obras completas en prosa,* ed. Luis Astrana Marín (Madrid: Aguilar, 1945).

43 Jammes, "Notes sur la *Fábula de Píramo y Tisbe*," concurs with Salazar Mardones's suppositions (p. 25) that it refers to his own obscurity or, more likely, to Lope; in her edition, Alicia Galaz Vivar (*Romances, Letrillas, Sonetos y Canciones. Fragmento de la Soledad Primera* [Santiago de Chile: Editorial Universitaria, 1961]) cites Eunice Joiner Gates's indication of Lope (p. 115); Guilllermo Araya "Shakespeare y Góngora parodian la *Fábula de Píramo y Tisbe*," differs, stating that "se trata de una autoalusión irónica o satírica" (p. 33); Ball pinpoints Lope as the target (p. 618).

44 Quoted from the edition of Ife, *Dos versiones de "Píramo y Tisbe."*

45 Text of the poem "Historia de Píramo y Tisbe" appears in the *Inventario,* ed. Francisco López Estrada, II (Madrid: La Gelindense, 1956), p. 25. Subsequent references are to this edition and will be incorporated in the text.

46 As translated by Paul Alpers, *The Singer of the "Eclogues"* (Berkeley and Los Angeles: University of California Press, 1979), p. 55. Varius and Cinna were prominent poets, contemporaries of Virgil, and *Anser* may be a punning reference to another poet. See the commentary of Robert Coleman, *Vergil: Eclogues* (Cambridge: Cambridge University Press, 1977), p. 264. For the *topos* of the swan and its association with Apollo and the Muses, see p. 262, n.29.

47 "Situación de la *Fábula de Píramo y Tisbe*," p. 481.

48 *Obras escogidas,* ed. Federico Carlos Sainz de Robles, II (Madrid: Aguilar, 1946), p. 1518. The "Respuesta" is discussed by Emilio Orozco Díaz, *Lope y Góngora frente a frente,* pp. 294-311, and the sonnet "Canta, cisne andaluz, que el verde coro" on pp. 164-66.

49 Jammes, "Notes sur la *Fábula de Píramo y Tisbe*," p. 43.

50 *Obras escogidas,* II, p. 1442.

51 Araya, "Shakespeare y Góngora parodian la *Fábula de Píramo y Tisbe*," p. 30.

52 "Góngora's Parodies of Literary Convention," pp. 606-07.

53 "Epistolario," *OC,* "Carta de Don Luis de Góngora en respuesta de la que le escribieron," p. 896.

54 *Landscape in Ovid's "Metamorphoses": A Study in the Transformations of a Literary Symbol* (Wiesbaden: Franz Steiner Verlag, 1969), p. 50.

55 Discussed by Jammes, "Notes sur la *Fábula de Píramo y Tisbe*," p. 19, n.16.

56 *Romances, Letrillas,* p. 111.

57 In Jammes, "Notes sur la *Fábula de Píramo y Tisbe*," p. 46.

58 "Góngora's Parodies of Literary Convention," pp. 593-95.

59 From *Odi et Amo. The Complete Poems of Catullus,* trans. Roy Arthur Swanson (Indianapolis: Bobbs-Merrill, 1959) and from *Catullus,* trans. Reney Myers and Robert J. Ormsby (London: George Allen and Unwin Ltd., 1972) respectively. The Loeb edition, trans. F. W. Cornish (1913; rpt. Cambridge: Harvard University Press; London: William Heinemann Ltd., 1976) offers the more modest "All in vain: as you plot against me, I'll have at you first." Just as a point of interest, Góngora's reference to the underarm odor of the go-between in the verses beginning "Abrazóle sobacada" is also of Catullan inspiration (Poems 69; 71). This specific portion of the poem is discussed by Lázaro Carre-

ter, "Dificultades en la *Fábula de Píramo y Tisbe*," in *Estilo barroco y personalidad creadora* (Salamanca: Anaya, 1966), pp. 105-07.

60 Quotations from Wayne Booth, *A Rhetoric of Irony* (Chicago and London: University of Chicago Press, 1974), p. 40, n.4 and p. 22, n.16. He describes the "reconstruction" necessary for the correct reading of irony (discussed especially in the first two chapters).

61 In the *Antídoto*, p. 139 in Gates's *Documentos gongorinos*.

III Quevedo

Quevedo, too, writes burlesque poems of mythological themes. The difference in "tone" between the parodic *romances* of Góngora and of Quevedo is manifest. Quevedo's *romancillo* "Hero y Leandro en paños menores" (III, #771), for instance, has been characterized as "quizá la más cruel y sangrienta de cuantas contrahechuras burlescas se han escrito de las fábulas mitológicas."[1] Góngora's versions, as we have seen, rich in metaphoric elaboration, have been adjudged to have a mixed and contradictory tone that points to a new aesthetic of parody, granting greater stature to a genre traditionally held in low esteem.[2] A closer analysis reveals a radical difference in their intertextual nature, a difference that affects the imagery and therefore the "tone."

In a larger sense, the difference in these poems corresponds to the opposing literary interests and intentions of their authors. Góngora's aesthetic delight in classical poetry, particularly Ovid, permits him an increasingly deeper appreciation of the irony, eroticism, and innuendo inherent in the classical texts.[3] Quevedo, on the other hand, remains largely unimpressed by these qualities, appearing to share Quintilian's view of Ovid as somewhat frivolous (*Institutio oratoria*). The Olympian gods of *La hora de todos y la fortuna con seso* are a motley lot, worthy only of derision and scorn. His contempt of these frolicsome deities, enterprising only in their sexual antics involving grotesque transformations into bulls and swans and cows, among other things, is clearly evidenced in the sarcastic mythological examples of the *romance* "Anilla, dame atención" (II, #682). Quevedo's troubled spirit inclines him rather toward Epictetus and Seneca.[4]

Quevedo's longest mythological burlesque, "Hero y Leandro en paños menores" (III, #771), is marked for negative parodic conversion in the very title, perhaps to distinguish it from his earlier compositions, a sonnet, "Describe a Leandro fluctuante en el mar" (I, #311), and a *romance*, "Hero y Leandro" (I, #210), which Cossío considers "aún más de un tanto afectado y artificioso."[5] If we compare Quevedo's parody to Góngora's on the same theme using the distinction made by Cervantes in the *Coloquio de los perros*, we may conclude that Góngora treated these star-crossed lovers with "un poco de luz"; Quevedo, on the other hand, chose the path of "sangre," not heeding the counsel to the narrator regarding satire: "quiero decir que señales, y no hieras ni des mate a ninguno en cosa señalada."[6] The result is that the comic detachment of Góngora turns into deadly serious excoriation.

Alatorre's conviction that Quevedo's *romancillo* postdates both of Góngora's poems generally has been taken for granted.[7] Though in no way vital to the appreciation of the poem, I would like to suggest that, while there is textual evidence that Góngora's earlier *romance* was known to Quevedo (particularly as seen in the development of the egg *chiste*), there is no convincing evidence to assume knowledge of the later poem. In contrast to the 1610 version, but in keeping with the 1589 poem as well as with the *romance* tradition in general, Quevedo deals exclusively with the final sequence of the tale, and even echoes some verses of the extant *romances*: Quevedo's vision of the distraught heroine "y por él se arranca/todos los cabellos,/y se mete a calva" (vv. 122-24) recalls the lines "Mesándose sus cabellos,/la torre abajo se ha echado";[8] the pun on "nada"/"nadar" in the verses "Mas pues todo amores/fue ese pecho y nada,/a nadar contigo/este mío vaya" (vv. 137-39) is anticipated in the verses "y entre ellas el triste amante/nada y nada . . . , es todo *nada*."[9] In sharp contrast to Góngora's second poem, there is no indication whatsoever of Boscán's text as a model, nor is any one of the numerous *romance* progeny of this prolific translation cited in particular. Quevedo reveals his literary model only at the end— "aunque más jarifa/Museo la canta" (vv. 183-84)—but this model is inoperative and remains external to the production of his own poem. He mentions his model but to reject it; he himself assumes an unequivocal position of authority ("La verdad es ésta,/que no es patarata" [vv. 181-82]).

Quevedo's narrative stance is different: Góngora assumes a distanced, mock-epic pose and describes the actions in the preterite, maintaining a constant awareness that their only reality is a literary one, as filtered through "las obras de Boscán"; Quevedo, on the other hand, assumes the lyrical stance of a speaker, an "I" directly addressing a "you" (Leander), and presents a vivid discourse, or diatribe, in the present tense. He is the mocking witness to Leander's dramatic performance of drowning, which at the end he applauds—"No habrá habido ahogado/que mejor lo haga,/ni con menos gestos,/ni con mayor gracia" (vv. 117-19). The result of this narrative stance is paradoxical. Although Quevedo's poem is structured, at least potentially, as dramatic discourse where an "I" addresses a "you," it is in essence an authorial monologue. In contrast to this, the result of Góngora's narrative stance is dialogical, as Boscán's "history" is counterposed to Góngora's own rewriting.

In Góngora's poem (especially the 1610 version), many features of the Boscán translation/amplification are incorporated in the new text, placed in ironic juxtaposition or negated through reversal of meaning. Góngora's imagery is thus deliberately derived from his model. Although Quevedo does incorporate some of the images found in the preexistent versions, he develops them in a surprisingly autonomous fashion. For example, the motif of the lover as boat, present in Musaeus ("His own oarsman, his own escort, himself his ship" [v. 255]) and in the multiple subsequent versions, is also included in Quevedo's poem, "de bajel se zarpa" (v. 6). However, this omnipresent traditional metaphor is immediately disarticulated, and by means of an associative process based not on semantic likeness but on their presumed contiguity in a liquid habitat, Leander, already a boat, is then called a "rana" (v. 8) and a "pescado" (v. 9). This, in turn, begins a new associative chain as Leander, this creature from the sea, is named an "hijo de cabra" (v. 10), which in its literal sense develops the previous animal categorization, and in its figurative sense of "rana" as prostitute adds to the pejorative transformation of the tale. Thus, too, Quevedo makes mention of Hero's famous burning lamp, but develops his specification of "mecha" in two senses (vv. 61-64): as the expected "candle wick" and then as the unexpected "bandage," which leads naturally to the mention of Leander's "llagas," caused, one assumes, by syphilis. These polysemous words and subversive associations occur at such a dizzying, as well as dazzling pace, that the reader is hard pressed to follow them, but they do have their logic, or their rhetorical pseudologic at least.

Góngora's conversion of Hero into a "Maritornes" figure, as Alatorre so aptly phrased it,[10] by means of the deliberate reversal of all the positive connotations of this figure — her beauty, chastity, loyalty — into their antonyms, is a predictable parodic procedure. The unusual effect of a "frenesí de destrucción"[11] is caused by a saturation of ironic reversals within the text itself, by a continuous series of puns veering toward Gracián's "corrección irónica."[12] Words and phrases lose semantic stability in this *danse macabre* of linguistic auto-destruction. For example, Quevedo's use of the cliché Petrarchan metaphor for Hero, "una perla toda," undergoes semantic displacement through contextual proximity to the verb "ensartar," in the verses "una perla toda,/que a menudo ensartan" (vv. 19-20). As mediated through the set metaphorical phrase "ensartar perlas" meaning "to cry," both substitutions for "perla," Hero and tears, are conflated, producing the new, surprising, and obviously sexual meaning for the phrase "ensartar a Hero." Similarly, in the zeugma "derribada de hombros,/pero más de espaldas" (vv. 39-40) the textual proximity of the adjectival sense of "derribar" ("Dícese de las ancas de una caballería cuando por el extremo son algo más bajas de lo regular") to the verbal sense ("Tirarse a tierra, echarse al suelo," *Dic. de la lengua española*) creates a surprising, and effective, sexual innuendo.

Quevedo's parody is not textual, but linguistic.[13] His poem is, therefore, not a parody, but rather a satire. His wit is a searing instrument against deception, against the "jarifa" of the myth as developed poetically through the ages. In command of the truth ("La verdad es ésta"), Quevedo views his plain diction and vulgar language as antidotes against the rhetorical ills of the past. His reduction of romance to vulgarity by means of obscenity is fully consistent with this satirical intent: "The author of satire always portrays the grotesque and distorted, and concentrates to an obsessive degree on the flesh."[14]

Another of Quevedo's burlesque series, "A Apolo siguiendo a Dafne" (II, #536) and "A Dafne, huyendo de Apolo" (II, #537) reveals a similar satiric, rather than parodic, process.[15] Once again, the negative transformation is accomplished by means of a displacement of emphasis, as Quevedo concentrates on the flesh, or lust.

With this tale we enter fully into the world of the fabulous, where, freed from logical restraints, miraculous transformations occur. Thus Ovid announces his project in the opening of Book I of the *Metamorphoses*: "My mind is bent to tell of bodies changed into new forms" (*In nova fert animus mutatas dicere formas/corpora*). The first tale of love is that of Apollo and Daphne, caused not by chance, but by "the malicious wrath of Cupid" (*sed saeva Cupidinis ira* [I. 453]), whom Apollo had insulted by addressing him as a mere "wanton boy" (*lascive puer* [I. 456]), unfit to bear manly arms. The victimization of Apollo is inherently comic, for here we see the great warrior, still relishing his conquest of the awful Python, deflated to the status of a forlorn lover, smitten with the golden dart of love. His visible desire and pathetic pleas are of no avail, for Daphne, smitten with Cupid's lead dart, covets only perpetual virginity, disdaining all lovers. After all, writes Brooks Otis, the gods are incongruous as lovers, with the result that:

The majesty of the gods and of the epic code of behavior, and of the epic style itself, is now subjected to the unbearable strain of the ridiculous. Even the effort to maintain it increases the comedy, the classic comedy of the pompous deflated and abased.[16]

The description of the metamorphic process is particularly vivid in Ovid's account and exudes a pervasive sensuality.[17] Even as a tree,

Daphne continues to be an object of erotic attraction; Apollo "embraced the branches as if human limbs, and pressed his lips upon the wood" (*conplexusque suis ramos ut membra lacertis/oscula dat ligno* [I. 555-56]). There is indeed a disturbing quality in the transformation, at once fascinating and repelling, for a grotesque image is created, resulting from the "fusion of incompatible elements from mutually exclusive kingdoms of the physical world,"[18] here a tree-woman, or woman-tree.

Garcilaso's Sonnet XIII, "A Dafne ya los brazos le crecían/y en luengos ramos vueltos se mostraban," describes only the portions from the *Metamorphoses* pertaining to the transformation of Daphne into a laurel, excluding such elements as the vengeance of Cupid, the ludicrous chase, or the subsequent continuing love of Apollo for his tree. The pictorial plastic vividness of the sonnet, which Herrera praised for its "perspicuidad"[19] and Rafael Lapesa for its "extraordinario poder de representación vital . . . acaso inspirada en alguna pintura,"[20] may indeed have been inspired by the typical drawings of the popular "illustrated Ovids," where this climactic moment of transformation was included in the illustrations. The violence perpetrated upon the body is pictorially dramatic, as seen in this engraving portraying the Daphne and Apollo myth in an early edition of the *Metamorphoses*: Quevedo

Fig. 2. "Daphne and Apollo." Ovid. *Metamorphoses* (Venice, Georgius de Rusconibus, 1517). *Rare Books and Manuscript Library, Columbia University.*

himself had written a presumably early poem in *quintillas*, "De Dafne y Apolo" (I, #209) which includes a description of the metamorphosis rendered in graceful conceits, based on rather standard visual metaphorical associations, as evidenced in the stanza:

De la rubia cabellera
que floreció tantos mayos,
antes que se convirtiera,
hebras tomó el Sol por rayos,
con que hoy alumbra la esfera.

(vv. 81-85)

In the later burlesque series, as in the poem of Hero and Leander,
Quevedo's narrative stance is that of a dramatic monologue in which he
addresses the figures, his "victims," directly, thereby divorcing them
completely from their literary matrix. In characteristic fashion, he
ignores the pictorial plastic qualities emphasized by Garcilaso, restricting the actual metamorphosis to a mere final mention—"y en cortezas
duras/de laurel se ingirió contra sus tretas" (#537, vv. 12-13). Instead,
the poem is dedicated to the inherently comic human drama, the chase.
But, while the Ovidian text stresses the theme of hopeless love or
desire, saying of Apollo "so was the god consumed with flames, so did
he burn in all his heart, and feed his fruitless love on hope" (*sic deus in
flammas abiit, sic pectore toto/uritur et sterilem sperando nutrit amorem* [I.
495-96]), Quevedo's text reverses this tragicomic code to a negative one
of prostitution—"si la quieres gozar, paga y no alumbres" (#536, v. 4), he
mockingly advises Apollo.

Quevedo's satiric conversion entails a negativization of the sun's connotative marker, "golden." If in the "serious" poem this is a characteristic shared with Daphne's blond hair ("rubia cabellera"), in the burlesque
version it will be semically related to money, also marked characteristi-
cally as "golden." Once the field of identification has been changed, all
the traditionally positive connotations of the marker, typical of the Renaissance ideology, suffer a conversion to a negative code of venality,
cynical and contemporary. Thus the classical "ninfa" is debased to yet
another "daifa" among the many who inhabit Quevedo's literary world
and exacerbate his misogynistic tendencies, inherited from his Latin
mentors in satiric verse, Juvenal and Martial.[21]

As at the lexical level Quevedo uses semic identity to create a conceit, so at the conceptual level he seeks correlations based on shared
semantic markers. In mock-imitation of the oratorical technique of
emphasis through examples, he argues by analogy to the Ovidian tales
of Mars and Jupiter, both of whom share at least one connotation in
common, that of "lust." The selection entails not Mars as god of war,
but Mars as the ridiculed lover of Venus, whom the wily Vulcan
ensnared in a finely spun web and exposed to all *flagrante delicto*,
whereupon "The gods laughed, and for a long time this story was the

talk of heaven" (*superi risere, diuque/haec fuit in toto notissima fabula caelo* [IV.188-89]).

Jupiter is not here the highest of the gods, wielder of the mighty thunderbolt, but the erotic, wife-deceiving master of many disguises (as a bull, a swan, a flame, a snake, etc.), among which was his consummation with Danaë in the guise of a golden shower, from which she bore a son, Perseus (*quem pluvio Danae conceperat auro* [IV.611]). By a simple shift in functional categorization, from "golden" as an adjective to "gold" as a noun ("golden shower" vs. "shower of gold"), and a swift synecdochic substitution of name of material for thing made (money is made of gold), Quevedo produces the highly relevant punning phrase "lluvia de dinero" (#536, v. 11) to describe this particular exploit of the lusty god. He thus echoes here not the Ovid of the *Metamorphoses*, but rather the Ovid of the *Ars amatoria*, who cynically disarticulates the *topos* of the "golden age" by reminding the hopeful lover that "Now truly is the age of gold" (*Aurea sunt vere nunc saecula* [II. 277]).[22] In Quevedo's own words, "Poderoso caballero es don Dinero" (II, #660)!

The address to Daphne (#537) is based on a breakdown of literary clichés. In the "serious" version (I, #209), the typical Renaissance hyperbole is developed regarding Daphne's beauty – more radiant than that of the Sun itself – which culminates in a conceit of paradox:

> Si el sol y luz aborreces,
> huye tú misma de ti.
>
> (vv. 44-45)

In the burlesque poem, on the other hand, the negative reversal of this conceit occurs, as Daphne's flight from the Sun reduces her to the status of a nocturnal bat:

> Vos os volvéis murciégalo sin duda,
> pues vais del Sol y de la luz huyendo.
>
> (vv. 3-4)

The final paradox of the poem, "el Sol se quedó a escuras" (v. 14), is but a continuation of the verbal gymnastics surrounding the careworn light/dark antithesis of the Petrarchan code.

Once again, the vulgarity of the chase and its meretricious implications are stressed, particularly in the description of Apollo:

> su aljaba suena, está su bolsa muda;
> el perro, pues no ladra, está muriendo,
>
> (vv. 7-8)

where the latter verse disarticulates the expression "dar perro muerto" ("Hacer alguna burla o engaño bastante pesado, como ofrecer dinero y no darlo," *Dic. de la lengua española*), and the meaning of the punning "literal" verb, "no ladra," is made clear through its contextual contiguity with the expression "bolsa muda."

There is a further disfiguration of a previous tradition in Quevedo's rendition of this metamorphosis. The *locus amoenus* of the pastoral tradition, the place of shady groves, crystalline water and shepherds' melancholic longings, that world which "is but a utopian projection of the hedonistic instinct,"[23] is transformed into a hostile scene of violent physical desire – "El os quiere gozar, a lo que entiendo" (v.5). As ridiculous a figure as Apollo is – the "Buhonero de signos y planetas" (v. 9), the "alquimista" (v. 1) to whose magical arts Daphne is impervious, remaining virginal or "cruda" (v. 2) (as opposed to "cocida"!)[24] – his threatening sexuality casts a symbolic shadow on the sylvan scene, which becomes a "selva tosca y ruda" (v. 6). Daphne, but a helpless victim of the god's lubricity, manages to outwit him by means of her paradoxically triumphant metamorphosis. As, for instance, in Calderón's tragedy, *El Alcalde de Zalamea*, where the rape scene occurs in a deserted mountainous terrain, the contrast between "wild" nature and "civilized" society reflects the opposition between disorder/order, instinct/reason.

If Góngora managed to capture, with irony and wit, the erotic ambivalence of Ovid's mythological narrative, Quevedo's unifocal, searing satire penetrates the brutal interiority of these tales. Charles Segal, differing with Brooks Otis's characterization of the *Metamorphoses* as an "epic of love," suggests this more "Quevedesque" description: "But we may wonder if it is not rather an epic of rape. Its very subject, metamorphosis, implies violence."[25]

A radical revision of perspective is again apparent in Quevedo's "Califica a Orfeo para idea de maridos dichosos" (III, #765). The poet's misogyny is deep-seated, and we can imagine his readily concurring with the following Stoic appraisal, as it appears in his own translation of the *De remediis fortuitorum*, attributed to Seneca:

Entre los acontecimientos del matrimonio, sólo el de la pérdida de la mujer no puede ser afrentoso, porque si la mujer es mala, se gana con perderla; si es buena, con perderla se asegura de que no lo deje de ser.[26]

It is not surprising, therefore, that Orpheus's traditionally tragic loss of his beloved wife, Eurydice, is interpreted by Quevedo as a positive gain.

This is a tale of undying love and inconsolable loss, and Orpheus concedes that no strength of will can conquer his passion: "Love has overcome me" (*vicit Amor* [X.26]). Suffering even greater guilty anguish after his wife's paradoxical double death, following his abortive attempt to rescue her from the underworld, Orpheus eschews the love of women altogether: "He set the example for the people of Thrace of giving his love to tender boys, and enjoying the springtime and first flower of their youth" (*ille etiam Thracum populis fuit auctor amorem/in teneros transferre mares citraque iuventam/aetatis breve ver et primos carpere flores* [X.83-85]). This latter development in Orpheus's sexual preference was avoided by the Spanish poets, much to the relief of Menéndez Pelayo, for whom it was a "rasgo repugnante, el cual basta para quitar toda poesía a la leyenda."[27] In more recent times, Pablo Cabañas comments that "Naturalmente este rasgo, de mal gusto, fué rechazado por los poetas españoles y Garcilaso, Jáuregui, Lope, Solís etc.... se apartaron en éste como en tantos otros puntos de Ovidio."[28]

The lack of precise dating for the poetry of Quevedo is especially troublesome in the discussion of this particular *romance*, which Astrana Marín suggests was written in 1635. This tentative date is at least psychologically plausible in view of the notoriously vitriolic temperament that Quevedo manifested in literary disputes. His roster of enemies included the names of Jáuregui and Montalván, so inextricably associated with poetic versions of Orpheus.[29]

There is no doubt that the tale of Orpheus attained literary notoriety in the first quarter of the seventeenth century, at least in the circles of the *cognoscenti*, and it is unlikely that the pugnacious Quevedo was not aware of this, nor involved, however tangentially.[30]

When Juan de Jáuregui published his *Orfeo* in 1624, he was already known as the author of the "anonymous," pointedly anti-Góngora *Antídoto contra las "Soledades"* and the more generalized anti-*culterano Discurso poético*, with the result that the appearance of this *culterano* poem was treated as a betrayal of the cause of the *llanistas*, as extant anonymous verses indicate.[31] Thus one sonnet says of Jáuregui "Que inculto y culto hermafrodita eres"; another sees him as a contradiction, "Pues si algo en prosa acertáis,/en verso lo confundís."[32] In one "Coloquio entre Eurídice y Orfeo" Eurydice indicates that she returned to Hell to escape from Orpheus's demonic *culto* style of speaking![33] Góngora, too, enters the fray and relishes his enemy's "slip" into florid obscureness in his sonnet beginning "Es el Orfeo del señor don Juan" (MG LXXXI, 1624).

Jáuregui's *Orfeo* was shortly followed by the *Orfeo en lengua castellana*, the critical intention of which is obvious in the malice of its title. Purportedly written by Juan Pérez de Montalván, it is most generally assumed to be the work of Lope de Vega.[34] These two *Orfeos* are linked in the satires; in Góngora's sonnet (MG LXXXI) it is stated that:

> Es el Orfeo del señor don Juan
> el primero, porque hay otro segundo.
> Espantado han sus números al mundo
> por el horror que algunas voces dan.
>
> (vv. 1-4)

The anonymous verses read as follows:

> A un tiempo salen á luz
> Dos Orfeos, Silvia hermana;
> Uno en lengua castellana
> Y otro en latín andaluz.[35]

The febrile battle between *cultos* and *claros* provided a suitable breeding ground for the microbes of Quevedo's virulent wit. Both the Jáuregui and Montalván versions of the myth, notwithstanding their much publicized linguistic and syntactic divergences, concur in their heroic treatment of the myth, with the result that their significance is the same. They are of epic dimensions (Jáuregui's five cantos having 1,488 verses, Montalván's four cantos, 1,872 verses!) and both are written in the noble *octava real*, the only noticeable difference in narrative treatment being the disproportionate attention given by Jáuregui to Orpheus's power of musical seduction, which occupies most of the fourth canto. Of the many meanings inherent in the Ovidian tale, it is the concept of marital love and fidelity that is stressed in both versions. The love of Orpheus and Eurydice is for Jáuregui "la union mas amorosa," unprecedented in its fidelity:

> bien que ignoravan Siglos anteriores
> tan regalado exemplo de amadores.[36]

Montalván's Orpheus sings "a la felicidad de su Hymeneo" and vows:

> Yo te amarè, diuina prenda mia,
> con amor tan leal, con fe tan rara,
> que diga Amor, que solo yo podia
> suceder en su fuego, si el faltara.[37]

It is this interpretive stress that is reflected in the title of Lope's play, *El marido más firme* (1630) and allows for the transformation of the tale "a lo divino" in Calderón's *auto sacramental, El Divino Orfeo*, where, as Orpheus rescues Eurydice from Hell, so Jesus Christ redeems mankind through his own sacrifice, his celestial instrument of salvation being the cross rather than the lyre: "pues Cithara de Jesus/es la Cruz."[38]

In Quevedo's hands, the significance of the myth will suffer dramatic negation and reversal. As one might expect from the author (at least in part) of the lengthy and vicious "Riesgos del matrimonio en los ruines casados" (II, #639), which includes such verses as

> A los hombres que están desesperados
> cásalos, en lugar de darles sogas:
> morirán poco menos que ahorcados,
>
> (vv. 43-45)

Quevedo will convert the basic seme of positive quest (the sign of marital fidelity and sacrifice) into its opposite, the worthless, ridiculous quest. Thus the myth is both condensed (the sole narrative element is the descent to Hades) and displaced in its focus. As in all parody, of course, the reader's comic perception will depend upon his recognition of the subverted model, which exists in juxtaposition to Quevedo's version.

In addition to the intertextual contradiction between the model and its parody, there exists (more noticeably in this poem than in others) a parallel to the theatrical device of intratextual contradiction. The antithetical *gracioso/noble* pairs of the Spanish *comedia* provide a collision of universes of discourse, whereby the spiritualized, idealized vision of the noble *galán* is parodied by the physical and materialistic vision of the *gracioso*. The comments of Menéndez Pelayo on the *gracioso* Fabio in Lope's play on the same topic, *El marido más firme*, attest to the dissonance created by the disparate discourses within the *comedia*:

Tal acontece con lo inoportuno de los chistes y de las alforjas de Fabio: no porque el *gracioso* del Teatro español sea en sí mismo condenable, puesto que no sólo suple con ventaja al enfadosísimo *confidente* de la tragedia francesa o a la *nodriza* de las tragedias de Eurípides, sino que muchas veces desempeña con superior sentido una función análoga a la del coro antiguo, restableciendo la armonía de los afectos, perturbada por la pasión del protagonista, sino porque, dado el carácter especial de la fábula mitológica de Orfeo, se destruye el efecto de su bajada a los infiernos haciéndole acompañar por un criado chistoso, cuyas sandias ocurrencias quitan toda poesía y majestad a estas escenas.[39]

Fabio's reductive comments do indeed provide a sharp contrast to Orpheus's elevated style of thought and speech. Flabbergasted by his

master's happiness in love, he offers the opinion that a wife is far worse
than any form of physical illness:

> Eso es lo peor que tiene,
> porque todo el daño viene
> de no poderla perder.
>
> La calentura se quita
> curándola, y el dolor
> con medicinas, señor,
> que el médico solicita.
>
> Pero la propia mujer
> solamente con la muerte,
> porque es la cosa más fuerte
> que un hombre puede tener.
>
> (II, p. 157)[40]

On another occasion he states that

> Son mujeres
> gente que sólo en interés repara.
> Llámalas con dinero si las quieres;
> enséñales la bolsa,
>
> (III, pp. 170-71)

and predictably considers Orpheus's descent to Hades in search of his
wife incredible:

> Tú serás el marido más notable
> que haya tenido el mundo, pues que quieres,
> una vez muerta tu mujer amable,
> volverla a ver.
>
> (III, p. 171)

At the end of the play, however, he finally considers himself ready to
marry:

> Quiero
> casarme; que bien podré,
> pues he estado en el infierno.
>
> (III, p. 184)

The same corrosive vision is present in the *gracioso* Anfriso of a later comedy, the *Erudice [sic] y Orfeo* of D. Antonio de Solís y Rivadeneyra. Hell in the myth acquires a unique meaning in the context of the noble quest of the lone and suffering hero, Orpheus; the *gracioso*, by inappropriately, indeed incorrectly, drawing analogies between the unique heroic man and the common man, causes the concept of Hell to suffer a semantic reversal. Thus, when Orpheus says after Eurydice dies

> que yo me ofrezco baxar,
> y enternecer con mi voz
> à los dioses del Infierno,

Anfriso rejoins

> Y no seràs tu, señor,
> el primero que al infierno
> por su muger caminò.

> (II, p. 22)[41]

Needless to add, these signs of marital fidelity seem quite unreasonable to the puzzled servant:

> que aya hombre, que neciamente tierno
> por su propia muger baxe al infierno?
> Si fuera por su dama, aun esso fuera
> para el demonio cosa llevadera.

> (III, p. 26)

This *galán/gracioso* interaction is mirrored in Quevedo's rendition, where the *gracioso*'s view in the poem is implicitly counterpoised to the familiar elevated and tragic voice of literary heritage, alluded to in the verbs "cuentan" and "dicen." As in the *comedia* examples, semantic reversals deliberately invert, and therefore distort, original meanings.

The fundamental pun of the poem is created by the bisociation of the incompatible positive and negative markers of the word "Hell," between Hell as the object of Orpheus's unique sacrificial quest and Hell as the place of castigation within a typical Christian framework.[42] So the poem commences:

> Orfeo por su mujer
> cuentan que bajó al Infierno;

> y por su mujer no pudo
> bajar a otra parte Orfeo.
>
> (vv. 1-4)

The punitive connotations of Hell are reinforced by the subsequent wordplay involving the sexual role of women. In the verses concerning the return of Eurydice,

> pero con ley se la dieron
> que la *lleve* y no la mire:
> ambos muy duros preceptos,
>
> (vv. 22-24)

as well as the following ones,

> porque es muy cierto
> que, al *bajar*, son las mujeres
> las que nos conducen, ciegos,
>
> (vv. 26-28)

the "innocent" literal sense of the verbs "llevar" and "bajar" (here in italics) is diabolically loaded with sexual meaning, reminding us that woman the temptress, the daughter of Eve, truly belongs in the infernal regions.

The basic poetic procedure is one of modification and displacement of narrative suppositions: Orpheus sings here, not to persuade Pluto to return his beloved, but to celebrate his current status as a "single" man, fortunate enough to have lost his wife!

> Dicen que bajó cantando;
> y por sin duda lo tengo;
> pues, en tanto que iba viudo,
> cantaría de contento.
>
> (vv. 5-8)

The traditionally tragic significance of the final loss of Eurydice is interpreted as decidedly suspicious:

> Volvió la cabeza el triste:
> si fue adrede, fue bien hecho;
> si acaso, pues la perdió,
> acertó esta vez por yerro,
>
> (vv. 29-32)

and the final paradox of a "twice-dead wife" provides an excellent
opportunity for the inversion of the cultural code favoring marital love:

> Dichoso es cualquier casado
> que una vez queda soltero;
> mas de una mujer dos veces,
> es ya de la dicha extremo.

(vv. 37-40)

Thus Orpheus, the erstwhile singular example of marital fidelity, is
debased to the lot of the common man, an example of nothing more
than yet another "casado tan necio."

"When a fiction concomitantly presents two domains of reality as a
set of voices in conflict with one another, irony results."[43] The *gracioso*,
whose discourse coincides and collides with that of the *galán*, provides
this ironic perspective within the *comedia*.[44] This split within the text is
echoed at the lexical level in one of the most salient characteristics of
the *gracioso*'s speech – the pun. As irony undermines the stability and
integrity of any univocal and complete meaning by exposing it as nothing more than mere "interpretation" rather than absolute "truth," so the
pun, which creates an intertextual contradiction by splitting at the
semantic level the seemingly integral word at the acoustic level,
reveals the word as unstable.[45] Neither word nor world are fixed and
eternal: "What before was considered to be a matter of course now
becomes a matter of discourse, subject to ongoing, ragged-edged interpretation."[46] Quevedo, too, in his parody of myth (and other forms of fiction) and in his parody of words defies the absoluteness of the dominant
pattern of language and literature. His challenge exposes the existing
modes as arbitrary, relative, and subject to change.

There is, however, a significant difference between the *comedia*
structure of explicit contradiction and Quevedo's burlesque of implicit
contradiction. In the *comedia*, the juxtaposition of voices is maintained
until the end; there is neither a dialectical synthesis or merging in a
higher unity, nor is there the "defeat" of one discourse by another. The
plurality of different voices remains intact. In Quevedo the polemic
(however hidden it may be) seeks resolution in defeat of the contradictory voice and leads to its victimization. The *comedia* is parodic in the
refined and complex sense that *Don Quijote* is parodic, as defined in an
essay by Dorothy Van Ghent:

But it is possible for parody to be much more complex than debate. Instead of
confronting two opposing views with each other, in order that a decision

between them be arrived at, parody is able to intertwine many feelings and attitudes together in such a way that they do not merely grapple with each other antagonistically but act creatively on each other, establishing new syntheses of feeling and stimulating more comprehensive and more subtle perceptions. Parody – except that of the crudest kind – does not ask for preferential judgments and condemnations. It is a technique of *presentation*; it offers a field for the joyful exercise of perception and not a platform for derision.[47]

Although Quevedo defies the absoluteness of another discourse, he strives to erect his own inflexible and absolute system. The coexistence of contradictory voices of true ironic discourse is not countenanced, with the result that instead of a "joyful exercise of perception," there emerges "a platform for derision." The satiric force of Quevedo's verse does not permit such equivocation. "It is scarcely surprising," writes Wayne Booth, "that such a powerful and potentially deceptive tool as stable irony should have been deplored by moralists."[48]

The didactic intent of these poems is most clearly evidenced in their organizational structure, which is generally pyramidal. They commence at the narrow apex, with reference to a specific narrative event of a mythological character, and broaden towards closure at the base, where the personal is expanded to the general, and the particular event is given universal significance. The poem of Orpheus is typical in this respect, for it has a clear sententious formulation at the end:

> Dichoso es cualquier casado
> que una vez queda soltero;
> mas de una mujer dos veces,
> es ya de la dicha extremo.

> (vv. 37-40)

Thus, once again, myth becomes a vehicle for moral-allegorical interpretation, the harsh impact of which is mitigated by wit. In the short, pithy epitaph "A Faetón" (III, #822), none of the splendid pictorial possibilities of the myth are explored, nor is the metamorphosis of Phaëthon's mourning sisters into amber-dropping trees even alluded to (II.345-66). The sole focus of the poem is the moral significance of the tale, and then only its negative facet. The ambiguous Ovidian epitaph combines the heroic quality of risk with the tragic one of death:

HERE PHAËTHON LIES: IN PHOEBUS' CAR HE FARED,
AND THOUGH HE GREATLY FAILED, MORE GREATLY DARED.

(*HIC•SITVS•EST•PHAETHON•CVRRVS•AVRIGA•PATERNI*
QVEM•SI•NON•TENVIT•MAGNIS•TAMEN•EXCIDIT•AVSIS)

(II.327-28)

In Quevedo's version, only the pejorative connotation remains. Based on a pun combining the literal "burning" of Phaëthon in the tale (he is scorched by the sun, and killed by Zeus's thunderbolt) and on the metaphorical "burning" of love, the poem quickly severs itself from the Ovidian context and recontextualizes itself as an abstract generalization. Phaëthon's fate is a negative *exemplum* of the risks of fire – of any kind:

> No los pises ni ultrajes,
> caminante, sus huesos sepultados,
> pues más de cuatro prueban sus linajes,
> por imitalle, con morir quemados.
>
> (vv. 5-8)

Thus Ovid's colorful tale of heroic risk and sentimental bereavement is reduced, in length and in meaning, to a didactic warning.

Except for the few examples of youthful poetic exercises, Quevedo's rejection of mythological fantasy and pathos is a fundamental characteristic of his *poiesis*. This can be considered a predictable facet of his attack on *culterano* poetry and its vogue of mythological subjects, referred to in one of his many lampoons against Góngora (III, #836), deliberately and exaggeratedly obscure:

> huye, no carpa, de tu Dafne Apolo,
> surculos slabros de teretes picas,
> porque con tus perversos damnificas
> los institutos de su sacro Tolo.
>
> (vv. 5-8)

Góngora's perversion of the language is such, suggests Quevedo, that Apollo, as god of music and poetry, flees from his Daphne (his poetic product) rather than pluck her branches ("súrculos"). Góngora's penchant for neologisms is parodied in the Quevedesque creation, "carpa," from the Latin *carpo, carpere*, meaning "to seize," "to pluck off," and the phrase "teretes picas," may refer to the expression "helvecias picas" of the *Polifemo* (v. 428), meaning the "cerdas erizadas del jabalí."[49] Because a descent into pornography is a constant feature of Quevedo's diatribe against Góngora, the absence of the accent on "súrculos" may well be deliberate. This results in yet another Quevedesque neologism, *surculos*, which becomes the key to an obscene reading of the verse whereby Quevedo manages to combine accusations of both linguistic and sexual perversion. Furthermore, Quevedo the moralist would

undoubtedly share one of Jáurequi's objections to Góngora's verse —
that its lack of substance beneath such excessive verbiage amounted to
"much ado about nothing":

> Aun si allí se trataran pensamientos exquisitos i sentencias profundas, sería to-
> lerable que dellas resultase la obscuridad; pero que diziendo puras frioneras, i
> hablando de gallos i gallinas, i de pan i mançanas, con otras semejantes
> raterías, sea tanta la maraña i la dureça de el dezir, que las palabras solas de mi
> lenguaje castellano materno me confundan la inteligencia, ¡por Dios que es
> braba fuerça de escabrosidad i bronco estilo![50]

In his satires, Quevedo followed the example of his mentors, Martial
and Juvenal, who had exiled mythological beings from their verse, in
favor of "reality," or so they claimed.[51] Thus Martial urges his readers to
avoid the vanities of mythology and to concentrate on the life portrayed
in his epigrams:

> Why does the vain twaddle of a wretched sheet attract
> you? Read this of which Life can say: " 'Tis my own."
> Not here will you find Centaurs, not Gorgons and Harpies:
> 'tis of man my page smacks.

> *(quid te vana iuvant miserae ludibria chartae?*
> *hoc lege, quod possit dicere vita "Meum est."*
> *non hic Centauros, non Gorgonas Harpyiasque*
> *invenies: hominem pagina nostra sapit.)*[52]

(X.iv)

So does Juvenal, in his poetic manifesto, Satire I, repudiate the reign-
ing fashion of mythology. It is not only dull and hackneyed, but point-
less:

> Why fool with those frivolous
> stories,
> All about Diomed's horses, Hercules, and the Minotaur's bellow,
> Icarus drowned in the sea, and Daedalus flying above him?

> *(sed quid magis? Heracleas*
> *aut Diomedeas aut mugitum labyrinthi*
> *et mare percussum puero fabrumque volantem.)*

(I.52-54)

Instead, his subject will be everything "human" (*quidquid agunt homines* [I.85]), in particular, man's foibles and faults, a fertile subject indeed, for "When was there ever a time more rich in abundance of vices?" (*et quando uberior vitiorum copia?* [I.87]).[53]

Both Juvenal and Quevedo are conversant with the philosophy of the Stoics;[54] as "conservative revolutionaries" they espouse the simplicity and austerity of its doctrine, with clear stylistic implications.[55] Rhetorical elaboration is avoided as deceitful; only a plain and blunt style can express the truth of the sinful ways of man in the world. As Juvenal specifies, "No fictive music now, but the facts" (*non est cantandum/res vera agitur* [IV.34-35]), Quevedo affirms in his poem on Hero and Leander (III, #771):

> La verdad es ésta,
> que no es patarata,
> aunque más jarifa
> Museo la canta.

(vv. 181-84)

Their poetry is that of moral persuasion (albeit witty), not, clearly not, that of lyrical vagaries. Not for them the divine comedy of Ovid, whose sweet wit and lightness lead Shakespeare to call him "a most capricious poet" (*As You Like It* [III.iii.9]). The elegy written by Carew for the English metaphysical poet John Donne is equally valid for his spiritual counterpart, Quevedo:

> But thou art gone, and thy strict lawes will be
> Too hard for Libertines in Poetrie.
> They will repeale the goodly exil'd traine
> Of gods and goddesses, which in thy just raigne
> Were banish'd nobler Poems, now, with these
> The silenc'd tales o' th'Metamorphoses
> Shall stuffe their lines, and swell the windy Page,
> Till Verse refin'd by thee, in this last Age
> Turne ballad rime, Or those old Idolls bee
> Ador'd againe, with new apostasie.[56]

Notes

1 Alatorre, "Los romances de Hero y Leandro," p. 29.

2 Jammes, *Études*, suggests a chronological development in Góngora's parodies towards an increasing aesthetic elaboration as well as tonal ambiguity: "que pour Góngora, et dès 1604 au moins, le burlesque peut être beau, et donc prétendre d'une certain façon à la dignité de genres littéraires réputés plus nobles" (p. 160).

3 Samuel L. Guyler, "Góngora's *Polifemo*: The Humor of Imitation," *RHM*, 37, no. 4 (1972-73), 237-52, points out the irony and humor in the key passages in this major work of the poet.

4 Recent studies on this aspect of Quevedo's work include, among others, A. Rothe, *Quevedo und Seneca: Untersuchungen zu den Frühschriften Quevedos* (Geneva: Droz, 1965); Henry Ettinghausen, *Francisco de Quevedo and the Neostoic Movement* (Oxford: Oxford University Press, 1972); Michèle Gendreau, *Héritage et création: recherches sur l'humanisme de Quevedo* (Lille: Université de Lille, 1977).

5 *Fábulas mitólogicas*, p. 254.

6 In the *Novelas ejemplares*, ed. Francisco Rodríguez Marín, II, p. 224.

7 See n.41, chap. 1 on Góngora's *Hero and Leander*.

8 Alatorre, "Los romances de Hero y Leandro," #5, p. 8, "Romance compuesto por Juan de Boraualias Mayayo."

9 Alatorre, #9, p. 15, from *Obras de diuersos recopiladas*, MS. 3294, fols. 17v-18r. (Italics in original.)

10 "Los romances de Hero y Leandro," p. 30.

11 Ibid., p. 29.

12 *Agudeza y arte de ingenio*, *Obras completas*, Discurso XXXIII, "De los ingeniosos equívocos," p. 401.

13 See Emilio Alarcos García, "Quevedo y la parodia idiomática," *Archivum*, 5, no. 1 (1955), 3-38 and Lía Schwartz Lerner, *Metáfora y sátira en la obra de Quevedo* (Madrid: Taurus, 1983), who decodes Quevedo's metaphoric "transgressions" in his satiric prose. Lerner shows that, while in most satirists the referent (object of attack) remains central, in Quevedo language itself assumes increasing importance and independence. He is, in fact, as obsessed with language as is his archenemy, Góngora (pp. 186-87).

14 Alvin Kernan, *The Cankered Muse. Satire of the English Renaissance* (New Haven and London: Yale University Press, 1959), p. 11.

15 For an analysis of these poems and a comparison with their earlier serious counterpart, see Mary E. Barnard, "Myth in Quevedo: The Serious and the Burlesque in the Apollo and Daphne Poems," *HR*, 52 (Autumn 1984), 499-522.

16 *Ovid as an Epic Poet*, p. 102.

17 Noted by Fränkel, *Ovid: A Poet Between Two Worlds*, p. 220, n.73, and developed by Segal, *Landscape in Ovid's "Metamorphoses,"* who stresses the ambiguity and contradiction in the text: "Like Scylla, the reader finds the divine and the monstrous closely and disturbingly intermingled" (p. 93).

18 James Iffland, *Quevedo and the Grotesque* (London: Tamesis, 1978), I, p. 48, thus summarizes the observations of Willard Farnham, *The Shakespearean Grotesque: Its Genesis and Transformations* (Oxford: Clarendon, 1971), which he applies to the work of Quevedo.

19 In the *Comentarios*, p. 326, of *Garcilaso de la Vega y sus comentaristas*, ed. Antonio Gallego Morell.

20 *La trayectoria poética de Garcilaso*, p. 166.

21 Amédée Mas, *La caricature de la femme, du mariage et de l'amour dans l'ouevre de Quevedo* (Paris: Ediciones Hispano-Americanas, 1957) takes for granted Quevedo's misogyny, a thesis which is combatted by Otis H. Green (author of *Courtly Love in Quevedo* [Boulder: University of Colorado Press, 1952]) in a review article of Mas's book in *HR*, 28 (January 1960), 72-76. Mas points out the influence of Juvenal (especially on Quevedo's caricatures of marriage [pp. 85 ff.]), as well as the predominant role of Martial in his misogynistic verse (pp. 199-214). The censure of women is one of the thematic coincidences outlined in B. Sánchez Alonso's study, "Los satíricos latinos y la sátira de Quevedo," *RFE*, 11 (1924), 33-62 and 113-53. For further discussion on the relation between Quevedo and Martial see Lía Schwartz Lerner, "Martial and Quevedo: Recreation of Satirical Patterns," *Antike und Abendland*, 23 (1977), 122-42, who focuses on Quevedo's translations of Martial's epigrams (*Imitaciones de Marcial*), indicating ideological and rhetorical coincidences.

22 Quoted from the Loeb Classical Library edition, trans. J. H. Mozley (1929; rev. and rpt. Cambridge: Harvard University Press; London: William Heinemann Ltd., 1962).

23 Renato Poggioli, *The Oaten Flute* (Cambridge: Harvard University Press, 1975), p. 16.

24 As in (II, #586) "Diálogo de galán y dama desdeñosa":
Galán: ¿Por qué conmigo siempre fuiste cruda?
Dama: Porque no me está bien el ser cocida.

(vv. 12-13)

25 *Landscape in Ovid's "Metamorphoses,"* p. 93.

26 "De los remedios de cualquiera fortuna," in the *Obras completas en prosa*, p. 871. Gendreau, *Héritage et création*, states that most critics agree that this work (*De remediis fortuitorum*) is not authentic, but rather a medieval compilation of Senecan materials (p. 109). (In his prefatory comments to the translation, Quevedo insists on the authenticity of the work.)

27 *Estudios sobre el teatro de Lope de Vega*, II, ed. Enrique Sánchez Reyes in the *Obras completas de Menéndez Pelayo*, vol. 30 (Santander: Aldus, 1949), p. 231.

28 *El mito de Orfeo en la literatura española* (Madrid: C.S.I.C., 1948), pp. 30-31.

29 See D. José Jordán de Urríes y Azara, *Biografía y estudio crítico de Jáuregui*, pp. 47-50, for the feud between Jáuregui and Quevedo. For the feud between Montalván and Quevedo see J. H. Parker, *Juan Pérez de Montalván*, pp. 77-79 and Agustín González de Amezúa y Mayo, "Dos estudios sobre el Doctor Juan Pérez de Montalbán," in *Opúsculos histórico-literarios*, II (Madrid: C.S.I.C., 1951), pp. 48-94. Amezúa y Mayo concentrates on Montalván's publication of the *Para todos* (1632) and Quevedo's bitter attack in his *Perinola*.

30 Camille Pitollet, "A Propos d'une 'Romance' de Quevedo," *BH*, 6 (1904), 332-46, suggests this contextual motivation for Quevedo's poem on the theme.

31 Eunice Joiner Gates, "New Light on the *Antídoto* Against Góngora's 'Pestilent' *Soledades*," *PMLA*, 66 (September 1951), suggests the probable date as 1614 (p. 747). Urríes, n.2, p. 38, believes that the *Antídoto* was written, even

published, shortly before the *Orfeo*, and that all these works were known in manuscript form before the actual date of publication.

32 Both included in Urríes, p. 39, n.1.

33 Urríes, p. 106, n.4ª cont.

34 See above, n.23 of the Introduction.

35 Urríes, p. 106, n.4ª cont.

36 *Orfeo*, canto I, p. 13, v. 10 and p. 15, vv. 1-2 respectively. Cited from the ed. of Pablo Cabañas (Madrid: C.S.I.C., 1948).

37 *Orfeo en lengua castellana*, canto II, p. 46, v. 15 and p. 64, vv. 9-12 respectively. Cited from the ed. of Pablo Cabañas, (Madrid: C.S.I.C., 1948).

38 Cabañas, *El mito de Orfeo en la literatura española*, p. 159, quotes from the *loa* to *El Divino Orpheo*, which is included as an appendix to his volume, pp. 243-87.

39 *Estudios sobre el teatro de Lope de Vega*, II, p. 239. (Italics in original.)

40 Quoted from the *Obras de Lope de Vega*, ed. D. Marcelino Menéndez Pelayo, XIV in the *BAE*, vol. 190 (Madrid: Atlas, 1966). The corresponding acts and page numbers are cited in parentheses.

41 In the *Comedias* (Madrid: Melchor Alvarez, 1681). The corresponding acts and page numbers are cited in parentheses.

42 Ragnar Johnson, "Two Realms and a Joke: Bisociation Theory of Joking," quotes on p. 203 Arthur Koestler's definition of the act of bisociation: "the perceiving of a situation or idea L, in two self-consistent but habitually incompatible frames of reference M1 and M2. The event in which the two intersect is made to vibrate on two different wavelengths as it were." See *The Act of Creation* (London: Hutchinson, 1964), p. 35.

43 Susan Stewart, *Nonsense: Aspects of Intertextuality in Folklore and Literature* (Baltimore and London: Johns Hopkins University Press, 1978), p. 20.

44 Jakob Kellenberger, *Calderón de la Barca und das Komische* (Bern: Herbert Lang/Frankfurt/M: Peter Lang, 1975), analyzes the parodying function of the *gracioso* figure and concludes that "Trotzdem ist der GRACIOSO für Calderón die wichtigste Möglichkeit, um eine *ironische Perspektive* einzuführen" (p. 145). (Italics in original.)

45 For an analysis of puns, see Milner's article, "Homo Ridens: Towards a Semiotic Theory of Humour and Laughter."

46 Stewart, *Nonsense*, p. 20.

47 *The English Novel: Form and Function* (New York: Rinehart & Co., 1953), p. 13. (Italics in original.)

48 *A Rhetoric of Irony*, p. 30.

49 Antonio Vilanova, *Las fuentes y los temas del "Polifemo" de Góngora* (Madrid: C.S.I.C., 1957), II, p. 618, cites the source of this simile as Ovid, *Metamorphoses*, VIII.284-86.

50 "Antídoto contra la pestilente poesía de las *Soledades*," in *Documentos gongorinos*, pp. 96-97.

51 On this particular aspect of Martial's and Juvenal's artistic intent, see H. A. Mason, "Is Juvenal a Classic? An Introductory Essay," *Arion*, 1 (Spring 1962), especially 8-14. The article is continued in *Arion*, 1 (Summer 1962), 39-79.

52 I quote from the Loeb edition of Martial's *Epigrams*, trans. Walter C. A. Ker (1920; rpt. New York: G. P. Putnam's Sons; London: William Heinemann, Ltd.,1927), II.

53 The Latin is quoted from *Fourteen Satires of Juvenal*, ed. J. D. Duff (1898; rpt. Cambridge: Cambridge University Press, 1940). The English is quoted from *The Satires of Juvenal*, trans. Rolfe Humphries (Bloomington and London: Indiana University Press, 1958).

54 Although Juvenal is usually related to the moral philosophy of the Stoics (see, for example, Kernan, *The Cankered Muse*, p. 118), Gilbert Highet, "The Philosophy of Juvenal," *TAPA*, 80 (1949), 254-70, argues that the poet in his later satires espoused the doctrines of the Epicureans. Quevedo's sensitivity to the "Senecan style" is obvious in his prose works and is particularly alluded to in such passages as

> Que no es natural la cólera prueba Séneca. Más mostramos noso-
> tros, que es contra naturaleza, *no tan agudamente, pero con más faci-*
> *lidad.*
>
> (*La cuna y la sepultura*, chap. III, p. 1074 in
> the *O.C. en prosa* [italics added].)

In his prefatory comments to *De los remedios de cualquiera fortuna*, where he insists on the authenticity of Seneca's authorship (against the opinion of Justus Lipsius), Quevedo writes:

> Yo no sólo afirmo ser de Séneca todas las sentencias y palabras,
> sino este mismo estilo: porque en Séneca hallamos, primero que en
> el Petrarca, el estilo de repetir una palabra muchas veces, y conso-
> larla, y declararla repetidamente en diferentes maneras.
>
> (p. 859 in the *O.C. en prosa*)

On the "Senecan" as opposed to the "Ciceronian" prose style revolution, see Morris W. Croll, *Style, Rhetoric, and Rhythm: Essays*, ed. J. Max Patrick, *et al.* (Princeton: Princeton University Press, 1966), in particular " 'Attic Prose' in the Seventeenth Century," and "The Baroque Style in Prose," pp. 51-101 and 207-33 respectively.

55 Kernan, *The Cankered Muse* (p. 41) uses this paradoxical term to describe the stance of the typical satirist.

56 "An Elegie upon the death of the Deane of Pauls, Dr Iohn Donne," in *The Poems of Thomas Carew*, ed. Rhodes Dunlap (Oxford: Clarendon Press, 1949), p. 73.

Minor Poets

The gods and goddesses of the *Metamorphoses* were not destined, however, to "swell the windy Page." On the contrary, in accordance with Otis Green's observation concerning religious parody that "With the Renaissance the gusto for malicious parodies increased, finally reaching its height in the seventeenth century,"[1] mythological treatment *a lo burlesco* increased rather than decreased during the course of the century, as a coterie of minor poets exercised their craft in this genre.

From among these, we have selected three authors to discuss: Polo de Medina and Castillo Solórzano, because both are noted for their substantial contributions to this genre (to which so many dedicated at least an "occasional" verse), and Solís y Rivadeneyra, because he developed, in a rather lengthy poem, a tale avoided by his predecessors—that of Salmacis and Hermaphroditus.[2] Although more original than most of the later seventeenth-century purveyors of parodic verse, they too suffer the fate of most "followers": to state it simply, they are not originators. Their reading of Ovid (albeit in preparation to "attack") is not innocent and fresh, for they read him through the already performed transformations of Góngora and Quevedo. They weave their tapestries with brilliantly colored threads, spun with amazing cleverness, but their representations lack texture or depth. They capture the attention, but not the imagination, of the reader.

Of the differing models available—Góngora's subtle and ironic reading of the erotic narrative tales, and Quevedo's satiric reduction of the tales to examples of sexual vice—it was the Quevedesque example that predominated. Exposure through verbal wit, modelled after the Roman satirists, Martial and Juvenal, was preferred to the Ovidian ambiguity and suggestive comedy. This does not imply that the traditions were antithetical, for they shared an attitude of cynical debasement of any form of idealized human love. In addition, both modalities contradicted the continuing tradition in Spain of moral-allegorical interpretations of myth. Francisco de Castro, in his *Metamorphosis a lo moderno* (1641), satirizes such readings:

Dizen otros más entonados: las fábulas son corteças, y el meollo de dentro gran filosofía. ¿Y no se pudiera ello filosofar sin estos testimonios? Yo por fábulas las vendo; cómanse el meollo los que tienen más sesso.[3]

Polo de Medina, praised in his lifetime as the "Quevedo murciano," acquired fame as the most notable practitioner of the art of mythological burlesque, and his formula was to provide the model for many other poets.[4] Specific satirical motifs, inherent since the inception of the genre and made manifest by Góngora's ironic self-consciousness, are continued and intensified by mid-century.

The old battle between the Italianate and Spanish school is continued as the *cultos* are condemned as heretical obscurantists, a "secta" responsible for the current "Babel de confusión" that Apollo is called upon to rectify in the *romance* "A Apolo":[5]

> Haya pues, Apolo, en esto
> Debida reformacion,
> Y vuélvase á cada lengua
> La voz que se le usurpó.
>
> (p. 189)

One salient characteristic of these poems is the satiric exploitation of the reified Petrarchan banalities associated with the *culteranos*. The extended portrait of Daphne in the "Fábula burlesca de Apolo y Dafne" is a highly self-conscious exercise parodying the well-known clichés. Polo de Medina initially intrudes in the text to assert a rebellious independence by reversing the sacrosanct order of traditional portraiture:

> Y pienso comenzar por los talones,
> Aunque parezca mal al que leyere;
> Que yo puedo empezar por do quisiere.
>
> (p. 207)

He proceeds with the description by fits and starts—interjecting, doubting, and correcting himself—making the reader conscious of the "literariness" of the text as well as of his own creative process as author. It is the describing, rather than the description, of Daphne that is significant, with the result that her portrait is a mere word heap. For example, of her foot he writes:

> Era, en efecto, blanco y era breve...
> ¡Oh, qué linda ocasion de decir *nieve*,
> Si yo fuera poeta principiante!
>
> (p. 207)

His description of her mouth includes the following parenthetical comment:

> (Vamos con tiento en esto de la boca;
> Que hay notables peligros carmesíes,
> Y podré tropezar en los rubíes,
> Epítetos crueles).

(p. 207)

Continuing upward to her cheeks, he exclaims:

> Y mi pluma describa
> Sus mejillas hermosas;
> Jesus, Señor, ¡qué tentación de rosas!
> ¡Qué notable vocablo!
> Tentarme de botica quiere el diablo;
> Apolo sea conmigo,
> Y me libre de modos tan perversos.

(p. 207)

The standard characteristics of vulgarization and Hispanification, present from Góngora's first mythological parody, are continued and exaggerated. Physical description occupies a much greater portion of narrative space than in previous parodic poems, as the ugliness and deformity of the heretofore classical beauties are stressed. To give but one example, in "A Vulcano, Vénus y Marte" Venus is hardly the standard Renaissance beauty:

> Era pues madama Vénus
> Moza redomada al uso,
> Con mas panza que un prior,
> Mas enaguas que un diluvio;
> . . . .
> Es mujer de pelo en pecho,
> Muy varonil y forzudo,
> . . . .
> A lo jinete, estevadas
> Son sus piernas y sus muslos,
> Frisadas de vello, y gordas
> Como las letras de algunos.

(p. 204).

The principle of negative conversion is evident: Venus, familiar to the readers as Ovid's goddess of love and beauty or Botticelli's exquisitely delicate figure, is here transformed into a deformed and masculine hussy.

Ovid's swift and succinct tale, a mere prelude to the story of the Sun's ill-fated love of Leucothoë by means of which Venus obtains her revenge, is expanded into a raucous courtship drama. While Ovid's narrative relates Apollo's disclosure of deceit and Vulcan's witty punishment (see *Fig. 3*), Polo de Medina's poem adds as a lusty preamble Mars's rhetoric of wooing, rife with erotic *double entendres*. His *requiebros*, for example, include the verses,

> «Permite que mis deseos
> Dén fondo en tu mar profundo,
> Si acaso de él no heredaste
> Sus borrascas y reflujos.»
>
> (p. 204)

Here "mar" is used in the sense of "female pudenda," a metaphor continued in the following verses:

> «Consiente pues, diosa bella,
> Que sea de tus ondas buzo,
> Si no quieres verme en ellas
> Infelice Palinuro.»
>
> (p. 204)

She is then explicitly called a prostitute or "manfla" ("Serás, oh Vénus, mi manfla" [p. 204]), while he characterizes himself as a carnivorous bird feasting upon her delectable flesh ("Que si vengo á verme cuervo/ De esas bellas carnes" [p. 204]). In proper Quevedesque fashion, the unsentimental and unromantic Venus capitulates to the power of money:

> Y al fin venció sus desdenes
> Con las armas de un escudo.
>
> (p. 205)

The tale of Pan and Syrinx as developed by Polo de Medina well exemplifies his poetic techniques in treating the episodes from the *Metamorphoses*. It is, like the tales of Apollo and Daphne, and Mars and Venus, a brief tale, fraught with somewhat grotesque comic innuendos.

Fig. 3. "Venus and Mars." Ovid. *Metamorphoses* (Venice, Georgius de Rusconibus, 1517). *Rare Books and Manuscript Library, Columbia University.*

As Apollo continued to love "his" tree, so too does Pan succumb to the charm of "his" reeds: "Touched by this wonder and charmed by the sweet tones, the god exclaimed: 'This converse, at least, shall I have with thee'" (*arte nova vocisque deum dulcedine captum/"hoc mihi colloquium tecum" dixisse "manebit"* [I.709-10]).

While the kernel elements of dynamic action are retained (discovery of deceit and revenge in the case of Mars and Venus; the chase and vegetable metamorphoses in the other two tales), these are considerably expanded by the static elements of dialogue and description. The effect is one of greater "psychologizing," as issues of subjectivity and attitude are incorporated. This does not by any means imply a greater "depth"; on the contrary, the Ovidian tale is undermined and trivialized by lighthearted chatter and caricatural portraits.

It does signify a change in the manner of representation. In Ovid, for example, the reasons for the nymph's rejection of her suitor are not mentioned, while in Polo de Medina they merit considerable attention. These are "pseudo-causes," not "real" or extraliterary, but firmly bound to the poem's lexicon, here a play on the name of the protagonist, Pan, described as follows:

> Pan, un cierto satirillo,
> Y deidad tan desmedrada,
> Que, en lo menudo del cuerpo,

No era pan, sino migaja.

(p. 211)

This double meaning (as proper name and common noun) is the kernel for further clusters of wordplay, particularly in Syrinx's refusal of Pan, where Polo de Medina takes full advantage of the many proverbial sayings or set phrases concerning bread ("migaja de pan"; "mendrugo de pan"):

> «No me ha de querer, ni quiero
> Sátiro que Pan se llama;
> Gente honrada, no es paniega,
> Y yo siempre he sido honrada.
>
> «Ese mendrugo de talle
> Délo á un pobre que demanda,
> Y ese mollete de huesos
> Délo á sopas abahadas.
>
> «Pan es cosa de muchachos,
> No quiero yo sus hornadas;
> Que mujer que adora pan,
> Mucho mas que adora, amasa.
>
> «No soy año estéril yo,
> Para que el pan me haga falta;
> A la alhóndiga del pueblo
> Puede ofrecer esta manda.
>
> «No quiero pan que es mas duro
> Que un miserable de casta,
> Negro mas que suele ser
> La maldicion de las pascuas.»

(p. 211)

Such a derivative sequence is typical of Polo de Medina's humor. Plays on words, expressions, and proverbs develop a life of their own in these derivative series, one pun leading to another in a string of associations of either the literal or figurative meanings. The punning discourse is an absurd one and basically incompatible with the "subtext" of Ovid, for his Pan has nothing to do with our daily bread. The incongruity is a source of amusement; it is also a literary stance of the author, whose poem is thus nothing more (or less) than wordplay.

Ovid is only a pretext; in reality, the text is Polo de Medina's joyful playing as he knowingly and deliberately dismantles clichés ("No quise decir alfange,/Porque si alfanje nombrara,/Sin decir lo damasquino,/ Los alfanjes se enojaran" [p. 212]) and stereotypes ("La belleza de Siringa/si fué Siringa bellaca" [p. 211]). Polo de Medina is not really involved with Ovid; he is involved with language.

The expansion of mythological parodies to incorporate Ovidian tales dealing with the darker side of love is well exemplified in the poem "Hermafrodito y Salmacis," a *silva burlesca* by Antonio de Solís y Rivadeneyra, friend and follower of Polo de Medina.[6] This is the last of the tales told by the disobedient daughters of Minyas, who immediately thereafter are punished for their defiance of Bacchus by being converted into hideous bats. While the previous tales can be characterized as pathetic (Pyramus and Thisbe; Leucothoë and Clytie) or humorous (Mars and Venus), Alcithoë's story of Salmacis and Hermaphroditus recounts a diseased and turbulent love, pervaded with "a touch of sultry sensuality,"[7] a case, indeed, of a perverted female libido. Ovid's description of the nymph stresses the relentless furor of her desire for the virginal, reluctant Hermaphroditus: "Scarce can she endure delay, scarce bear her joy postponed, so eager to hold him in her arms, so madly incontinent" (*vixque moram patitur, vix iam sua gaudia differt,/iam cupit amplecti, iam se male continet amens* [IV. 350-51]). The grotesque literal union achieved between the maiden and the youth in the pool of Salmacis is poisonous in its unnaturalness. The fountain is condemned to be enfeebling to man, who will emerge from its waters no more than a half-man, a *semivir* (v. 386), a retribution exacted from the gods by Hermaphroditus, himself doomed to be eternally half a woman.

In this highly self-conscious exercise, the Spanish poet immediately specifies his debt to the *Metamorphoses* – "al gran poeta Ovidio,/à quien, no lo Nason, lo culto embidio" (p. 299, vv.16-17). These verses, as well as the mocking reference to his "instrumento" ("tomando el pulso à mi instrumento" [p. 299, v.21]) clearly echo similar verses in the romance "La ciudad de Babilonia" (no. 74) of Góngora, the implicit parodic target of the opening verses:

> Hablando con perdon, yo tengo gana
> (vergonçoso lo digo) de hazer versos,
> obscuros no, si candidos, y tersos.
>
> (p. 299, vv. 4-6)

Distancing himself from the reified text, the poet disarticulates even the Ovidian place names in playful puns ("ido de Ida" [p. 300, v. 43]; "de

Ida, ò de venida" [p. 303, v. 22]), or carelessly feigns ignorance about a location, urging the reader to "ponerle en la Provincia que quisieres" (p. 301, v. 11). He develops an extended portrait of Salmacis, not present in the *Metamorphoses*, which is in no way referential, but rather a meta-linguistic statement that exposes and destroys Petrarchan portrait cli-chés (such as golden hair, crystal forehead, arched brows, green eyes, pearly teeth, etc., *ad nauseam*) as well as the pompous periphrases typi-cal of *culteranismo*:

> Y assi la dixo vn culto,
> destos, que hablan à bulto,
> silabizando de sus pies lo breve,
> que pisava con Dactilos de nieve.
>
> (p. 302, vv. 20-23)

Although Antonio de Solís diverges from the *Metamorphoses* account at various junctures, he is faithful to the ambiguous characterization of the protagonists presented by Ovid, who stresses the extraordinary, quite uncanny beauty of the young man, as well as his chastity. Thus the poet describes the youth of fifteen, brought up entirely among women to the point where he finds himself "Enninfado" (p. 300, v. 39), as "bonito" (p. 303, v. 24), an epithet usually reserved for women. Salmacis, on the other hand, is initially characterized as "bizarra" (p. 301, v. 15). The etymological provenance of this word is the Italian *biz-zarro* ("iracundo," "furioso," "fogoso"), although Corominas (*Dic. crítico etimológico*) includes the mistaken supposition that it derived from the Basque *viçarra*, "hombre de barba o pelo en pecho." Its various uses in the sixteenth and seventeenth centuries made it synonymous with "ele-gante," "hermoso," "gallardo," "garboso," among others, but also with "valiente," and later with the pejorative sense of "extraño, fantástico, caprichoso, desusado." This ambiguous characterization of the nymph, so much more colorful than the effeminate youth, suits her role as sex-ual aggressor in this tale of frustrated love. It is she who succumbs to his beauty ("à essa beldad me rindo" [p. 303, v. 42]), even offering pay-ment for his "services" ("tambien lo pagarè, como qualquiera" [p. 304, v. 7])! The sight of his nude body bathing in the pool is more than she can bear—"Viòle encueros, en fin, y tan hermosa/la vista fuè, que rabia de amorosa" [p. 305, v. 43-p. 306, v. 1]). Ovid had also specified this sight as a turning point, for "Then did he truly attract her, and the nymph's love kindled as she gazed at the naked form" (*tum vero placuit, nudaeque cupidine formae/Salmacis exarsit* [IV.346-47]).

Although this tale, with its innuendo of nymphomania, offers the opportunity for lurid sensationalism, its critical importance lies in the fact that it makes manifest what was a latent concern in previous tales, in particular Pyramus and Thisbe. A sexually aggressive woman in juxtaposition with a passive male is a motif both disconcerting and fascinating. We may recall that even the existence of female sexual desire, so freely admitted in classical texts, was intolerable to Boscán, who sublimated erotic willingness into Christian modesty in his rendition of Musaeus's *Hero and Leander*. While Antonio de Solís freely admits and develops this dimension of the sexual experience, in other ways he negates the Ovidian tone, diluting eroticism with facile wordplay. He is silent, for example, where Ovid is most openly graphic in his depiction of Salmacis's watery lust, comparing her embraces to the coils of a serpent, the vines of ivy, the tentacles of a sea-polyp (IV.362-67). Even more significant is his openly condemnatory view of Salmacis as "viciosa" (p. 303, v. 25), "lasciva" (p. 306, v.2), accusing her of cupidity in a punning play between the Latin *cupido* ("longing," "desire") and its personification, Cupid:

> aunque fuera muy feo,
> su Cupido en Latin desnudo hiziera,
> que Cupido en Romance pareciera.
>
> (p. 306, vv. 3-5)

While Ovid stressed the fatal beauty of Hermaphroditus and his own frigidity as causative factors in the tragedy, Antonio de Solís rejects such irony and ambiguity.[8] He adopts, though with levity, the blunt voice of the Christian moralizer and eagerly takes advantage of this tale as yet another version of the perils of Eve, against whom neither Adam nor Hermaphroditus can prevail.

Alonso de Castillo Solórzano, known mainly as a novelist (albeit of the type of "purveyed literature"[9]), is, in Quevedesque fashion, no less of a determined *anticulterano* than Polo de Medina. His "Fábula de Polifemo" is a brilliant parodic exegesis of Góngora's notorious exercise in which he displays an intimate comprehension of his "enemy's" lexical and syntactical calisthenics, as seen in the following verses:

> Donde el mar espumoso de Sicilia,
> Ponlebies le calça al Lilibeo,
> ya taller de la Ciclople familia,
> ya prensa de los huessos de Tifeo:
> señas se ven aqui (que no en Panfilia)
> de aquel suplicio, al sacrilegio feo,

y del oficio de aquel Dios sufrido,
Turquesa para todo buen marido.

(p. 86r)[10]

Though less obviously laden with the motif of *anticulteranismo* than
Polo de Medina, his mocking mythological poems in the *Donayres del
Parnaso* (1624) contain intrusive authorial commentary which disrupts
the narrative discourse anchored in the Ovidian tales. In the "Fábula de
Marte y Venus" allusion is made to the "lenguaje biforme" and with
ironic modesty the poet comments that

Solo me falta saber
aquestas modernas vozes,
que a la Catolica lengua
son opuestos Vgonotes.

(p. 53r)

The narrative description *a lo culto,*

Brillantes contempla luzes,
claros dislumbran fulgores
de Deidad suma, que haze
sus crepusculos las noches,

(p. 56r)

is written only to be destroyed in the following verses:

Que en nuestra Christiana lengua
dize, que miraua entonces
los bellos ojos, que Venus
todas las noches recoge.

(p. 56v)

A satirist at heart, Castillo Solórzano shifts the perspective from the
world of mythology to that of contemporary society in order to comment negatively upon modern ways. The virility of Actaeon constitutes
an implicit criticism of contemporary male effeminacy:

no vieron sus guedexas
jamas rizos postizos,
ni el hierro de rizar ostentò rizos,
que tiene intentos viles
quien se precia de intentos mugeriles,

(p. 23v)

and the innocence of the nymph Syrinx provides Castillo Solórzano with the opportunity of berating the deceitfulness of makeup, much in the spirited manner of Quevedo:

> Que en aquella pura edad
> no se exercitaua el vso
> del afeyte pernicioso,
> de las bellezas verdugo.
>
> Mas en esta, que el engaño
> haze lisonjas al gusto,
> para embelecar los hombres
> está cometiendo insultos.

(p. 71r)

Castillo Solórzano, like his predecessors, chooses the typical tales of heterosexuality (the rape of Europa, Pan and Syrinx, Mars and Venus, Actaeon and Diana, Apollo and Daphne, avoiding the tales of lust that involve incest or homosexuality (such as Byblis's love for her brother, Myrrha's passion for her father, the homosexual *amores* of Orpheus, Apollo's love for Cyparissus and Hyacinth, Jupiter's love for Ganymede) or tales of unusual cruelty, such as that of Tereus and Philomela. Also like his predecessors *a lo burlesco*, he treats the theme of *amor deorum* with lightness, wit, and irreverence.

The difference in Castillo Solórzano's poetry lies in his sensitivity to a facet of the *Metamorphoses* captured also by Góngora—the inherent sensuality of the tales. García Lorca characterized Góngora's *Polifemo y Galatea* as "un poema de erotismo puesto en sus últimos términos. Se puede decir que tiene una sexualidad floral."[11] Paradoxically, similar erotic qualities emerge in Castillo Solórzano's parodic discourse; instead of the grotesque transformation of the goddesses and nymphs into ugly and deformed creatures, they appear as "objects of desire." Actaeon is visibly affected by Diana's nude beauty:

> tan gustoso de ver el exercicio,
> que ponia el cuydado
> en ser curioso, mas que bien criado,

(26v)

and the description of Syrinx's beauty stops coyly at the "dos pomos maduros," leading to the familiar *double entendre* of sexual consummation and death:

Me quedo, en cuya mansion
sè que se quedara alguno
sepultado para siempre,
por gozar de su sepulcro.

The landscape promises voluptuous pleasures. Water is associated
with sexuality, as in the description of Diana's bath:

Iugaua con los liquidos cristales,
que acuden presurosos
a tocar en sus partes celestiales,
dexando a los remotos embidiosos,
de auer perdido alli por negligencia,
de llegar donde pueden con licencia,

(25v)

and sylvan settings provide a symbolic landscape for erotic escapades.
The passion of Venus and Mars is played out in a natural scene fraught
with erotic overtones:

Exemplares les ofrecen,
ya las plantas, ya las flores,
para gozar en su sitio
de venereas ocasiones.

La vid al olmo se abraça,
los jazmines trepadores,
con las hayas se ceñian,
la murta troncos escoje.

(p. 58r)

The final scene of consummation in the rape of Europa is situated in a
secret and lovely *locus amoenus*:

Entranronse [*sic*] a vn bosquecillo,
a quien el Florido Abril
hizo Opaco con las plantas,
del olmo, y del tamariz.

La nunca pisada yerua,
el cantuesso, el torongil,

por hazer ameno al suelo,
le dio vistoso telliz.

(pp. 41r-41v)

In Ovid, Jupiter is no ordinary bull, but one of exceeding attractive-
ness: "His colour was white as the untrodden snow, which has not yet
been melted by the rainy south-wind. . . . His brow and eyes would
inspire no fear, and his whole expression was peaceful" (*quippe color
nivis est, quam nec vestigia duri/calcavere pedis nec solvit aquaticus
auster. . . . nullae in fronte minae, nec formidabile lumen:/pacem vultus
habet* [II. 852-53, 857-58]); the same incongruous combination of bestiality and beauty is retained in Castillo Solórzano's description:

La piel que cubre su cuerpo
no es armiño valadi,
porque con la misma nieue
puede muy bien competir,

(p. 40r)

as is the playful seductiveness of the beast with the nymph, foreplay to
the flight and rape.

In a very modern way, Castillo Solórzano absorbs and reflects the
sensuality of the landscape of the *Metamorphoses*, the eroticism of the
love tales. Charles Segal points out that this is a characteristic derived
by Ovid from the pastoral tradition and suggests that "The woods and
groves of pastoral may themselves express a certain degree of erotic
wish-fulfilment and libidinal freedom."[12] The dangerous and menacing
aspects of the Ovidian world, which in effect constitute an inversion of
the pastoral idyll,[13] are absent from the world of Castillo Solórzano, for
the possibilities of horror and suffering are dissipated by the parodic
treatment. What remains in Solórzano's landscape corresponds to that
"*inner landscape*, a realm where normally repressed impulses are made
visible and possible."[14]

Ovid's delicate world of marvels was not destined to prosper in the
following centuries. The rationalistic spirit of neoclassicism exiled the
gods from poetry because of their lack of verisimilitude, and Luzán's
uninspired *Leandro y Hero. Idilio anacreóntico* and allegorical *Juicio de
Paris renovado entre el Poder, el Ingenio y el Amor* (commemorating Fer-
dinand VI's entrance into Madrid in 1746) signalled the already evident
demise of the mythological genre;[15] while Spanish romanticism cultivated the medieval and oriental worlds, it eschewed its classical heritage.[16] The allusive eroticism and tantalizing beauty of such a world

will again be appreciated only by such poets as García Lorca and Cernuda in our own century.

Notes

1 "On Juan Ruiz's Parody of the Canonical Hours," *HR*, 26 (January 1958), p. 12., n.1.
2 For a fuller discussion see Cossío, *Fábulas mitológicas*, chap. XXV, "Fábulas burlescas en el siglo XVII," pp. 679-727, and chap. XXVI, "Romances mitológicos burlescos," pp. 728-62.
3 In "*Metamorphosis a lo moderno*" *y otras poesías*, ed. Kenneth R. Scholberg (México: Colegio de México, 1958), p. 31. I am grateful to Dr. Theodore S. Beardsley, Jr. for drawing my attention to this author, mentioned in his *Hispano-Classical Translations Printed Between 1482 and 1699: A Study of the Prologues and a Critical Bibliography* (Ph.D. diss., University of Pennsylvania, 1961), pp. 244-45, n.147. The published version (Pittsburg: Duquesne University Press, 1970) does not include this particular reference.
4 The citation is from *Obras escogidas de Salvador Jacinto Polo de Medina*, ed. José María de Cossío, Los clásicos olvidados, vol. 10 (Madrid: Compañía General de Artes Gráficas, 1931), p. 55, quoted from Inés de Padilla's praise of *El buen humor de las musas* (Madrid, 1637). For a discussion of Polo de Medina see Cossío's Introduction to this volume, as well as "Apuntes biográficos," pp. LIX-LXIII in *Poetas líricos de los siglos XVI y XVII*, vol. II, ed. Adolfo de Castro, *BAE*, vol. 42, 2d ed. (Madrid: Rivadeneyra, 1875), and Cossío, *Fábulas mitológicas*, pp. 680-85.
5 The text used is that of the *BAE*, vol. 42, pp. 176-214. The "Fábula burlesca de Apolo y Dafne" appeared in 1634 and was published again with the "Fábula de Pan y Siringa" (and other works) in 1636. The "Romance a Apolo" and "A Vulcano, Venus y Marte" appeared in *El buen humor de las musas* (1637). All the poems were included in the 1664 Zaragoza edition of Polo de Medina's works, *Obras en prosa y en verso* (see "Noticia bibliográfica," pp. 25-37 in Cossío's edition of the *Obras escogidas*).
6 Included in *Varias poesías sagradas y profanas*, ed. Manuela Sánchez Regueira, Clásicos hispánicos, serie II, vol. 16 (Madrid: C.S.I.C., 1968), pp. 299-306. See also "Apuntes biográficos," pp. LXXIV-LXXV of vol. 42 of the *BAE*, and Cossío, *Fábulas mitológicas*, pp. 686-88.
7 Fränkel, *Ovid: A Poet Between Two Worlds*, p. 217, n.49.
8 For Ovid's focus see Otis, *Ovid as an Epic Poet*, pp. 156-57; Segal, *Landscape in Ovid's "Metamorphoses,"* pp. 24-26, 52-53; and Keach, *Elizabethan Erotic Narratives*, p. 195.
9 Alan Soons, *Alonso de Castillo Solórzano* (Boston: Twayne Publishers, 1978), pp. 72-76. See also Peter N. Dunn, *Castillo Solórzano and the Decline of the Spanish Novel* (Oxford: Blackwell, 1952). Cossío, *Fábulas mitológicas*, discusses Solórzano's mythological parodies on pp. 694-704.
10 All citations are from *Donayres del Parnaso* (Madrid, Diego Flamenco, 1624), courtesy of The Hispanic Society of America. Soons, *Alonso de Castillo Solórzano*, includes "El robo de Europa" with a prose translation into English in his anthology of Castillo's verse, pp. 108-11 of chap. 7.

11 "La imagen poética de Góngora," *Obras completas*, ed. Arturo del Hoyo, 13th ed. (Madrid: Aguilar, 1967), p. 80.

12 Segal, *Landscape in Ovid's "Metamorphoses,"* p. 9.

13 Ibid., p. 74.

14 Ibid., p. 12 (italics in original).

15 Cossío, *Fábulas mitológicas*, pp. 824-32 (on Luzán). This is also the age of translations, including José Antonio Conde's Musaeus translation (1797) and Dionisio Alcalá Galiano's incomplete *Faetón* (pp. 832-37).

16 Ibid., "Epílogo," pp. 843-50.

A Carnival Play: *Céfalo y Pocris*, "comedia burlesca"

The vitality of the ancient gods continues intact throughout the seventeenth century, achieving special prominence in the theatre. Calderón's works alone include no fewer than ten *autos* and nineteen plays on mythological subjects, performed on the stages of the court palaces, where biweekly representations were the norm, in addition to the performances on special occasions and holidays.[1] Written largely after 1651, when Calderón was ordained as a priest, they correspond to the period when the playwright had ceased to write for the *corrales* and dedicated himself exclusively to court performances and to the *auto sacramentales* for the *Corpus Christi* celebrations.[2]

King Philip IV's passion for the theatre, coupled with the Conde-Duque de Olivares's dedication to his King's diversion, afforded munificent, if not excessive, theatrical support. A special theatre, the Coliseo, was completed at the Palacio del Buen Retiro in 1640, expert Italian stage craftsmen were hired in succession to produce the technically complex *comedias de tramoyas*, small orchestras were incorporated and expanded.[3] Calderón's mythological dramas were, in fact, theatrical spectacles; his *comedias de música* are considered prototypes of the *zarzuela* (so named after the Palacio de Zarzuela) as well as of the opera.[4]

There were, of course, many other playwrights likewise charged with satisfying the seemingly insatiable court appetite for theatre. As the century progressed, a bevy of minor authors produced a plethora of mythological plays for palace representations, indicating a vogue for such subject matter that reflects the rather degenerate elitism of the court.[5] In fact, the court's ever greater intrusion in the theatre and the concomitant demise of public theatre signals the decadence of the Spanish drama after the death of Calderón. This process, seemingly inevitable, is described by Shergold and Varey:

El impacto del teatro de corte, así como el de las prohibiciones, fue, no obstante, a lo largo del tiempo, grave. La gente frecuentaba menos los corrales, cansados sin duda de asistir a funciones que a último momento se cancelaban. El número de las compañías empezaba a disminuir. Los dramaturgos volvían sus ojos, y su talento, cada vez más hacia el Rey y el Palacio, que ofrecía mejores recompensas financieras y sociales y mayores atractivos que el sencillo corral.[6]

As previously mentioned, Calderón continues the medieval tradition of Christian interpretation of pagan myths, clothing the stark moral truths in magnificent clothing as he transforms theological doctrine into drama.[7] Their sumptuous staging, singing, and musical accompaniment helped maintain the beauty of the myths, even as the process of allegorization dispelled their mystery.

The play that concerns us is the "opera" *Celos aun del aire matan* (1660), which, like *La púrpura de la rosa* (earlier in 1660), was sung in its entirety. It was to be Calderón's last venture in plays written completely as recitative.[8] Its exceptional nature is further increased by the fact that it forms the basis for a rare example of a parodic mythological play, *Céfalo y Pocris*, a "comedia burlesca" (1661 or 1662?) dubiously attributed to Calderón himself.[9] Before discussing its burlesque reversal, however, the model – Calderón's elaboration of his source material – must be taken into account.

The tale of Cephalus and Procris, a pathetic account of a wife (Procris) mistakenly killed by the spear of her loving husband (Cephalus) as she spies on him in a state of suspicious jealousy, appears both in the *Ars amatoria* (III.685-746) and in the *Metamorphoses* (VII.661-862), although its significance varies in the two texts. In the piquant, pseudo-didactic *Ars amatoria*, never too serious in its advice on the whims and wiles of love, the tale is invoked rather craftily as a warning against overly hasty jealousy. Emotionalism has no place in this treatise's concept of love as artifice; sentiment only interferes in the proper pursuit of the beloved by the desirous lover.

It is not the craft of love, but the pathos of love that dominates the version of this tale in the *Metamorphoses*. Joined in wedded bliss with Procris, Cephalus remembers with grief his pristine happiness: "I was called happy, and happy I was" (*felix dicebar eramque* [v. 698]). It is once again the meddlesome, lustful gods who interfere with the human condition: the goddess Aurora desires the handsome Cephalus, whisks him away, and then vows revenge because of his devotion to his own wife. It is she who encourages Cephalus's unjust distrust of his wife during his absence and helps him trick his wife into infidelity by changing his form. Procris, shamed by her husband for having succumbed to a "stranger's" advances, flees to the woods and joins Diana. When she is finally induced to return, she bears the gifts of a magic javelin and hound for her husband, and they resume their peaceful existence. External influence again intrudes upon the lovers' harmony, when a "rash tell-tale" (*temerarius index* [v. 824]) informs Procris that the name of "Aura" is uttered by her husband as he rests from his hunting. Although he is only invoking a cooling breeze, Procris thinks that it is the name of a nymph, and the linguistic confusion proves fatal. As Procris spies on Cephalus in the woods, her rustling noise is mistaken for that of an animal, and she is lanced by her husband with his javelin. In spite of the tragedy, she dies happily. Made aware of her confusion, she is satisfied in the knowledge of her husband's faithfulness and love: "But she seemed to die content and with a happy look upon her face" (*sed vultu meliore mori secura videtur* [v. 862]). Throughout the tale emphasis is placed upon marital harmony – "Mutual cares and mutual love bound us together" (*mutua cura duos et amor socialis habebat* [v. 800]) – which is destroyed only by the malice of others, Aurora and the gossip. Equal emphasis is placed upon the tender vulnerability of lovers, which makes them so susceptible to doubt: "and besides, we lovers fear everything" (*sed cuncta timemus amantes* [v. 719]); "A credulous thing is love" (*credula res amor est* [v. 826]) [*Fig. 4*].

Fig. 4. "Cephalus and Procris." *Las transformaciones,* trans. Jorge de Bustamante (Anvers, Pedro Bellero, 1595). *The Hispanic Society of America.*

It is precisely this stress upon mutual marital love that Brooks Otis considers unique to Ovid. Ovid has mitigated, or even eradicated, details of covetousness or perversion that appear in the sources. In Hyginus, for example, Cephalus obtains the wondrous spear and dog by consenting to a homosexual solicitation by Procris, disguised as a young man; in Apollodorus, Procris is found to have been unfaithful to Cephalus in exchange for a golden crown.[10] In the *Metamorphoses*, the homosexual encounter is alluded to only very subtly — when Phocus asks about the provenance of the beautiful weapon, it is written that "Cephalus told what the youth asked, but he was ashamed to tell at what price he gained it" (*quae petit, ille refert, sed enim narrare pudori est,/qua tulerit mercede* [vv. 687-88]); Procris's capitulation to bribery is softened to a hesitation, a mere possibility — "and by adding to my offer I finally forced her to hesitate" (*muneraque augendo tandem dubitare coegi* [v. 740]). In contrast to the tales of lustful violence, this tale, among others, represents the positive side of the love experience:

> It is Pyramus and Thisbe, Procris and Cephalus, Ceyx and Alcyone who represent the Ovidian ideal: their tragedy arouses sympathy and pity, not horror or disgust. . . . In this sense, indeed, the conjugal love of husband and wife is the most adequate instance of Ovid's amatory ideal.[11]

Calderón's treatment of the tale shows a tendency towards incorporation of extraneous material and plot complication, necessitated by the transformation from "epic" narration to dramatic representation.[12] For example, an historical incident — Herostratus's burning of the temple of Diana in Ephesus in 356 B.C. — becomes the dramatic climax in the second act that determines Diana's revenge; the inclusion of the Furies provides for spectacular scenic effects as the Furies and Diana, dressed in black gauze adorned respectively with flames and stars, stand on a boulder, which then divides into four parts as the characters disappear from view (Act III). The Ovidian narrative concentration on one main action (Cephalus/Procris) becomes dispersed by the addition of the other pairs typical of the *comedia* (the *nobles* Aura/Eróstrato and the *graciosos* Rústico/Floreta, with Clarín as a comic complication). While this mitigates the tragic intensity of the story, it allows for much greater movement and variety, creating a richer texture of dramatic, vocal, and choreographic play.[13]

Ovid's amatory tale remained totally human, its pathos not alleviated by a metamorphosis. Calderón, on the other hand, provides a final metamorphosis that is an apotheosis: Procris is resurrected and converted into a star and Cephalus is transformed into a breeze; together (with Aura) they ascend to the heavens. The significance of the tale in Christian terms can be stated as follows:

[L]ove (Christ/Venus) will prevail over hate and destruction (Satan/Diana) for true disciples (Christians/Aura, Céfalo, and Pocris). Such belief may in fact lead to great hardship while on earth, even to ostracism by an unfriendly society (Eróstrato), but the rewards are great in the end.[14]

Calderón's proximity to the meaning of the Ovidian tale is impressive. Elements of contrast are a primary structural feature in both versions: placed at the end of book VII of the *Metamorphoses*, the tale of Cephalus and Procris serves as a counterpoint to the tale of Medea's vindictive passion that begins this section;[15] in *Celos aun del aire matan* the love of Céfalo and Pocris contrasts with the revengeful cruelty of Diana and with the bestiality of Eróstrato, whom vengeance has reduced to an infrahuman condition of which he is aware, tragically:

> me an dejado tan sin mí,
> de mí, ¡ay de mí!, tan ajeno,
> q*ue* de quién soy olvidado,
> de lo q*ue* fui no me acuerdo.
>
> (II, vv. 1334-37)

Calderón stresses Ovid's "miracle of mutual love" by deleting all references to the seduction scene, and by adding an element of altruism to Pocris's death — her death is not sheer accident, for she has moved out from the bushes in an effort to prevent her husband from pursuing the dangerous beast ("Porq*ue* tan horrible monstro/no siga, al paso le salga" [III, vv. 2240-41]).[16]

This exaltation of such noble lovers, proclaimed "prodijios de amor" who will inspire "castos amores" in the future (III, vv. 2384-85), is noticeably absent in the versions of the mythographers. Pérez de Moya comments, for example, that:

Que Procris muera a manos de su marido, significa que la poca prudencia nos guía las más veces a buscar lo que no querríamos hallar, y así quedamos muchos de nosotros muertos del dardo de la poca continencia, esto es, de la pasión que encerramos en nosotros mismos, por haber loca y desvanecidamente creído a palabras ajenas.[17]

Baltasar de Vitoria shows himself more sensitive to the lovers' innocent victimization as he notes the role of Aurora in the catastrophe:

pero nunca falta vn azar en las mayores prosperidades. Y el que estos amantes tuuieron en las suyas, fue que como el era tā hermoso, se enamoro della Aurora.[18]

He does not, however, exalt the couple and is much less subtle than Ovid in his account of the disguised Cephalus's painfully successful seduction of his wife, now proven unfaithful:

la vino à rendir, ofreciendole vna gran promessa, con la qual ella le ofrecio su voluntad, y cama.[19]

In his elaboration of the myth, Calderón is much closer to the moral complexity of Ovid than to the simplistic moralization of Christian interpreters. He chose to stress not the self-destructiveness of love, but rather its transcendent power.

The seeds of parodic transformation in this and other plays are implanted within the work itself, in the figure of the *gracioso*, which Calderón developed in a unique way from Lope's crystallization of the type.[20]

In keeping with classic Aristotelian class-bound decorum, the comic function in the *comedia* is relegated to the "common" man, whose words and actions provide the audience with humorous diversion while allowing the *damas* and *galanes* to maintain their dignity.[21] The inversion of the noble hero, the *gracioso*'s common sense and proximity to everyday reality are a foil for the exalted pride and exaggerated ceremoniousness of the nobility. Removed from spiritual considerations, from the niceties of platonic love, from the nobility's "vertical" aspirations towards a higher good, the *gracioso* consistently represents the "horizontal" materialistic perspective.[22] Thus, for example, in *Celos aun del aire matan*, Céfalo, upon hearing Aura's laments, must act in accordance with his code and go to her rescue; the *gracioso*'s code, a satiric inversion of the noble's, allows for flight:

> Zéfalo [Dentro.]
> ¿Cómo, [oyendo su] queja,
> podrá el balor de un hombre
> no ir a faborezerla?
>
> Clarín [Dentro.]
> Yendo por otra parte.

(I, vv. 104-07)

Contrasting scenes with an obvious parodic function are common. In this play, for instance, Céfalo's lofty floral offering to the virginal Pocris is mimicked by Clarín's offering to Floreta, the *graciosa villana* described as a "nimfa de escalera abajo" (I, v. 597). Céfalo gives Pocris flowers laden with symbolic significance:

> Céfalo [Aparte.]
>   —¡O si ablara sin vozes el suspiro!—
>   De azuzena y rosa [v]es
>   [u]n yris, cuya velleza
>   símbolo es de la pureza,
>   y sangre de Venus es;
>   y assí [a] tus pies,
>   rosa y azuzena, infiero
>   lisonjero
>   don, pues una es del candor
>   ymagen, y otra en verdor,
>   de una púrpura teñido.
>   ¡Muera el amor y viva el olvido!
>
>   (II, vv. 930-41)

Clarín offers his "lady" a mere hound, a gift made doubly outrageous by the fact that the dog is in reality her transformed husband, Rústico:

> Clarín   Estrafalaria beldad
>   q*ue* ni turba ni enbaraza,
>   este lebrel para caza
>   en nombre mío tomad.
>
> Rústico [Aparte.]
>   ¡Qué maldad!
>   ¿Yo lebrel de mi muger?
>
>   (II, vv. 955-60).

     The contrastive function of Calderón's *gracioso* corresponds to the prototype; it is the emphasis on the metacritical function of his *gracioso* that provides the novelty of the playwright's treatment. Ironically distancing himself from the play and players, the *gracioso* breaks the comic illusion and with the self-parodying author assumes a critical stance towards commonly accepted theatrical ideals and procedures.[23] In *Auristela y Lisidante*, for example, the *gracioso* Merlín deliberately disrupts the illusion of an exotic setting in far-away Athens by referring to commonplace localities in Madrid (the Retiro and the Parque de la Vega) and then comments upon his breach of decorum in an *aparte*:

> (Señor crítico, chitón;
> que nadie quita que en Grecia
> haya Vegas y Retiros.)
>
>   (II, p. 2028)[24]

Another striking instance occurs in *Eco y Narciso*, when the *gracioso* Bato concludes the tale of wondrous metamorphosis by saying,

> Y habrá bobos que lo crean.
> Mas, sea cierto o no cierto,
> Tal cual la fabula es
> Esta de Narciso y Eco.
>
> (III, vv. 3227-30)[25]

This passage leads the critic Charles V. Aubrun to observe that

Calderón lui-même ridiculise la crédulité vulgaire de spectateurs encore soumis à l'illusion comique de type lopesque. Un an après la représentation d'*Eco y Narciso*, il fait représenter *Céfalo y Procris*, sorte d'opéra bouffe, de parodie burlesque d'*Auristela y Lisidante* et de *Celos aun del aire matan* que les mêmes comédiens allaient donner le lendemain. Plus encore, il prend ses distances avec ses propres oeuvres dans maints passages où il démonte en public les artifices de la construction dramatique.[26]

We know that *Céfalo y Pocris* is of doubtful attribution. Nevertheless, it is precisely this disconcerting intratextual parodic dialogue that makes a full-blown Calderonian parody, or "opéra bouffe," possible. The increasing autonomy of the *gracioso*, as he assumes a metatextual stance vis-à-vis the theatrical discourse, creates a strong "second" voice that subverts the "principal" voice (the characters' dialogue) of the official text. Often addressing the audience by means of *apartes*, he ridicules and undermines theatrical and societal conventions and even threatens to usurp the role of the main characters in his ever-increasing ascendancy. A parodic play is a logical outcome of this tendency; it merely represents the successful usurpation of power by the *gracioso*.

The "comedia burlesca" *Céfalo y Pocris* is designated as a "Fiesta que se representó a Sus Majestades, día de carnestolendas, en el Salón Real de Palacio."[27] It clearly formed part of the carnival festivities celebrated during the three days preceding Lent, in all likelihood on its principal day, Shrove Tuesday ("Martes de Carnaval"), the culmination of the merrymaking prior to Ash Wednesday, which signals the onset of abstinence.[28]

Gaspar Lucas Hidalgo noted in his *Diálogos de apacible entretenimiento que contienen unas Carnestolendas de Castilla* (1606) that carnival diversions were class-related: the lower classes ("gente vulgar y callejera") indulged in "burlas" and "apacibles y donosas picardías"; the decent folk in "discretas y alegres conversaciones"; the "caballeros de poca edad" were prone to celebrate with "máscaras, juegos de sortija y otros disfraces con que alegran sus personas y las calles de la ciudad."[29]

Although certain popular customs such as the "corrida del gallo" pene-trated court circles,[30] the courtiers and kings generally shared the tastes of the "caballeros de poca edad," and a variety of performances were staged. To give but one example, for the Carnival of 1676, no fewer than four plays were performed in addition to a *mojiganga* and *entremeses*.[31] Many of these were amateur performances, done by the ladies of the court, the Queen's servants, even the courtiers them-selves.[32]

From its early literary manifestation in the Arcipreste de Hita's per-sonification of the battle between Don Carnal and Doña Cuaresma, the dramatic representations of the carnival ritual emphasized the crea-turely exuberance of the body as opposed to the penitent severity of the spirit. Cotarelo y Mori describes one of Juan del Encina's *Representa-ciones hechas en la noche del Carnal* (end of the fifteenth century), as fol-lows:

En la segunda de ellas, en que lo jocoso y bufonesco adquiere caracteres rabele-sianos, se describe una ridícula batalla de la Cuaresma con sus atributos, y el Carnal auxiliado de los suyos, aunque en vano, pues vencido y roto por las hor-talizas y pescados, tiene que apelar á la fuga.[33]

The carnival spirit does indeed correspond to Mikhail Bakhtin's description of Rabelaisian medieval humor as the "drama of bodily life (copulation, birth, growth, eating, drinking, defecation)".[34] Sexual activ-ity is, in fact, central to the meaning of Carnival, as symbolized in the games (and representations) of the *corrida de gallos*, wherein the lusty rooster is killed in order to make way for the period of abstinence, in accordance with the following definition (Alexo Venegas, 1565):

Carnestollendas quiere dezir privación de carnes, y a esa causa se corren los gallos, que son muy lascivos, para significar la luxuria, que deve ser reprimida en todo tiempo, y especial en quaresma.[35]

This aspect too was included in the festive theatrical productions, as revealed in the erudite Cotarelo y Mori's comments upon an *entremés* of the first half of the seventeenth century:

El Carnaval, pieza que gana en gracejo é intención á las antecedentes, pero también en desvergüenza; de modo que no ya representarse, pero ni aun imprimirse será posible. Varias parejas se sitúan para ver pasar las máscaras y figuras del Carnaval, y en tanto, unos charlan y meriendan, otros retozan, se besan y palpan con el mayor desahogo. Lo que sigue es aún menos decoroso.[36]

The basic characteristic of Carnival is the celebration of "el mundo al

revés," a period during which, often with the help of liberating cos-
tumes and masks, normally repressed aggressive and sexual behavior
can seek gratification in wild diversions, noisemaking, private and public vituperations, satires against the authorities.[37] The most literal manifestation of this topsy-turvy world is a reversal of sexual roles, best
exemplified, perhaps, in the description of the *mojiganga* by that same
title – *Mojiganga del mundo al revés* (late 1600s or beginning of the
1700s):

El mundo al revés son las mujeres con espada y broquel y los hombres hilando
y demás menesteres domésticos; dos mal casados que salen bailando con la
cabeza hacia abajo y los pies en alto; una dama que obsequia con comida y lo
demás de la casa á un galán afeminado que la recibe con abanico en la mano y
mucho melindre y se esconde al aparecer una rival. . . . Sale luego un doctor con
la mula á cuestas; el toreador á caballo sobre un toro y luego todas juntas en
pandorga.[38]

In Calderón's *entremés Las Carnestolendas*, the "mundo al revés" is typi-
fied by role reversal, according to the "Vejete":

Al reves anda ya el mundo.
Por San Dimas, que no falta
Sino andar de hombres las hembras,
Y los hombres con enaguas.

This statement is followed by the entrance of a man, *la mitad de mujer,
y la otra mitad de hombre, puesto al reves y andando hacia atras*.[39]

Even the court theatricals indulged in such "scandalous" role reversals, as witnessed by descriptions of a carnival *mojiganga* of 1623 in the
Alcázar, and the *Mojiganga de la Boda*, performed on the "martes de
Carnestolendas" of 1638 at the Buen Retiro.[40] Jesuit correspondence on
the subject of the *Mojiganga de la Boda*, in which several titled noblemen appeared as women, reveals official and church disapproval of
what was apparently considered a "debasement":

A algunos no ha parecido tan ajustado a la decencia el traje, aun para burlas, a
las personas que le llevaban; mas como fue fiesta otros lo excusan, y esto entre
solos los de Palacio y criados de SS. MM. que estuvieron, y así no hizo tanta
disonancia a algunos.[41]

The carnival spirit is, therefore, one of lusty defiance of hierarchy,
one of repudiation of officially recognized custom and discourse –
noblemen "play" women, the common man "plays" king; prudent behavior is replaced by wild and raucous acts (throwing eggs, or water, or

flour; robbing; chasing and mistreating animals, etc.); polite conversation is substituted by shouts, insults, and obscenities. An incident occurring during the 1642 carnival festivities in Mérida, adjudged a "caso feísimo," clearly illustrates the mocking aggression directed against sanctities, guaranteed to shock the "bourgeoisie":

Desnudóse en carnes un hombre y púsose una corona de papel a la cabeza, y un cetro o bastón en la mano, y una cadena como Jasón al cuello, y su espada en un tahalí, y dos pajes con hachas encendidas delante y otros pocos con gran copia de chirimías tocando delante por las calles principales, y los que oían el sonido salían a sus ventanas, entendiendo que era el Santísimo Sacramento para adorarle; y como la figura veía las mujeres a las ventanas, volvíase a ellas, y así él como los acompañantes les decían muchas desvergüenzas, y llegando a la puerta de la señora Virreina, como su Alteza es tan devota, y sus damas, salieron con su celo cristiano con mucha prisa a las ventanas a hacer la divina adoración, y en viéndolas fueron sin cuento las desvergüenzas de palabras y hechos que hicieron con ademanes y meneos.[42]

This procession of parodic profanation reveals the intimate connection between the carnival spirit and the "unmasking" essence of parody. The mock crownings central to Carnival are echoed in parody, for it too, in the words of Mikhail Bakhtin, "is the creation of a *double which discrowns its counterpart*...it is that same 'inside-out world.'"[43] The parodic vision shares with the spirit of Carnival a continuously "ambivalent" and "bilevelled" focus, which celebrates relativity rather than certainty:

Carnivalistic laughter is also directed toward a higher order—toward the change of authorities and truths, toward the change of world orders. Laughter encompasses both poles of change, and it relates to the very process of change, to *crisis* itself. In the act of carnival laughter death and rebirth, negation (ridicule) and affirmation (joyful laughter) are combined. This is profoundly ideological and universal laughter.[44]

The jolliness of Carnival is perfectly expressed in this parodic play *Céfalo y Pocris*, where the intratextual polemic established in other Golden Age plays between the ironic *gracioso* and the exalted *galán* is expanded to an intertextual polemic between this "unofficial" text and previous "official" (serious, authoritative) plays. The voice, in both cases, is a double one, whereby two diametrically opposed points-of-view are juxtaposed and encompassed, poised in a festive carnivalesque relativity. The play, which includes a blindfolded "carrera de gallos" (in act II) in which the "princesses" participate and Céfalo is the "gallo," ends with guitar playing and dancing. "El Gigante con las dueñas/salga el guineo a bailar," sings the King, and the final stage directions indicate "*Hacen un torneo en forma de matachines, y dan fin*" (III, p. 91). The *guineo* is defined in the *Diccionario de la lengua española* as "Cierto baile de movimientos violentos y gestos ridículos, propio de los negros," which the *Diccionario de autoridades* describes as "poco decentes"; the *matachines* is a "baile grotesco":

> Lo característico de los *matachines* era su traje extravagante sin responder á ninguna idea determinada, á veces de salvajes, y los movimientos descompuestos y exagerados, aunque siempre rítmicos y coordinados entre los que los ejecutaban al son de la música.[45]

The Dionysian character of Carnival is fittingly reenacted in the final moments.

The supposition that the play is based upon both *Celos aun del aire matan* and *Auristela y Lisidante* seems correct.[46] In addition to the title, certain kernel narrative events explicitly recall the mythological *fiesta*: Aura's conversion into air (in this case to escape her father's wrath, rather than Diana's); Céfalo's marriage to Pocris and final "accidental" killing, this time knowingly and intentionally committed. The desire for vengeance is the main motif that determines the sequence of events: in *Celos aun del aire matan*, Aura, her love for Eróstrato having been denounced to the goddess Diana by the nymph Pocris, condemns her erstwhile best friend to fall in love, though it is actually the stern Diana who contrives the final revenge; in *Céfalo y Pocris*, Aura, her tryst with Prince Polidoro having been discovered, is thrown out of the palace by Pocris and subjected to her father's castigation of her "dishonor." She reappears as a veiled figure in the final scene, lures Céfalo away from his wife, and hands him not the spear ("venablo") of Diana, but a less exalted crossbow ("ballesta") for his "hunting."

These elements are combined with plot events of the second play, a "comedia caballeresca" set in Athens, where a veritable paroxysm of "doubling" occurs, ending in "cuatralvas bodas" of noble ladies and gentlemen, all of them, of course, princes and princesses, and all of them, at the end, destined to live and reign "happily ever after." In *Auristela y Lisidante*, the twin sisters, Auristela and Clariana, vie for the Kingdom of Athens after their brother Polidoro dies in a duel; these become Pocris and Filis in *Céfalo y Pocris*, twin daughters of the aging King, who in grotesque mimicry of Basilio (*La vida es sueño*) is "learned," heeds dire heavenly prognostications upon his daughters' birth, and raises them in isolated secrecy. His son Polidoro is killed during his escapade with Aura and transformed into a jasmine, in distorted imitation of the Echo and Narcissus myth:

MÚSICA. [*Dentro.*]

Vengan noramala,
noramala vengan,
a ser jazmín él,
y a ser aire ella;
que pues quiere Ovidio
que, aquesto suceda,
vengan noramala,
noramala vengan.

(II, p. 48)

The basic motif of *Auristela y Lisidante* is honor: Auristela's conflict is between her love for Lisidante and her family honor (Lisidante is responsible for her brother's death); Prince Arsidas, shipwrecked and then mistakenly apprehended for Polidoro's death, refuses to flee imprisonment when the possibility is offered to him by the loving Clariana, for his honor is at stake, and honor, he explains,

es un fantasma aparente,
que no está en que yo le tenga,
sino en que el otro lo piense.
Alhaja es tan mal hallada
con los honrados, que a veces,
sin perderla lo que éste obra,
lo que aquél juzga la pierde.

(III, p. 2040)

Such nobility of thought is intolerable to the *gracioso*, Arsidas's servant:

Señores, ¿hay quien tolere
un honrado a todas horas?

(III, p. 2041)

Lisidante, too, must resolve a question of honor; responsible for Polidoro's death, he ironically finds himself, in disguise, as guard to the wrongfully accused Arsidas.

In the parodic text *Céfalo y Pocris*, the basic semes of honor (*Auristela y Lisidante*) and transcendent marital love (*Celos aun del aire matan*), sacred to the ideological ethos of the period, are inverted with defiant irony. They are revealed as mere banalities, stock motifs within the theatrical repertoire, expected by an audience fully versed in the conventions.

The question of honor concerns Aura's nonvirginal "condition" and is subjected to unexpected treatment in the father/daughter exchange on the subject. Its importance is diminished — Aura claims that she has lost "Sólo el honor," whereupon her relieved father asks "¿No más?" (II, p. 41); its significance is reduced to profanatory physical details, as Antistes requests that a doctor verify the situation, "Pues el médico es un tras/de cámara a verte venga" (II, p. 37); the requisite paternal revenge is presented as nothing more than a formal code of societal and theatrical expectations of a "manly" man; Antistes, about to offer his daughter ("as a lesson") nonpoisonous poison, explains that

> ¿Qué padre que honor sustenta
> y tiene sangre en el ojo,
> pelo en pecho, y canas peina,
> puede andar sin un veneno,
> teniendo una hija doncella,
> que la pesa el serlo tanto,
> que parece que se huelga?
>
> (II, p. 42)

The positive love quest is subjected to a process of pejoration, primarily by means of the humorous reduction of women to objects, devoid of any physical attraction and certainly of any spiritual qualities. When the King asks Céfalo to choose between the sisters for a wife, the Prince of Trapobana objects and with unseemly metaphoric comparisons requests a minute inspection of the "wares," preferably, he later adds, in the nude:

> ¿Qué hombre compra una tinaja,
> que antes de dar lo que vale,
> no la mire si se sale?
> ¿Qué hombre a una bodega baja
> a concertar algún vino,
> que antes que a casa le lleve,
> si es bueno o malo no pruebe?
> Melón compra, y es pepino,
> el que calarle no quiera;
> y en fin, ¿quién da su dinero
> por un potro, que primero
> no repase la carrera?
>
> (III, p. 66)

The debate is expanded to include Rosicler, Prince of Picardía, who makes a bid to Céfalo for Filis that is hardly devoid of sexual innuendo:

> vengo a valerme de vos,
> y a suplicaros que si
> vos no la habéis menester,
> que me la dejéis a mí,
> porque la he menester yo
> para cierta cosa.
>
> (III, p. 73)

They merrily proceed to expose courting for what it is—a game—and play dibs ("taba") for the women, who are won piecemeal: "Bien que dos cuartos de infanta/ganando estoy," comments Rosicler (III, p. 77), until Aura interferes and assures the marriage of Pocris to Céfalo. The disparagement of love reaches its apogee with the death of Pocris, when Céfalo expresses annoyance at her meddlesomeness rather than dismay and exaltation:

> ¿Y es justo, por apurar
> recelos, aguar venturas?
> ¡Qué condición infernal
> de mujer!
>
> (III, p. 88)

This response is applauded by Pocris's father, the King, for

> ¿Quién la metió en ser curiosa?
> Muy bien empleado está.
>
> (III, p. 89)

All seriousness is diluted in this celebration of an upside-down world, where princesses squabble and tear out their hair (III, p. 69) and noblemen do not use handkerchiefs but, as the stage directions indicate in the case of Antistes, "*Suénase con los dedos*" (II, p. 50), where not the *graciosos* but the *nobles* admit unabashedly to fear ("Mamá, coco," says Céfalo; "Coco, taita," quakes Rosicler [I, p. 14]), where neither logic nor reasonable motivation exist. When asked by Céfalo, Rosicler, and their servants why he has condemned them to death, the Giant admits to no cause:

Por nada;
y así, yo quiero mataros. . .
Pero ahora no tengo gana.

(I, p. 16)

Reason does not exist, only whimsy. The Giant asks the King to enu-
merate the causes against him, whereupon the King responds blithely
that

Es la primera
ésta, la segunda la otra,
y la tercera es aquélla.

(II, p. 45)

As the customary plot devices of cause-effect relations are violated,
shattering the traditional attempts to achieve verisimilitude, so too are
stylistic and theatrical techniques "laid bare," exposed as mere literary
devices.[47] The authority and absoluteness of the conventional models
are thereby dislodged, their strength diluted by countering points-of-
view and differing perspectives.

No attempt is made to establish a semblance of "objective" reality. On
the contrary, the previous literary creation is not only alluded to but
actually flaunted, as the players recreate another text instead of creating a world. When Aura sings "Tinaja es aqueste reino/que diz que fué
ayer Trinacria" (I, p. 18), she refers to Cephalus's birthplace (Sicily) in
Celos aun del aire matan; in the following dialogue between Antistes
and the King concerning Aura's punishment, the reference to a previous play is explicit:

REY.—Pues dadla. . .
ANT. —   ¿Qué?
REY. —   Una fraterna.
ANT.—En la comedia de ayer
no se hizo.
REY. —   Que se haga en ésta.
¿Hay más de pedir prestado
ese paso a otra comedia?

(II, p. 40)

The comic illusion created by scenery and acting is deliberately violated, as illusion and reality are comically both exposed and juxtaposed: when Antistes comments "Y pues/Hemos llegado a esta

selva...," Aura expresses her disbelief:

> ¿A qué selva? ¿No quedamos
> en palacio, y esa puerta
> cerraste?
>
> (II, p. 43)

The uneasy misalliance of the real and the ideal is highlighted by Aura's confused portrayal of herself, in which the text of the play is subverted by the presence of a subtext, the actor's (author's) own voice in competition with the voice of the character. She sings

> Yo soy hija de Luis López...
> > [*Representa.*]
> Mas, ¡ay de mí! ¡Qué ignorancia!
> ¡Como si fuera en mi casa! [*Canta.*]
> Hija soy de Antistes, que hoy
> tiene del rey la privanza;
> y pues él es el privado,
> su hija será la privada. [*Representa.*]
> Mi nombre es María,...¿qué digo?
> Es Aura; que estoy turbada. [*Canta.*]
>
> (I, pp. 19–20)

It is possible that the choice of this particular mythological play, *Celos aun del aire matan*, as a target for parody may have been sparked less by its subject matter than by its musical uniqueness—the play as libretto, an experiment that apparently proved unpopular, for this play was not again produced in Spain, and the other "opera," *La púrpura de la rosa*, was repeated only once, in 1680. Portions of *Céfalo y Pocris* are sung, and after the first musical intervention by Aura, Céfalo and Rosicler are quick to criticize her singing: "que quien canta mal sus males,/ muy mal sus males espanta"; "Dinos ya de quién te quejas/con música tan amarga" (I, p. 18). In keeping with the pejorative intent, the conventional floral descriptive system of the *culto* style is supplanted by a fruit and vegetable system with quite different connotative properties; the wooing Céfalo sings,

> Trairéte
> de todos cortes
> rábanos y lechugas
> y alcaparrones,
>
> (I, pp. 29-30)

and one of the ladies-in-waiting suggests

> Haz de aquestas berenjenas
> un ramillete.
>
> (I, p. 26)

When the Petrarchan clichés are used, they are distorted into a grotesque image, as in Céfalo's description of Filis:

> Con las liendres parecen
> sus rubias trenzas
> de color de cilicio,
> blancas y negras.
> Iris es de colores
> su hermosa cara,
> amarillas y verdes
> y coloradas.
>
> (I, p. 29)

Certain stylistic traits necessitated by musical considerations are actualized in parodic mimicry.[48] For example, the stammered verse "Yo...si...quando..." (or "Yo...quando...si..."), repeated three times in *Celos aun del aire matan* (I, vv. 57, 325-26, 499), is reiterated by Aura (II, p. 42) in the inappropriate context of a discussion of her lost honor. The use of parallel constructions and repetition to add variety and interest to the musical recitative is very frequent in the libretto, such as in Céfalo's series of questions "¿No viste[i]s estrellas?"..."¿No viste[i]s flores?"..."¿No oíste[i]s aves?"..."¿Cristales no escuchasteis?" (II, vv. 1163-66). This type of sequence is the model for jesting imitations, such as in the following exchange:

> CLORI. – El rey, señora, ha venido.
> LESBIA. – El rey, señora, ha llegado.
> NISE. – El rey aquí se ha metido.
> FLORO. – El rey hasta aquí se ha entrado.
> POCRIS. – Catorce de reyes pido.
> CLORI. – El rey viene a verte hoy.
> LESBIA. – El rey, por nuevas te doy,
>   que llega.
> FLORO. – El rey está aquí.
> NISE. – El rey...
> LESBIA. –   Calla; que sin ti
>   a treinta con rey estoy.
>
> (II, p. 53)

A similar example occurs in the mockingly lyrical pseudoamorous dialogue between Céfalo and Pocris, all the stanzas of which begin with the same formula: "¿Ves esta fragante rosa...?"; "¿Ves aquel bello narciso...?"; "¿Ves esas parleras aves...?"; "¿Ves esos sauces...?" (III, pp. 80-81). Another typical construction of Calderonian poetry, the epiphoneme, appears in the mythological *fiesta, Celos aun del aire matan*, as in the following recitative portion of Aura:

> Soberanas esferas,
> poderosas deidades,
> cielo, sol, luna, estrellas,
> fuente, arroyos, mares,
> montañas, cumbres, peñas,
> árboles, flores, plantas,
> aves, pezes y fieras,
> compadezeos de mí,
> tened de mí clemenzia,
> no permitáis que digan
> ayre, agua, fuego y tierra,
> "¡Ay, infeliz de aquella
> que hizo verdad aver quien de amor muera!"
>
> (I, vv. 86-98)

This poetic summary is reduced to a chaotic and vulgar enumeration in Céfalo's concluding comments following Pocris's death:

> Expiró el mayor fanal
> del día, vino la noche.
> República celestial,
> aves, peces, fieras, hombres,
> montes, riscos, peñas, mar,
> plantas, flores, yerbas, prados,
> venid todos a llorar.
> Coches, albardas, pollinos,
> con todo vivo animal:
> pavos, perdices, gallinas,
> morcillas, manos, cuajar,
> Pocris murió: decid, pues,
> «Su moño descanse en paz.»
>
> (III, pp. 88-89)

The use of offstage voices, effective in the musical presentation and found thirty-nine times in *Celos aun del aire matan*,[49] is recalled in the absurd plethora of voices heard from offstage in the opening scene of the parodic text.

Calderón himself had expressed apprehension lest the audience find the Italianate opera form unacceptable. The allegorical figure Tristeza in the *loa* to *La púrpura de la rosa* warns,

> No mira quanto se arriesga
> en que colera Española
> sufra toda vna Comedia
> cantada?[50]

The playwright's misgivings proved to be correct, for not the opera, but the *zarzuela*, which combines singing and speaking, was destined to succeed in Spain. The parody in *Céfalo y Pocris* indicates excessive stylization and tedious repetition as prime reasons for this "failure."

We have seen that the carnivalistic treatment of the heroic (epic and mythological) material involves an "unmasking" of the exalted by means of a reductive process of degradation or mere familiarization. Bodily functions supersede spiritual concerns; sexuality and aggression have their heyday; nonsense overrides sense.

Similarly, the representation of the king in *Céfalo y Pocris* is a carnivalistic inversion of the dignified and authoritative image of the king, glorified in this genre of the *fiestas reales*, written especially for specific court occasions and performed in splendid social circumstances.[51] Thus, for example, *La púrpura de la rosa* was written in honor of the marriage of the Infanta María Teresa to Louis XIV; *Celos aun del aire matan* was a celebration of the birthday of Prince Philip Prosper. Encapsulated in a rigid system of protocol, their absolutism protected by an inflexible hierarchy, the later Hapsburg kings (Philip IV, Charles II) immersed themselves in the revels of theatre, ever more distant from the riddles of politics and power.[52]

The isolation of the monarchs is revealed in the arrangement of the theatre, whereby the monarchs are seated in an elevated and privileged position directly in front of the stage, while the other spectators (members of the court) occupy lateral positions on the two rows of benches on either side of the room. The time-consuming complications of the accommodations, strictly assigned according to the rules of court etiquette, are implied in the description of the representation of Calderón's *Hado y divisa de Leonido y de Marfisa* (1680).

Las bien aprendidas y respetuosas etiquetas de la Casa Real redujeron á tanta brevedad el acomodarse todas estas jerarquías de personas, que en un punto se halló el coliseo sin mas voz que la de la muda ansia con que esperaban la comedia.[53]

Removed physically from the other spectators, the monarchs are also emotionally and intellectually distanced, for these mythological *fiestas* serve an essentially panegyrical function: the kings see themselves represented in the allegorically interpreted fictions of the gods and goddesses of myth and are thereby magnified and exalted beyond the earthly realm. The theatre as "mirror of the King" is quite literally rendered in the stage setting for *Hado y divisa de Leonido y de Marfisa*:

En la frente del salon, ocupando el medio de la perspectiva, se hizo un trono cubierto de un suntuoso dosel, debajo del cual habia dos retratos de nuestros felicísimos monarcas, imitados tan al vivo, que como estaban frente de sus originales pareció ser un espejo en que trasladaban sus peregrinas perfecciones; y el ansia que desea verlos en todas partes, quisiera hallar mas repetidas sus copias.[54]

Spectator and spectacle merge to such an extent that, in the words of Shergold and Varey, a division between the two is difficult to establish:

En toda representación palaciega, los reyes constituyen un autoespectáculo, y el cortesano mira indistintamente al actor dentro del cuadro escénico, y al rey, al parecer tan teatral y consciente de su actuación como el actor propiamente dicho.[55]

As the ideological ethos of the period is crudely demythified, so too is the figure of the king radically humanized, which is appropriate to the festival occasion, as he himself states:

> Viendo que Carnestolendas
> son para que se hagan rajas
> estas tocas reverendas.
>
> (II, p. 54)

Wrested from heroic distance, the king is contemporized; wrenched from the protection of strict formality, he is treated in familar terms. His bodily functions are stressed: when the captain asks to kiss his hand, he answers, "Toma, como me la vuelvas,/porque ésta es con la que como" (II, p. 35); when he decides to walk instead of taking a carriage, he complains, "¡Qué canse el andar a pie!" (II, p. 44). Hardly a wise and discreet ruler, he prides himself on his irrationality, his "galante capricho" (II, p. 50) and expresses himself in such ridiculous rhymes as,

> Yo, pues, viendo que hacía
> tan fatal su dinguindux
> que era su vista primera
> para sus designios flux,
> dije, como jugador
> de manos: «Quirlinquinpuz,
> ¿veisla?, pues ya no la veis».

(II, p. 60)

He saves Céfalo's life so that he can enlist his help in killing the populace:

> No le matéis; que antes quiero
> que esté conmigo de hoy más,
> porque me vaya matando
> a toda mi vecindad.

(III, p. 90)

No longer treated with deference, the king is subjected to disrespectful comments: the Giant explains that he was unable to recognize the Prince at night because "De noche todos los reyes/son pardos" (II, p. 45), a mocking and witty modification of the *refrán* "De noche todos los gatos son pardos"; when the Giant demonstrates how he killed the Prince by hitting him on the head with his mace, he explains why the identical blow does not harm the king—"Como tienes la mollera/más cerrada que tu hijo" (II, p. 46).

This "upside-down" or "inside-out" representation of the monarch most clearly exemplifies how the official court theatre, which apotheosizes the king, is subverted by the egalitarian and aggressively parodistic spirit of Carnival, which respects neither legal nor moral sanctions and challenges official pomp and pretense.

There is yet another symbolic facet to this figure of the king in *Céfalo y Pocris*, who at the end of the play is rejuvenated, as indicated by the stage directions: "*Empieza a cantar, y por un alambre le quitan las barbas y cabellera cana al* REY" (III, p. 91). The old man must be removed; for not death, but life, is celebrated at carnival time; love and fertility are exalted, not abstinence and sterility. As Vicente Risco explains:

El *Entroido* es una época del año y una fiesta, que ocupa un lugar en el calendario usual cristiano; es también, como veremos, una personificación, sea del año viejo, sea del invierno, sea de algo menos asequible al entendimiento o a la memoria.[56]

Popular carnival customs include the making of a rag figure stuffed with straw (*monigote*), who is celebrated, then sermonized, killed, and buried on Shrove Tuesday, and to whom various names are assigned, such as *Entroido, Meco* and *Vello* (Viejo). Risco asks whether "Aludiría el de *Vello*, en relación con la frecuencia del disfraz de viejo, al 'Año Viejo'?"[57] In this play, death and burial are circumvented and springtime "resurrection" is affirmed, maintaining the lusty spirit of fun. Here, as in Calderón's *entremés, Las Carnestolendas*, or in the popular festivals with their caricaturesque masks of *vellos*, age (and its concomitant meanings of seriousness, severity, and self-denial) is derided.

Notes

1 N. D. Shergold and J. E. Varey, *Representaciones palaciegas: 1603-1699. Estudio y documentos,* Fuentes para la historia del teatro en España, vol. 1 (London: Tamesis, 1982), p. 15.

2 W. G. Chapman, "Las comedias mitológicas de Calderón," p. 51.

3 See Matthew D. Stroud's "Introduction" to Calderón's *Celos aun del aire matan* (San Antonio: Trinity University Press, 1981), pp. 3-25. For information on the Palacio del Buen Retiro, see Jonathan Brown and J. H. Elliott, *A Palace Fit for a King* (New Haven: Yale University Press, 1980).

4 José Subirá, *La participación musical en el antiguo teatro español*, Publicaciones del Instituto del Teatro Nacional, no. 6 (Barcelona: Diputación provincial, 1930), pp. 29-35.

5 N. D. Shergold and J. E. Varey, *Teatros y comedias en Madrid: 1666-1687. Estudio y documentos*, Fuentes para la historia del teatro en España, vol. 5 (London: Tamesis, 1974) lists mythological titles by such theatrical producers as Antonio (de) Escamilla, Agustín Manuel, Simón Aguado, Manuel de Mosquera, Matías de Castro, among others. For example (pp. 176-79): Agustín Manuel and Antonio Escamilla, *Los juegos olímpicos* (22 Dec., 1677-Palace), *Alfeo y Aretusa* (18 Jan., 1678-Palace); *La fragua de Vulcano* (26 July, 1678-Palace); *El laurel de Apolo* (4 Nov., 1678-Palace); Escamilla and Matías de Castro, *Dafnedis y Clori* (22 Dec., 1678-Palace); *Endimión y Diana* (18 Jan., 1679-Palace); *Celos son que al aire matan* (12 Feb., 1679-Palace); Manuel Vallejo, *Faetón* (22 Dec., 1679-Buen Retiro); *La púrpura de la rosa* (18 Jan., 1680-Palace; Salón). The last two plays are also included in *Representaciones palaciegas*, pp. 238-39.

6 *Teatros y comedias en Madrid: 1651-1665. Estudio y documentos*, Fuentes para la historia del teatro en España, vol. 4 (London: Tamesis, 1973), p. 42. They add that documents reveal that, after 1651, at least some of the palace plays were subsequently transferred to the *corrales*, where objections were voiced to the excessive cost of such productions (p. 43).

7 See Introduction, n.24.

8 See Stroud, p. 23; Shergold's and Varey's edition of Juan Vélez de Guevara's *Los celos hacen estrellas* (London: Tamesis, 1970), pp. lxxiii-lxxiv. Jack Sage, "Nouvelles lumières sur la genèse de l'opéra et la zarzuela en

Espagne," *Baroque*, 5 (1972), 107-14, notes that although the two operas (*entirely* sung) *Celos aun del aire matan* and *La púrpura de la rosa* were unsuccessful, the operatic style, based on Italian models, was the basis of the *partially* sung *zarzuela* form, of which Calderón's *El laurel de Apolo* (1658) is considered prototypical. He concludes that "La zarzuela espagnole du XVIIe siècle n'était qu'un développement de l'opéra de cour du type international, et la musique de cette zarzuela suivait par conséquent les lignes générales de l'opéra italien" (p. 114). The score has been published by José Subirá, *"Celos aun del aire matan," ópera del siglo XVII (texto de Calderón y música de Juan Hidalgo)* (Barcelona: Institut d'Estudis Catalans, Biblioteca de Catalunya, 1933).

9 *Céfalo y Pocris* appeared in vol. XIX of *Comedias nuevas escogidas de los mejores ingenios de España* (Madrid: Imprenta Real, 1663) along with *Celos aun del aire matan* and *Auristela y Lisidante*. Hartzenbusch, "Catálogo cronológico de las comedias de don Pedro Calderón de la Barca" (*BAE*, vol. 14, p. 679) had assigned a date of no later than 1662 to all three plays; Harry Warren Hilborn, *A Chronology of the Plays of D. Pedro Calderón de la Barca* (Toronto: The University of Toronto Press, 1938) suggests an earlier date for *Auristela y Lisidante* (ca. 1653-60) and assigns, with a question mark, the date of 1662 for *Celos* and *Céfalo y Pocris* (pp. 62, 69).

The date of December 5, 1660, has been firmly established for *Celos* (Stroud, p. 21). *Céfalo y Pocris* was performed after *Celos* and before the permission date of October 18, 1662, granted to vol. XIX of the *Comedias nuevas*, very possibly during the *Carnestolendas* of 1661 (rather than those of 1662, because of the immediacy of the references to the "other" play). A. Valbuena Briones does not include *Céfalo y Pocris* in his *Obras completas* of Calderón, doubting the authenticity of the play (see his *Perspectiva crítica de los dramas de Calderón*, p. 325). In his edition of the play (Salamanca: Almar, 1979) Alberto González Navarro maintains Calderón's authorship.

Extant mythological parodies are rare. Two plays (*Píramo y Tisbe* by Pedro Rosete Niño and *Hipómenes y Atalanta* by Francisco Antonio de Monteser) cited as mythological parodies in Salvador Crespo Matellán's *La parodia dramática en la literatura española*, Acta Salmanticensia, Filosofía y Letras, no. 107 (Salamanca: Ediciones Universidad de Salamanca, 1979), pp. 28 and 31 respectively, do not pertain to this genre. Frédéric Serralta, "La comedia burlesca: datos y orientaciones," in *Risa y sociedad en el teatro español del Siglo de Oro* (Paris: Editions du C.N.R.S., 1980), pp. 99-125, shows that *Píramo y Tisbe* is a tragedy, and *Hipómenes y Atalanta* a type of "fiesta musical" (p. 121). There is a record of a palace performance of *Progne y Filomena*, "burlesca," during the carnival period of 1687 (Shergold and Varey, *Teatros y comedias en Madrid: 1666-1687*, p. 192). The work, however, does not appear in Cayetano Alberto de la Barrera y Leirado, *Catálogo bibliográfico y biográfico del teatro antiguo español, desde sus orígenes hasta mediados del siglo XVIII* (1860; rpt. London: Tamesis, 1968).

Several short theatrical pieces are cited as mythological parodies: D. Emilio Cotarelo y Mori, *Colección de entremeses, loas, bailes, jácaras y mojigangas*, I, *NBAE*, vol. 17 (Madrid: Bailly y Bailliére, 1911), mentions *El marido hasta el infierno* (1656), based on the tale of Orpheus, by D. Francisco Bernardo de Quirós (p. XC); *Píramo y Tisbe* by Alonso de Olmedo [d. 1682] (p. CX); a *mojiganga, Andrómina y Perro viejo* (1748), probably based on Calderón's *Andrómeda y Perseo* (p. CCCV). Crespo Matellán lists (p. 57) a *Fábula de Orfeo*, a *baile* by Jerónimo de Cáncer (1675), as well as other *bailes* in manuscript form, and a *mojiganga, Las bodas de Proserpina* (ca. 1690), also in manuscript form (p. 63). When one considers that, according to Crespo Matellán (p. 17), there are some thirty *entremeses*, eleven *bailes*, eighteen *mojigangas*, and one *loa* that can be considered parodic in the baroque theatre, the number dedicated to mythology is small.

10 The sources are compared in the appendix, pp. 410-13, of *Ovid as an Epic Poet*.

11 Ibid., p. 270.

12 The sources of Calderón's play are discussed by Valbuena Briones, p. 361 and Stroud, pp. 30-31.

13 The "pairing principle" is mentioned by Charles V. Aubrun, *"Eco y Narciso,"* in *Homenaje a William L. Fichter* (Madrid: Castalia, 1971): "En effet, les personnages se groupent par paires qui s'opposent ou se réconcilient dans un jeu essentiellement dramatique (et choréographique)." This is mirrored in the thematic structure, for "Le dramaturge doit maintenant répartir entre ses paires de personnages des sentiments *doubles"* (p. 56). (Italics in original.)

14 Stroud, p. 36.

15 Otis, pp. 174-75.

16 These points are noted by Henry M. Martin, "Notes on the Cephalus-Procris Myth as Dramatized by Lope de Vega and Calderón," *MLN*, 66 (April 1951), 238-41. Lope's play on the same subject is *La bella Aurora* (1635).

17 *Philosophia secreta*, II, p. 238.

18 *Theatro de los dioses de la gentilidad*, libro IIII, capítulo XXIIII (Salamanca, Antonio Ramírez 1620), I, p. 632. Courtesy of The Hispanic Society of America.

19 Ibid., p. 634.

20 Charles David Ley, *El gracioso en el teatro de la Península (Siglos XVI-XVII)* (Madrid: Revista de Occidente, 1954) considers Lope's Tristán of *La Francesilla* the prototype of the figure, whose antecedents are the slaves in Plautus and Terence. According to Ley, Calderón's *graciosos* are less complex, highly stylized, because of the playwright's rigid, aristocratic code: "Para Calderón, la sociedad está hecha, y bien, con paredes de hierro" (p. 212).

21 The class distinction is fundamental to the contrastive roles of *galán* and *gracioso*, as stated by José F. Montesinos, "La figura del donaire en el teatro de Lope de Vega," *Homenaje a Menéndez Pidal*, I (Madrid: Hernando, 1925), pp. 469-504: "Carne y espíritu. No es posible entenderse. Lo impide la contextura espiritual de ambos. Es la nobleza o la plebeyez, la sangre" (p. 489). It is mentioned in the works of Ley (p. 40), of Amelia Tejada, *Untersuchungen zum Humor in den Comedias Calderóns: unter Ausschluss der "Gracioso"—Gestalten* (Berlin and New York: Walter de Gruyter, 1974), pp. 4-5, 22, and in the study of José María Díez Borque, *Sociología de la comedia española del siglo XVII* (Madrid: Cátedra, c. 1976), pp. 239-53. Miguel Herrero, "Génesis de la figura del donaire," *RFE*, 30 (1941), 46-78, posits the historicity of the type, originating from a university context of master and servant.

22 Jakob Kellenberger, *Calderón de la Barca und das Komische*, p. 28.

23 Ibid., pp. 145-46. See also Claire Pailler, "El gracioso y los «guiños» de Calderón: apuntes sobre «autoburla» e ironía crítica," in *Risa y sociedad en el teatro español del Siglo de Oro*, pp. 33-48.

24 In the *Obras completas*, ed. Angel Valbuena Briones, II, 2d ed. (Madrid:

Aguilar, 1960). All subsequent references to the play are to this edition.

25 Quoted from the edition of Charles V. Aubrun (Flers: Imprimerie Folloppe, 1961), p. 74. Aubrun compares this Calderonian procedure to Brecht's "distancing effect" (p. 74, n.1, also p. XI, n.27).

26 "Preface," *Eco y Narciso*, p. XI. Bato's "distancing" role is also mentioned by Aubrun in his article on this play in the *Homenaje a William Fichter*, p. 54.

27 All references to the play are to the edition of Alberto Navarro González (Salamanca: Almar, 1979).

28 Julio Caro Baroja, *El Carnaval* (Madrid: Taurus, 1965), pp. 39-45, outlines the many variations in time designations for the carnival period. Although he judges that, from the point of view of folklore, this three-day designation is too restricted, theatrical records specify these days as the relevant period. Listings appear as follows (Shergold and Varey, *Representaciones palaciegas*): "Domingo, lunes y martes de Carnestolendas de 1680" (p. 239); "Domingo, Lunes y Martes de Carnestolendas de 1685" (p. 248).

29 In *BAE*, vol. 36 (Madrid: Rivadeneyra, 1855), pp. 278-316. Quotes from p. 279.

30 Caro Baroja, pp. 72-73, n.19, quotes from a letter dated February 28, 1634, according to which "El marqués de Oropesa se desposa hoy con la hija del Alburquerque; y halláronse los reyes al desposorio, después de haber corrido los gallos en el gallinero, donde hoy están. Las Carnestolendas se han celebrado como otros años." Quoted from *Cartas de algunos PP. de la Compañía de Jesús sobre los sucesos de la Monarquía entre los años de 1634 y 1648*, I, Memorial Histórico Español, vol. 13 (Madrid, 1861), p. 26.

31 Shergold and Varey, *Representaciones palaciegas*, p. 238. The plays listed are *Del mal lo menos*, *El caballero de Olmedo*, *Los tres mayores prodigios*, and *El Pastor Fido*.

32 Hannah E. Bergman, "A Court Entertainment of 1638," *HR*, 42 (Winter 1974), 67-81, describes the anonymous *Mojiganga de la Boda*, with a cast of titled nobility including the Conde-Duque de Olivares. The participation of courtiers is also established in another *mojiganga* of 1623 by J. E. Varey, "La creación deliberada de la confusión: estudio de una diversión de Carnestolendas de 1623," in *Homenaje a William L. Fichter*, pp. 745-54. Bergman (p. 67, n.1) mentions the court ladies' performance of Villamediana's *La gloria de Niquea* (1622) and Antonio de Mendoza's *Querer por solo querer* (1623). The play for the Carnival of 1650 was performed by the queen's servants (Shergold and Varey, *Representaciones palaciegas*, doc. no. 18, pp. 52-56).

33 In *Colección de entremeses, loas*, I, p. LX.

34 *Rabelais and His World*, trans. Hélène Iswolsky (1965; Cambridge: M.I.T. Press, 1968), p. 88.

35 Caro Baroja, p. 82, as quoted from Samuel Gili, *Tesoro lexicográfico...*, fascicle III, p. 491, *c* and *Agonía del tránsito de la muerte*, in *Escritores Místicos Españoles*, I, *NBAE*, vol. 16 (Madrid, 1911), p. 292.

36 *Colección de entremeses, loas*, I, p. CXXVII.

37 These various activities are described by Caro Baroja, *El Carnaval*, in pt. 1, chaps. III ("Actos propios del Carnaval"), IV ("El gallo de Carnestolendas"), V ("Los agravios de Carnaval"). On the "Martes de Carnaval" of 1637 (February 29), a *mojiganga* was performed in which Philip IV's and the Conde-Duque de Olivares's taxation policies and expenditures were openly criticized (pp. 84-85).

38 Cotarelo y Mori, *Colección de entremeses, loas*, I, p. CCCIV.

39 In vol. IV of the *Comedias de Don Pedro Calderón de la Barca*, ed. D. Juan Eugenio Hartzenbusch, *BAE*, vol. 14 (Madrid: Rivadeneyra, 1850), p. 634 (italics in original). For a discussion of this facet of Calderón's work see Evangelina Rodríguez and Antonio Tordera, *Calderón y la obra corta dramática del Siglo XVII* (London: Tamesis, 1983). The "mundo al revés" is considered a *topos* of this festive genre (p. 187). These authors are also responsible for an edition of Calderón's *Entremeses, jácaras y mogigangas* (Madrid: Castalia, 1983).

40 The former is described in Varey's "La creación deliberada de la confusión: Estudio de una diversión de Carnestolendas de 1623"; the latter is the subject of Bergman's "A Court Entertainment of 1638."

41 In Bergman, p. 77, as quoted from *Cartas de algunos PP. de la Compañía de Jesús*, Memorial Histórico Español, vol. 14, pp. 336-37.

42 Caro Baroja, *El Carnaval*, p. 91, n.26, as quoted from *Cartas de algunos padres de la Compañía de Jesús sobre los sucesos de la Monarquía entre los años de 1634 y 1648*, IV, Memorial Histórico Español, vol. 16 (Madrid, 1862), pp. 268-69.

43 Bakhtin, *Problems of Dostoevsky's Poetics*, p. 105 (italics in original).

44 Ibid., p. 104 (italics in original).

45 Cotarelo y Mori, *Colección de entremeses, loas*, I, pp. CCL and CCLIII-CCLIV respectively.

46 According to Hartzenbusch in his edition of the play, vol. 12 of *BAE* (Madrid: Rivadeneyra, 1849), p. 489, n.1; repeated by D. Marcelino Menéndez Pelayo, *Estudios sobre el teatro de Lope de Vega*, II, p. 246. Menéndez Pelayo mentions a subsequent version by Calderón's disciple, D. Agustín de Salazar y Torres, *El amor más desgraciado, Céfalo y Pocris*, included in *Cythara de Apolo*, vol. II (Madrid, 1681). Ley, *El gracioso en el teatro de la Península*, suggests that *Céfalo y Pocris* is a parody of a play by Salazar (p. 224). Thomas A. O'Connor, "The Mythological World of Agustín de Salazar y Torres: Is *El amor más desgraciado, Céfalo y Pocris* a Tragedy?" *RomN*, 18, no. 2 (1977), p. 1, n.2, suggests that the play was presented between 1667 and 1669 and therefore postdates that of Calderón.

47 Concept developed by Victor Shklovsky (*ostraneniye* – "making strange") to explain aesthetic perception. See "Art as Technique" and "Sterne's *Tristram Shandy*: Stylistic Commentary," pp. 3-24, 25-57 respectively, in *Russian Formalist Criticism: Four Essays*.

48 For an analysis of these traits, see Matthew D. Stroud, "Stylistic Considerations of Calderón's Opera Librettos," *Crítica Hispánica*, 4, no. 1 (1982), 75-82.

49 Ibid., p. 77.

50 In the facsimile edition of the *Comedias*, ed. D. W. Cruickshank and J. E. Varey, vol. VIII of the *Tercera parte*, 1664 (London: Gregg Int. Publishers Ltd. and Tamesis, 1973), p. 206v. Unfortunately, the Aguilar volume of the *OC* in which *La púrpura de la rosa* appears (I [1966]), does not include the *loa*.

51 Neumeister, *Mythos und Repräsentation* stresses this contextual aspect of the *fiesta* genre as vital to the understanding of such plays. See in particular "Die 'Okkasionalität' der Gattung Fiesta," pp. 11-22.

52 Ibid., pp. 25-27.

53 In vol. IV of the *Comedias de Don Pedro Calderón de la Barca*, *BAE*, vol. 14, p. 357.

54 Ibid., p. 358. Neumeister stresses the mythological *fiestas* as "die Selbst-

bespiegelung" or "die Selbstdarstellung des Herrscherpaares" (p. 282), summarized in chap. VII, "Die Fiesta, der Spiegel des Herrschers," pp. 257-92, and
considers it the result of the "fatal solipsism" of the Hapsburgs (p. 26).

55 "Introducción," *Los celos hacen estrellas*, p. lxxi.

56 "Notas sobre las fiestas del Carnaval en Galicia," *Revista de Dialectología y Tradiciones Populares*, 4 (1948), p. 176.

57 Ibid., p. 346.

Velázquez: His Mythological Paintings

It was a painter, not a poet, who expanded the rigid hierarchical boundaries reflected in the mythological *fiestas reales*, where a bridge between king and gods was forged with the subtle instrument of allegory. Velázquez, painter to the court from the age of twenty-four until his death, recipient of many court honors, including the coveted position of *aposentador* in 1652 and, towards the end of his life, successful petitioner for entry in the noble and prestigious military order of Santiago, executed a painting in 1656 in which neither gods nor kings are central to the action of the composition. It is the painter, Velázquez himself, who usurps that central function in the work that has become known as *Las Meninas*.[1]

The painting did not appear with this title until the 1843 Prado Catalogue. A previous inventory had listed it as "Her Highness the Empress with her ladies and a dwarf" (1666) and a later one as "Family of King Philip IV" (1734).[2] Philip IV and his queen, Mariana of Austria, are presented indirectly, dimly reflected in the mirror on the rear wall, a symbol perhaps of their exemplary role as "mirror to the Realm" for their subjects "en quien se miren y se compongan las costumbres" – truthful, prudent, and wise.[3]

A description of a version of the painting, written before 1696 by Félix da Costa, reveals the disconcerting effect of this displacement of focus: the author states that "The picture seems more like a portrait of Velázquez than of the empress."[4] This early insight has been ratified by the art historian Jonathan Brown, who has linked this work to the struggle to ennoble the status of painting by changing its classification from a mechanical art, or craft, to a more noble "liberal" art, a matter of theoretical as well as practical concern to the ambitious Velázquez, a courtier aspiring to knighthood as well as a painter:

Las Meninas is not only an abstract claim for the nobility of painting, it is also a personal claim for the nobility of Velázquez himself.... He meant to demonstrate once and for all that painting was a liberal and noble art that did not merely copy, but could re-create and even surpass nature. Painting was a legitimate form of knowledge, forever beyond the realm of craft, and therefore was a liberal art. Its lofty status was proved conclusively by the monarchs who visited the atelier to watch the painter work his special magic, and who remained there as perpetual guarantors of his claims.[5]

The kings still continue in their splendid isolation, untouched by their surroundings, but their mere presence in the atelier glorifies the artist.

Velázquez was, after all, no mere craftsman, but a knowledgable man, versed in the arts and sciences. As an apprentice to Francisco Pacheco, whose Academy was a center of humanistic learning in Seville, he was exposed to such leading intellectuals as Fernando de Herrera, Francisco de la Medina, and Pablo de Céspedes. Pacheco's *El arte de la pintura* (begun between 1600 and 1604; manuscript completed 1638; published 1649) was the leading theoretical treatise on art of the period; Céspedes's *Poema de la pintura* (only portions of which now remain, cited by Pacheco) also dealt with the theory of art. The "learned" painter was represented as the ideal,[6] and the inventory of Velázquez's library completed at the time of his death bears testimony to the artist's broad range of concerns and curious mind, steeped in the scientific and theoretical treatises relevant to his own work of painting, a science requiring intellectual vigor, not a mere craft.[7] Though less interested in literary (and not at all in devotional) works, Velázquez came into contact with principal writers of his day, as attested to by the portrait of Góngora (1622, at the request of Pacheco) and the portrait of Quevedo attributed to him (before Quevedo's imprisonment in 1639);[8] the composition of *The Surrender of Breda* (*Las Lanzas*) is thought to have been suggested by a scene in Calderón's play, *El sitio de Bredá* (performed in 1625).[9] In Gracián's *El Criticón*, the ship bearing the pilgrims to the "Isla de Inmortalidad" boasts sails that are "lienzos del antiguo Timantes y del Velázquez moderno,"[10] and the reference to the "galante pintor" in the praise of originality in *El Héroe* is thought to refer to Velázquez:

Vio el otro galante pintor que le habían cogido la delantera el Ticiano, Rafael y otros. Estaba más viva la fama cuando muertos ellos; valióse de su invencible inventiva. Dio en pintar a lo suave y pulido, en que podía emular al Ticiano, y satisfizo galantemente que quería más ser primero en aquella grosería que segundo en la delicadeza.[11]

In the section dedicated to seventeenth-century Spanish painters of Quevedo's *silva* "El pincel," the interpolated verses referring to Velázquez praise his mature style:

Y por ti el gran Velázquez ha podido,

diestro cuanto ingenioso
ansí animar lo hermoso,
ansí dar a lo mórbido sentido
con las manchas distantes,
que son verdad en él, no semejantes.
Si los afectos pinta
y de la tabla leve
huye, bulto, la tinta, desmentido
de la mano el relieve.
Y si en copia aparente
retrata algún semblante y ya viviente
no le puede dejar lo colorido,
que tanto le quedó lo parecido,
que se niega, pintado, y al reflejo
te atribuye, que imita en el espejo.[12]

Analogies have been drawn between the parodic mythological poems and Velázquez's treatment of mythological themes; in particular Polo de Medina's *romance* "A Vulcano, Venus y Marte" is mentioned in reference to Velázquez's painting of Mars.[13] In spite of his exposure to the leading literary figures of the day, it is difficult to ascertain whether Velázquez was seriously aware of, or in any way involved in, the current trends in mythological poetry. In his library, after all, contemporary Spanish works of prose and poetry are conspicuous by their absence, limited to one novel, *Auroras de Diana* by Pedro de Castro y Anaya, and another volume of poetry identified with the insufficient title of *Poetas*, which Sánchez Cantón suggests may be Pedro Espinosa's *Primera parte de las Flores de Poetas ilustres de España, dividida en dos libros*, although others consider it more likely to be a generic title, referring to various books by different poets.[14]

Current trends in mythological painting in Spain are curiously scarce, especially if one compares this situation with the wealth of mythological material in literature.[15] An aberration in this pattern of dearth was the rich collection of the royal family (which included Titian, Veronese, Tintoretto, Parmigiano, especially Rubens, among others), to which Philip IV added with passion. While in 1636 the royal collection included 58 mythological paintings (5 of which were by Spanish painters), by 1686 the number had risen to 165 mythological paintings, 40 by Spanish painters.[16]

Generally speaking, however, Spanish painters were inhibited from representing myths by the strong prohibitions of the Post-Tridentine Church against the depiction of nudes, which had become inextricably associated with the ancient fables.[17] Pacheco, whose proven morality merited him an Inquisitorial appointment as "Censor y Veedor de las Pinturas," admonishes the painters of lascivious nudes in his *Arte de la pintura*:

Dexo aparte los famosos pintores, que se han extremado con la licenciosa espresión de tanta diversidad de fábulas; y hecho estudio particular de ellas, con tanta viveza o lacivia, en debuxo y colorido; cuyos cuadros (como vemos) ocupan los salones y camarines de los grandes señores y príncipes del mundo. Y los tales artífices alcanzan no sólo grandes premios, pero mayor fama y nombre; que yo (séame lícito hablar así) en ninguna manera les invidio tal honra y aprovechamiento.[18]

Even the poets recognized the difference in the mediums of representation; while it might be permissible to write about Leda, Europa, Venus, or Diana, it was another matter to paint these women nude. Thus the poet Bartolomé Leonardo de Argensola laments the lack of "proper" decorum in the paintings of these goddesses and nymphs:

> que las tendría por figuras vivas
> quien jusgarlo a sus ojos permitiese,
> y en la descompostura son lacivas,
>
> pero, ¿qué ni unos pámpanos creciese
> el pincel descortés, ni otro piadoso
> velo que a nuestra vista estorbo hiciese?[19]

The Church dominated artistic patronage and, as Brown reminds us, "the Church's influence was not limited to works commissioned by its member organizations; its negative view of classical subject matter held sway over secular patrons as well."[20] Even the noble and royal patrons were bound to exercise caution, although they were, of course, less vulnerable to denunciation.

It is not surprising, therefore, that the rare examples that exist of Spanish mythological painting are clearly allegorical (not simply narrative) in their intent. Not Ovid, but the mythographers, in particular Pérez de Moya and his *Philosophia secreta* (1585), are the primary sources of interpretation. As in the case of Calderón's mythological plays, an orthodox, moral meaning is found in the characters and actions of the fables. The ceiling paintings in both the palaces of the poet Juan de Arguijo and the duke of Alcalá in Seville provide salient examples of such treatment. Arguijo's library ceiling (1601) is dominated by the figure of Jupiter (in an assembly of the gods) and depictions of Ganymede and Phaëthon. Jupiter (Wisdom) judges against Phaëthon (Arrogance) in favor of Ganymede (Prudence), thus contrasting improper and proper means of achieving knowledge; the duke of Alcalá's study ceiling (1604), fashioned after Arguijo's and executed by Pacheco and assistants, is dominated not by Jupiter, but by Hercules, exemplary hero of strength and fortitude and model for this noble family, admonishing against vice (exemplified in scenes of Phaëthon and Icarus) in favor of virtue (exemplified in scenes of Ganymede and Perseus).[21] The same allegorical intention accounts for Zurbarán's paintings (1634) in the Salón de Reinos of the story of Hercules, associated by tradition with the remote beginnings of Spanish history and considered an ancestor of the Spanish monarchs.[22]

Velázquez's mythological paintings defy such a unidimensional, allegorical exegesis: herein lies the artist's greatness, and his mystery. The ambiguity of his representations has led to contradictory interpretations, especially in regard to *Bacchus, The Forge of Vulcan,* and *Mars,* which some critics consider ironic (or satirical) in their interpretation, while others deny such a reading.[23] Ortega y Gasset has remarked upon this critical confoundedness:

Pero todas estas mitologías velazquinas tienen un aspecto extraño ante el cual, confiésenlo o no, no han sabido qué hacerse los historiadores del arte. Se ha dicho que eran parodias, burlas, pero se ha dicho sin convencimiento.

He suggests that the artist's own innovative "naturalism" is the source of his unconventional vision:

Es decir, que Velázquez busca la raíz de todo mito en lo que podríamos llamar su logaritmo de realidad, y eso es lo que pinta. No es, pues, burla, parodia, pero sí es volcar del revés el mito y en vez de dejarse arrebatar por él hacia un mundo imaginario obligarlo a retroceder hacia la verosimilitud. De este modo la jocunda fantasmagoría pagana queda capturada dentro de la realidad, como un pájaro en la jaula. Así se explica cierta impresión dolorosa y equívoca que estos cuadros nos producen. Siendo los mitos la fantasía en libertad, se nos invita a contemplarlos reducidos a prisión.[24]

Jonathan Brown reminds us that "Velázquez not only read the ancient texts, he also interpreted them";[25] nurtured in the Academy of Pacheco, "Velázquez represented the highest expression of the association between painting and letters that the academy fostered during the late sixteenth and early seventeenth century."[26] Any consideration of Velázquez's mythological works must look to literary as well as artistic influences.

An important key to Velázquez's treatment of mythology is Rubens, present at the Madrid court in 1628 on a special mission from Brussels. He may well have inspired Velázquez to paint his first mythological painting, *Los Borrachos* (ca. 1628), and in all likelihood provided the necessary incentive for him to undertake his first visit to Italy (1629-31).[27] For the renovations of the royal hunting lodge, the Torre de la Parada, undertaken in the 1630s, Philip IV commissioned Rubens to paint, among other subjects, mythological paintings, which Rubens himself designed and which he, as well as several other painters, completed for delivery in 1638. Of the total of sixty-three mythological works painted for the Torre, forty-one are directly based on the *Metamorphoses*.[28]

In her thorough study of the surviving paintings and sketches, Svetlana Alpers demonstrates the influence on Rubens of the woodcuts and engravings of the volumes of "illustrated Ovids," in particular the very popular and influential 1557 Lyons edition of *La métamorphose d'Ovide figurée* with woodcuts by Bernard Salomon, but also the 1582 Leipzig edition and the engravings of Antonio Tempesta, probably done between 1600 and 1606. Not related to the tradition of the *Ovide moralisé*, the illustrations are not allegorical in their intent.[29] The presentation of mythological stories as human dramas, with narrative rather than allegorical significance, is central to Rubens's conception;[30] the tales are as appropriate for the Torre de la Parada as the animal and hunting scenes because

Nothing in the hunting retreat was out of place. Ovidian myths provided the kind of light, licentious entertainment traditionally recommended for a pleasure house in the country.[31]

In his interpretation, therefore, Rubens is faithful not to the mythographers and the tradition of Christian moralization, but to Ovid:

In both Ovid and Rubens this emphasis on love corresponds to a de-emphasis on heroic action. Rubens's Torre de la Parada series, like Ovid's *Metamorphoses*, is essentially anti-heroic in attitude and effect. We have already seen that the basis of the comic treatment of the gods in both the *Metamorphoses* and the Torre works is the conflict between heroism and love – or to put it differently, the conflict between the ideal stance of the gods and the experience of the common human passions.[32]

In contrast to the "illustrated Ovids," Rubens's concentration on the humanity of the gods leads him to avoid scenes of physical violence and the actual metamorphoses themselves, so often quite grotesque; in contrast to the previous examples cited of the allegorical ceiling paintings in Seville, Rubens favors female amorous adventures as opposed to male heroic enterprises.[33]

As to literary sources, Velázquez had in his library, in addition to Pérez de Moya's *Philosophia secreta* (1585), two volumes of the *Metamorphoses*, one in an Italian translation by Lodovico Dolce, one in a Spanish translation listed vaguely as "en romance." Although Sánchez Cantón (1925) originally suggested the translation of Antonio Pérez Sigler (Salamanca, 1580; Burgos, 1609) or that of Felipe Mey (Tarragona, 1586), both in verse (as is the translation, with commentary, of Sánchez de Viana [Valladolid, 1589]), he later considered it more likely to be the very popular prose version of Jorge de Bustamante, first published in 1543(?) (Antwerp), and re-edited at least ten times in the sixteenth century and three in the seventeenth.[34] The Dolce translations were illustrated, although the illustrations differed depending on the edition;[35] the Bustamante edition of 1595 (Anvers, Pedro Bellero) includes illustrations based on Salomon's *La métamorphose d'Ovide figurée* (inverted and slightly enlarged) and has an addendum of "alegorías" that are Sigler's (which, in turn, correspond to the "Annotationi" of M. Gioseppe Horologgi in the Giovanni Andrea dell'Anguillara Italian translation.)[36]

The Bustamante translation is considerably "freer," some might even say less correct, than the others available, such as Sigler's or Viana's.[37] He is not averse to elaborating upon the Ovidian text, and, in order to make the original more accessible to his readers, he even adds in some instances details of "Hispanification." To cite but a few examples: the bacchic festival that describes the "matrons and young wives" obeying and worshipping the god (*parent matresque nurusque* [IV. 9]) is further specified in Bustamante as "A esta fiesta se juntaron, & yuan quantas auia en Grecia y en Castilla y en otras muchas partidas del mundo" (p. 53r); in the fable of Pallas and Arachne, it is stated that after the goddess removed her disguise, "The nymphs worshipped her godhead, and the Mygdonian women" (*venerantur numina nymphae/Mygdonidesque nurus* [VI. 44-45]). Bustamante, realizing perhaps that neither "nymphs" nor "Mygdonian women" were familiar entities in the Spain of his day, chose to render this as "Quando Arachnes la conoscio, luego se turbo: y las otras donzellas de casa quando la vieron honrraronla mucho" (p. 80r). This more "familiar" treatment is certainly characteristic of Velázquez's mythological approach.

Velázquez's Caravaggesque *Bacchus* (begun 1628) only later became known as *Los Borrachos* [*Fig. 5*].[38] The name reflects the impression given by the painting of a group genre scene, perhaps a picaresque costume party on a hot afternoon, with little reference to an Olympian god, indicative of Velázquez's naturalistic preference: "Su credo naturalista no le permite emplear el lenguaje heróico ni los modelos idealizados," writes Angulo Iñiguez.[39] Not in the tradition of the orgiastic "bacchanals," nor of Ribera's *The Drunken Silenus* (1628), a gross and obese figure (although these may have been sources of inspiration),[40] the painting has been interpreted as a *teoxenia* (the manifestation of a god to men): "As the lord of the vineyard—a secondary aspect—he [Dionysius] may also vouchsafe to churls a mocking delusion of equality with the gods; so he does in Velázquez's *Borrachos.*"[41] Others have pointed to a 1596 Flemish engraving, *The Worship of Bacchus* (by Jan Saenredam, after Hendrik Goltzius), "Inscribed with a Latin verse by the Dutch poet Cornelis Schonaeus (1540-1611)—a prayer to the god of wine to relieve the pains and worries of the humble suppliants—the suppliants being peasants and a soldier."[42]

In Ovid's description of the bacchic festival, Bacchus is hailed as "planter of the joy-giving vine" (*genialis consitor uvae* [IV.14]) and the women praise his beauty: "For thine is unending youth, eternal boyhood; thou art the most lovely in the lofty sky; thy face is virginseeming, if without horns thou stand before us" (*tu puer aeternus, tu formosissimus alto/conspiceris caelo; tibi, cum sine cornibus adstas,/ virgineum caput est* [IV.18-20]). In his train follow women, satyrs, glad

Fig. 5. Bacchus (begun 1628). Velázquez. *Museo del Prado.*

youths, and "that old man who, drunk with wine, supports his staggering limbs on his staff, and clings weakly to his misshapen ass" (*quique senex ferula titubantis ebrius artus/sustinet et pando non fortiter haeret asello* [IV.26-27]).

This celebration of youth and joy is described with even greater vividness by Bustamante, who amplifies upon the original text. Bustamante's women are even more lavish in their praise of this god of the vine: not satisfied with "O Baco que hermoso, y que fuerte y que blanco y que colorado, y que fresco eres," they continue with

O Baco tu siempre fueste y seras fresco, alegre y lindo mancebo en el cielo y en la tierra: sin duda no ay tan hermoso dios como tu. . . Tus paños y tus armas son rubias y algo vermejas y blancas. Viejos y mancebos pobres y ricos: coxos, mancos, y tollidos todos van detras de ti, y aman mucho tu compañia. Todos hazen contigo gran alegria. A los mudos hazes hablar, y a los coxos correr. Todas las gentes te honrran, sino Alcitoe y sus hermanas. (p. 53r)

In Velázquez's painting, the young god finds himself surrounded by these "Viejos y mancebos pobres y ricos: coxos, mancos, y tollidos."

The commentators are quick to point out the evils of inebriation.[43] Pérez de Moya, who displays a keen awareness of the pictorial qualities of mythological figures, notes the following:

Según Diodoro, a Baco pintan en dos maneras: una con figura muy severa y cruel, con barba larga y figura de viejo, con la cabeza calva, sin pelo; y otra con cara alegre y hermosa, de mozo, sin barba. Por la primera entendían que el vino bebido fuera de medida hace a los hombres terribles y airados, y porque el mucho beber atrae la vejez, por esto le pintan viejo, calvo, porque el vino, puesto que es húmido, es tan caliente en virtud y poder, que deseca y enjuga muy presto. Por la otra denotaban que bebido con templanza es de gran provecho y utilidad, porque usándolo con moderación dicen los médicos que consume la demasiada humedad de los manjares en el estómago, como bebido demasiado, con su sobrado calor amata el húmedo radical y enflaquece las fuerzas, y vuelve al hombre débil y tembloso. Hácenle niño o mozo, porque los que mucho se dan al vino, son siempre sin cuidado, como los niños, o porque como el niño es inocente, así el cargado de vino es sin culpa en todos sus hechos y dichos.[44]

He later adds that

Píntanle desnudo, porque el beber demasiado calienta de manera que no son menester vestidos; o porque quien dél es tocado, descubre todas las cosas y nada tiene encubierto; y por esto dice el adagio: en el vino está la verdad.[45]

The god may be young and handsome, appropriately sensuous rather than heroic, perhaps himself a little inebriated (as has been suggested in the case of Michelangelo's beautiful statue of Bacchus).[46] His admirers are decidedly not strapping examples of manhood. However, Bacchus is also "padre del olvido,"[47] and in this moment of ritualistic devotion, his poor, broken, and battered devotees briefly forget their infirmities—"A los mudos hazes hablar, y a los coxos correr," writes Bustamante—and in so doing they will undoubtedly hasten their decline.

It would seem that Velázquez, in his faithful rendition of the Ovidian text in the translated version, has conveyed the contradiction inherent in the worship of Bacchus, a contradiction implied in the literary text and fully developed by the commentators—the all-too transitory pleasures of wine; the silent will again cease to talk and the cripple will again cease to walk. Velázquez has captured the blissful present, the pause of illusion, pregnant with the inevitable *desengaño* of the future, unspoken, but known to all.

The Forge of Vulcan [*Fig. 6*] was painted in Rome in 1630, at the same time as *Joseph's Blood-Stained Coat Brought to Jacob*, and possible thematic coincidences have been suggested.[48] One of the briefest and most riotous stories of the *Metamorphoses* (IV.169-89), the linear narrative

Fig. 6.   The Forge of Vulcan (1630). Velázquez. *Museo del Prado.*

Fig. 7. "Venus and Mars." *Le trasformationi,* trans. Lodovico Dolce (Venetia, Domenico Farri, 1570). *Rare Books and Manuscript Library, Columbia University.*

sequence of the amours of Venus and Mars is clearly delineated in the illustration of Dolce's Italian translation [*Fig. 7*]: Apollo exposes the adultery of Venus with Mars to her husband, Vulcan, who then takes revenge by fashioning a nearly invisible net of bronze, in which he captures and exposes the lovers *flagrante delicto,* to the hilarity of the gods: "The gods laughed, and for a long time this story was the talk of heaven" (*superi risere, diuque/haec fuit in toto notissima fabula caelo* [IV.188-89]). In illustrations where a single action is selected for representation, as in the Salomon woodcuts, the moment of adultery and mockery is the preferred choice [*Fig. 8*].[49]

"The subject, Apollo announcing to Vulcan the adultery of his wife Venus with Mars, is an unusual choice for illustrating the story of Mars and Venus," comments Enriqueta Harris.[50] It is indeed an unusual choice and distances Velázquez's interpretation from that of the *cornudo* theme, dear to the mocking poets of parody such as Polo de Medina.[51] His choice may have been based on questions of taste and discretion, factors which must be taken into account in the case of this painter to the king; it also, however, reveals a particular reading of the story. Velázquez has displaced the interest from the end of the story to its beginning, to that narrative node from which all subsequent action is unleashed. His silence about the end is only apparent, not real, for his text is superimposed on the very familiar Ovidian text, and the outcome is known to his audience: the adultery is present, but *in absentia*; the armor on the floor of the forge is, after all, Mars's insignia.

The moment when Apollo divulges the secret to Vulcan constitutes in itself a crucial point of change—the transformation of ignorance to knowledge as Vulcan learns the "truth." The pain of the discovery is attested to in Ovid's text: "Then Vulcan's mind reeled and the work upon which he was engaged fell from his hands" (*at illi/et mens et quod opus fabrilis dextra tenebat/excidit* [IV.174-76]). As is his wont, Bustamante's version is more explicit and detailed:

Este Vulcano que era el mejor herrero del mundo quando oyo estas nueuas sintiolo tanto que quedo sin sentido: & con la gran turbacion y pesar se le cayeron de las manos las tenazas y el martillo. (56v)

While Ovid writes that "straightaway" (*extemplo*) he made his net of revenge, Bustamante allows for a suitable recovery time from the shock: "mas despues tornado en si para vengarse dellos luego haze vna red de hierro" (p. 56v). Bustamante's stress on the outward manifestations of an attitudinal transformation in Vulcan, symptomatic of his greater interest in the psychology of the characters, is also characteristic of Velázquez's painting of *The Forge of Vulcan* and constitutes a unique artistic contribution to the pictorial history of the portrayal of this tale.

Fig. 8. "Venus and Mars." *Las transformaciones,* trans. Jorge de Bustamante (Anvers, Pedro Bellero, 1595). *The Hispanic Society of America.*

Moral-allegorical interpretations have been posited for this painting,[52] and Charles de Tolnay has suggested an Allegory of the Arts, whereby Vulcan, a craftsman, is visited by Apollo, representative of the "noble arts," or *artes maiores*.[53] This does not, however, account for the reaction of Vulcan, otherwise so comprehensible within the narrative sequence. Spanish commentators such as Sánchez de Viana, though they include the astrological readings of the tale (according to which a daughter, Harmony, was the result of this unlawful conjunction of opposites), stress the moral connotations, defining Vulcan as the "fuego inferior," Venus as "el apetito concupiscible del hombre, el qual se deriua del Planeta Venus," Mercury as "el feruiēte desseo de la lasciuia, porque la desenfrenada luxuria es influencia de aquel planeta," the Sun as "clara razon humana."[54] Pérez de Moya's interpretations concur in general terms with these, suggesting that Apollo is "algún varón sabio que profundamente ve las cosas," who "viendo el desordenado deseo libidinoso de los viciosos, reprehéndelo y decláralo a Vulcano, que es el marido de Venus, queriendo tornar el ayuntamiento ilícito, al que es lícito."[55]

More obviously related to Velázquez's painting are the descriptions of pictorial representations included in Pérez de Moya's discussion. Of Vulcan he writes that

Pintaban a Vulcano, según Alberico, de figura de un herrero lleno de tizne, y ahumado, y muy feo, y cojo de una pierna, con un martillo en la mano, y la pintura mostrando como que los dioses con ímpetu le echaban del cielo.[56]

Pérez de Moya dedicates an explanatory passage to the significance and function of the Cyclopes, Vulcan's assistants in the forge, mentioning three (rather than Velázquez's four) by name.[57] The description of Apollo is particularly revealing, because it dispels certain impressions of impropriety in the too-boyish, somewhat feminine representation of this supposed ideal of manly beauty.[58] In addition to explaining one of Apollo's identifying features, the laurel wreath, Pérez de Moya includes a chapter entitled "Por qué pintan a Apolo sin barba":

Pintar a Apolo sin barbas, es porque por Apolo lo entendían los gentiles un solo Dios criador del Universo, para significar que Dios nunca envejecía, y que es inmortal, y siempre permaneciente en un ser. O píntanle sin barba y niño, porque el Sol nace cada día como los niños, y los niños no tienen barbas, y así no se las dan a Apolo, según dice San Isidoro.[59]

Velázquez's later portrait of *Mars* (1639-41) [*Fig. 9*], painted for the Torre de la Parada (along with the portraits of Menippus and Aesop) is

Fig. 9. *Mars* (about 1639-41). Velázquez. *Museo del Prado.*

obviously based on the same tale in the *Metamorphoses*. As in the Salomon illustration [see *Fig. 8*] the god of War is unarmed, and thus described in the 1772 inventory of the New Royal Palace at Madrid: "*Un quadro, que contiene a Marte con los Arneses Militares a sus pies.*"[60] Though his pose has been related to Michelangelo's *Pensieroso* and the *Ignudi* of the Sistine Chapel, as well as to the sculpture of *Ares Ludovisi*,[61] there is nothing epic or heroic about his demeanor, for he is sitting on a rumpled bed. His attitude and expression have been variously interpreted as melancholic and meditative; revealing the vanity of life,[62] or as bored and enervated, an implicit criticism of Spain's waning military glory.[63] The erotic overtones cannot, however, be overlooked.[64] The nudity and lassitude of Mars, as well as his pensiveness, can also be attributed to the adage, *post coitum, tristis*. After all, he has been vanquished by Venus in the battle of love. Svetlana Alpers has stressed that in the context of its location in the hunting lodge, Velázquez's disarmed Mars, an image of peace, is highly appropriate, as are Rubens's mythological paintings.[65] In the Salón de Reinos of the Buen Retiro Palace, the military achievements of Philip IV were celebrated, as in the case of Velázquez's own *The Surrender of Breda*; in the Torre de la Parada, peaceful relaxation and enjoyment were the keynotes:[66] hunting may be the training ground for war, but it is, as Don Quijote reminds us in his mocking of the Caballero del Verde Gabán's hunting pursuits, but a pale and tame imitation of the "real" battle (at this moment in the Knight's perilous existence he is confronting lions!):

-Váyase vuesa merced, señor hidalgo-respondió don Quijote-, a entender con su perdigón manso y con su hurón atrevido, y deje a cada uno hacer su oficio.[67]

It must be remembered, too, that humorous renditions of Mars are not a rarity; even Botticelli's *Mars and Venus*, laden with moral-allegorical significance, can be shown to have amusing erotic overtones, and Tintoretto's painting of *Venus and Vulcan* includes the cowering Mars hiding under the bed![68]

Velázquez never depicted the two main characters of this Ovidian episode together. However, in addition to the single portrait of *Mars*, he also painted *Venus at Her Mirror* (1644-48) [*Fig. 10*]. Exceptional because of the nude female figure, the painting was in all probability not commissioned by the king. It is known to have been in the collection of the Sixth Marquis of Carpio by June 1, 1651 (completed before Velázquez's second trip to Italy in 1649 or sent from Italy); its "unofficial" character, therefore, explains the greater license.[69] Related to the Venetian tradition of depictions of Venus, in particular Titian's *The Toi-*

let of Venus, part of the Spanish Royal collection at the time, as well as to figures of antique statuary, especially the reclining *Hermaphrodite* of which Velázquez had a bronze cast made, the painting's naturalistic treatment of the goddess distances it from the mythological world.[70] It was, in fact, long considered to be a portrait of the Marquis's mistress, the actress Damiana.[71] If it were not for the side of the mirror and Cupid, the identification of the figure would be dubious.

The association of beauty and a mirror is a common iconographical rendering of the theme of *vanitas*.[72] The painting, however, is in no way threatening – no spectres of old age or death lurk in the background of this scene that exudes the sensual tranquility of carnal perfection. In addition, Gállego has noted a peculiarity in the posture of Cupid, as he compares it with similar figures in Titian, Veronese, and Rubens:

Cupido se está arrodillando, bajando la cabeza con aire melancólico; no pone las manos separadas en el marco del espejo, como lo hubiera hecho sin duda de interesarle sólo sostenerlo; las tiene una sobre la otra, cruzadas, no como un devoto, sino como un preso, y sobre las muñecas le cae esa cinta que nunca ha servido para colgar el espejo. . .sino que es la ligadura con la que, voluntaria pero tristemente, el Amor se ata a la imagen de la Belleza. Cupido nos aparece así rendido y prisionero, pero sin rebelión, de esa fatal hermosura. . . . Y cabría proponer un título más para este cuadro emblemático: «El Amor vencido por la Belleza.»[73]

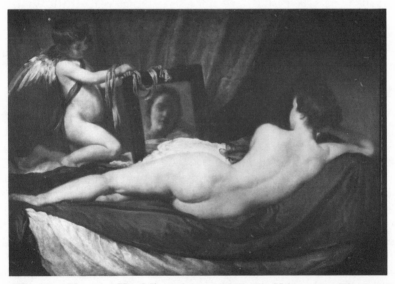

Fig. 10. Venus at Her Mirror (about 1644-48). Velázquez. *The London National Gallery.*

The "sadness" and "melancholy" of Cupid may exist, however, only in the eyes of the beholder.

The private commission of the painting, in addition to the great beauty of the model's body, lead one to believe that it is rather a celebration of the power of beauty. Velázquez's *Venus* may be related to the Neoplatonic concept of Beauty as "sacred," originating in God and equated with Goodness, the visible sign of the Divine in the earthly. It is thus described in Castiglione's very popular *Il libro del Cortegiano* (1528), a copy of which formed part of Velázquez's library:[74]

Therefore Beautie is the true monument and spoile of the victory of the soule, when she with heavenly influence beareth rule over martiall and grosse nature, and with her light overcommeth the darkenesse of the bodie. (p. 311)

(*però la bellezza è il vero trofeo della vittoria dell' anima, quando essa con la virtù divina signoreggia la natura materiale, e col suo lume vince le tenebre del corpo.* [p. 484])[75]

This holy perception of Beauty, in Castiglione's sense of a "spirituall beholding" (p. 306) (*contemplazion spirituale* [p. 476]) is radically distinct from the possession of Beauty, which is mere "bestial" sensuality. The prime instruments of this "proper" apprehension of Beauty were seeing, then hearing,

which have litle bodily substance in them, and be the ministers of reason, without entring farther towarde the bodie, with coveting unto any longing otherwise than honest. (p. 313)

(*i quali tengon poco del corporeo, e son ministri della ragione, senza passar col desiderio verso il corpo ad appetito alcuno men che onesto.* [pp. 486-87])

The sense of touch is perforce low on the value scale, associated with the material, as opposed to the spiritual, side of love.[76]

Velázquez's Venus sees herself in the looking glass, albeit "darkly." The mirror is also a symbol of the sense of sight. Castiglione reminds us that

And as a man heareth not with his mouth, nor smelleth with his eares: no more can he also in any manner wise enjoy beautie, nor satisfie the desire that she stirreth up in our mindes, with feeling, but with the sense, unto whom beautie is the very butte to level at: namely, the vertue of seeing. (p. 313)

(*e che così come udir non si po col palato, né odorar con l'orecchie, non si po ancor in modo alcuno fruir la bellezza né satisfar al desiderio ch'ella eccita negli animi nostri col tatto, ma con quel senso del qual essa bellezza è vero obietto, che è la virtù visiva.* [p. 486])

The dimness of the reflection of the face in the mirror makes the vision of beauty not a concrete and particular one, but one that is abstract and universal. The superiority of the sense of vision is further enhanced by the figure of Cupid, neither touching nor caressing Venus as in other paintings of this mythological pair, but removed and admiring. The painting thus becomes also a hymn in praise of painting, the art that is spiritual rather than material: it glorifies the sense of sight; its instrument is the eye. We are reminded of *Las Meninas* and its insistence on the nobility of the painter.

The spectator cannot yield entirely, however, to such an overly idealized Neoplatonic interpretation. This Venus is, after all, a very human testament to beauty—her flesh is so seductively appealing. Another more playful tradition, that of so-called "bedroom art,"[77] must be considered in relationship to this painting, especially in view of the fact that López-Rey mentions that this painting was placed on the ceiling of the mansion ("Jardín de San Joaquín") of the Seventh Marquis of Carpio, D. Gaspar de Haro y Guzmán—perhaps on the ceiling of a bedchamber.[78] We may recall also that Venus was considered the patron "saint" of prostitutes, thus embodying the contradictory coexistence of "Goddess of Beauty" and "Goddess of beauties," leaving the carnal and the sensual poised in an equivocal manner. It is difficult to see this painting as an allegory of vanity or lust; none of the emblems of lust mentioned by Pérez de Moya (such as doves, myrtle, the rose, the shell) are incorporated in this portrait.[79]

Velázquez's human emphasis in his representation of the gods of Olympus is also Arachne's in her tapestry-weaving dispute with Pallas, and this may account, at least in part, for the artist's attraction to the tale. Pallas depicts the majesty and power of the gods, their harsh castigation of arrogant mortals; the defiant Arachne chooses less exalted scenes of heavenly metamorphoses for the purposes of seduction (Europa and the bull, Leda and the swan, Danaë and the golden shower, etc.) [VI.70-128]. Ovid writes that "The golden-haired goddess was indignant at her success, and rent the embroidered web with its heavenly crimes" (*doluit successu flava virago/et rupit pictas, caelestia crimina, vestes* [VI.130-31]). Bustamante exaggerates and specifies more completely the causes of the goddess's outrage:

Palas quãdo vio que tãbiẽ auia texido, vuo dello grã pesar, no porque le parescio mal, ni vuo embidia de la tela, mas porque vio los dioses en ella pintados y descubiertos sus vicios cõ tã grãdes deshonrras: por cuya causa Palas tomo luego la tela, y rompiola toda: porq̃ jamas no paresciesse la afrenta manifiesta de los dioses. (p. 83r)

The emphasis shifts from the pride of workmanship to the honor of the gods.

Velázquez's *Fable of Arachne* (1644-48/1656-58)[80] [*Fig. 11*] was long thought to be a realistic view of the Royal Tapestry factory of Santa Isabel of Madrid, described in the inventory of the new Royal Palace of 1772 as "*Otro que expresa una fábrica de Tapices y varias mujeres hilando, y devanando. . .*,"[81] until accurately interpreted by Angulo Iñiguez.[82] The unique spatial disposition is responsible for the ambiguity of the painting: the significant unit of mythological meaning – here, as in Rubens's painting, Pallas Athena's gesture of striking Arachne – is relegated to a small background position, a fantasy in the distance as opposed to the proximity and reality of the foreground figures of the weavers. As in the case of Bacchus amidst the drinkers, or Apollo before the blacksmiths, the juxtaposition of two distinct realms is disconcerting.

Velázquez's transcription of the fable requires, in terms of chronology, not a linear reading but a reading in depth. The foreground incorporates the warning visit of Pallas Athena, in the disguise of an old woman, to the arrogant Arachne, described as being "low-born" (*de plebe* [VI.10]);[83] in the background the goddess, now in her helmet and shield revealed in her true identity, is lifting her hand to strike the mortal girl following their weaving contest: "and, as she held a shuttle of

Fig. 11. The Fable of Arachne (about 1644-48). Velázquez. *Museo del Prado.*

Cytorian boxwood, thrice and again she struck Idmonian Arachne's head" (*utque Cytoriaco radium de monte tenebat,/ter quater Idmoniae frontem percussit Arachnes* [VI.132-33]), writes Ovid, rendered in Bustamante as "y tomo la espada o lançadera cō que texia: y dio cō ella vn grā golpe en la frente de Aragnes" (p. 83r). In this way the discrete moments selected for illustration in the various "illustrated Ovids" are unified into one continuous narrative. The early Latin edition includes a sequential illustration, incorporating the scenes of advice (background), revelation and weaving (foreground) [*Fig. 12*]; the Anguillara edition illustrates the moment of advice [*Fig. 13*]; the Dolce edition chooses the dramatic moment of confrontation between the condemning goddess and the mortal [*Fig. 14*]. These illustrations assiduously avoid the grotesque transformation of Arachne into a spider, as do both Rubens and Velázquez.[84] In the background of Velázquez's painting is Titian's *The Rape of Europa*, the first of the fables woven by Arachne.

These narrative elements follow the Ovidian text, although loosely. Continuing questions in regard to this painting focus on the non-Ovidian ingredients: the presence of three elegant ladies, the musical instrument, the ladder.

Angulo Iñiguez has related the women to the presence of onlookers in the "illustrated Ovids" and has suggested that the damsels are a transcription of the Ovidian verses describing the reaction to the disguised goddess's revelation of herself: "The nymphs worshipped her godhead, and the Mygdonian women" (*venerantur numina nymphae/Mygdoni-*

Fig. 12. "Arachne." Ovid. *Metamorphoses* (Venice, Georgius de Rusconibus, 1517). *Rare Books and Manuscript Library, Columbia University.*

Fig. 13. "Arachne." *Le metamorfosi di Ovidio,* trans. Giouanni Andrea dell'Anguillara (Venetia, Alessandro Griffio, 1584). *Rare Books and Manuscript Library, Columbia University.*

desque nurus [VI.44-45]).[85] This becomes even more plausible in the light of Bustamante's contemporized translation of these verses as "Quando Arachnes la conoscio, luego se turbo: y las otras donzellas de casa quando la vieron honrraronla mucho" (p. 80r). In a previous passage Ovid had mentioned that "Often, to watch her wondrous skill, the nymphs would leave their own vineyards on Timolus' slopes, and the water-nymphs of Pactolus would leave their waters" (*huius ut adspi-*

Fig. 14. "Arachne." *Le trasformationi,* trans. Lodovico Dolce (Venetia, Domenico Farri, 1570). *Rare Books and Manuscript Library, Columbia University.*

cerent opus admirabile, saepe/deseruere sui nymphae vineta Timoli,/ deseruere suas nymphae Pactolides undas [VI.14-16]), described much more realistically in Bustamante as "muchas mugeres venian a marauilla por ver, la labor que ella texia en que se mostraua tan sabia" (p. 79v).

The strange presence of the viola da gamba is explained by Angulo Iñiguez in relationship to popular belief in the curative powers of music as an antidote to the poisonous spider bite.[86] As in the case of the armor on the floor of the forge in *The Forge of Vulcan*, this pictorial element completes by allusion the end of the tale, reminding us of Arachne's hideous metamorphosis into a spider.

Charles de Tolnay has noted that Pallas Athena, or Minerva, was considered a *dea lanificii*, viewed as a mechanical art, and suggests that the background scene represents Pallas as the Goddess of the Fine Arts (both Major and Minor) surrounded by personifications of Painting (Arachne herself), Sculpture, Architecture, and Music.[87] The painting, therefore, differentiates between the craft (spinning) and the realm of fine art (the background area is suffused with light, indicative of its higher prestige). Though they are distinct realms, they are intimately related: "Both, idea and craftmanship, together form the realm of art."[88] This significance of Minerva is also mentioned in Pérez de Moya:

Dícese Minerva, según San Isidoro: *Quasi manus, vel manus variarum artium.* Quiere decir: Mano o don de diversas artes. Llámase mano, porque las artes que ella halló (en cuanto fué mujer) eran mecánicas o manuales, como tejer, coser, hilar, según el mismo San Isidoro. Decir que es don de diversas artes, le conviene en cuanto es diosa del saber.[89]

It may well be that an allegory of the arts is intended. As has been discussed in the case of *Las Meninas*, the issues of the role and status of the painter were critical to Velázquez. It should be remembered, however, that the theme of the fable is not art *per se*, but *hubris*: Arachne is a *contemptor deum*.[90] The disguised goddess urges Arachne to "yield place to the goddess, and with humble prayer beg her pardon for your words, reckless girl" (*cede deae veniamque tuis, temeraria, dictis/supplice voce roga* [VI.32-33]) and her tapestry scenes are warnings of the punishment to come; Bustamante's translation insists that "nadie se deue ensoberuescer contra sus dioses" (p. 81v) and adds at the end of the tale that "todos ouieron gran miedo, y mas que de antes começaro a venerar y tener en mucho los dioses" (p. 83v). The commentators stress the moral significance of *soberbia*: Sánchez de Viana explains that the purpose of the punishment is a darles a entender su poquedad si carescen de la gracia de Dios, sin la qual no somos parte para hazer cosa intelectual, ni mecanica, que no sea fragil, y perecedera mas q̄ la debil tela de vna araña.[91]

Pérez de Moya's moral interpretation is that

Otrosí nos da ejemplo que por más excelencia que parezca que tenemos, no debemos igualarnos con Dios, ni ensoberbecernos de manera que por no reconocerlo todo de su bondad nos castigue y haga conocer lo que somos, siendo apartados de su gracia, y que todo cuanto sabemos es frágil como tela de araña, como experimentó Aragnes, vuelta en tan pequeño y vil animalejo.[92]

There is a tragic and complex quality to this tale. Arachne's artistry is perfection itself: "Not Pallas, nor Envy himself, could find a flaw in that work" (*Non illud Pallas, non illud carpere Livor/possit opus* [VI.129-30]). But the transcendence towards beauty is subjected to the envy and vengeance of the gods. The ladder, which Kahr interprets "as symbolizing the ascent from the material concerns of life to the heights of art,"[93] is also an attribute of Philosophy,[94] and therefore can be related to Pallas Athena as the figure of Wisdom. The beauty created through art can only come from knowledgable hands: only they can create the *concordia discors*, as alluded to in the following emblem:

QVAL LA MANO QVE ME TOCA.

Soy vn laud, de vozes estremado,
De euano, y marfil, con cuerdas de oro,
No se percibe, en quanto estoy colgado,
Quan excelente soy, y quan sonoro:
Si de algun ignorante, soy tocado,
Pierdo mi consonancia, y mi decoro.
Pero en manos de vn musico discreto,
Descubro quanto soy fino, y perfeto.[95]

The gap dividing mortals from the gods is bridged through art, for only by means of art can one approximate the gods' great gift of creation. The attainment of this gift by mortals requires wisdom and knowledge, qualities that distinguish and separate the artist from the mere craftsman. Nevertheless, bridging the gap is perilous, for it constitutes a transgression, for which Arachne, for example, suffered hideous punishment. The pagan tale is curiously close in meaning to the Christian exhortation to humility and reverence to God, as seen in the following emblem:

A QVO TREPIDABO.

Cest homme icy, prest a tumber en bas,
Et se froisser, au moins en apparence,
Monte tousiours, et rasseure son pas,
Sachant que Dieu le soustient d'asseurance.
Que tout Chrestien donc prie en confiance
Dieu, qu'il le tienne, et ne le laisse point.
Car s'il nous laisse, il n'y a esperance
D'aucun salut iusqu'a vn petit poinct.[96]

The tale following that of Arachne involves another example of *superbia*–Niobe. While emblematic literature chose her bloody tale as a caution against pride,[97] Velázquez chose Arachne's painful drama of the pride, achievement, and castigation of the artist.

It is difficult fully to understand or assess Velázquez's latest extant mythological painting, *Mercury and Argus* (ca. 1659) [*Fig. 15*]. Executed for the Hall of Mirrors in the Alcázar, it is but one of a series of four paintings placed between the windows of the room, the ceiling frescoes of which depict the Fable of Pandora. The other paintings (Venus and Adonis; Cupid and Psyche; Apollo Flaying Marsyas) did not survive the fire of 1734. The possibility exists that there was an overall allegorical program intended in the ceiling decorations, with the basic seme provided by "Pandora's Box" and the other fables adding related clusters of significance.[98]

The tale of Jupiter and Io is another example of divine *eros* (I.568-746): Jupiter, to circumvent the wrath of his jealous wife, Juno, converts the maiden Io (whom he has recently ravished) into a white heifer; Juno, still suspicious, requests the heifer as a gift and sends Argus, the many-eyed monster, to stand guard. In response to this, Jupiter summons Mercury, who, in the guise of a shepherd and with the help of a reed pipe and a magic rod, manages to lull Argus to sleep by telling him the apparently soporific tale of Pan and Syrinx, and finally decapitates him. Argus's eyes are transferred to the peacock's tail; Io, after much suffering and supplication, resumes her human shape and is worshipped as a goddess in Egypt (she has, in fact, been identified with Isis).

The story is fraught with connotations of erotic ridicule, for even as a heifer Io is beautiful (*bos quoque formosa est* [I.612]), and with overtones of pathos, for Io's human consciousness suffers in its bovine form. As did Rubens in his painting of this tale for the Torre de la Parada, Velázquez avoided the ludic or sentimental aspects and chose the moment of silence preceding the violence of the beheading of the sleeping Argus.

Fig. 15.   Mercury and Argus (about 1659). Velázquez. *Museo del Prado.*

When Mercury was going on to tell this story, he saw that all those eyes had yielded and were closed in sleep. Straightway he checks his words, and deepens Argus' slumber by passing his magic wand over those sleep-faint eyes. And forthwith he smites with his hooked sword the nodding head just where it joins the neck, and sends it bleeding down the rocks, defiling the rugged cliff with blood.

> (*talia dicturus vidit Cyllenius omnes*
> *subcubuisse oculos adopertaque lumina somno;*
> *supprimit extemplo vocem firmatque soporem*
> *languida permulcens medicata lumina virga.*
> *nec mora, falcato nutantem vulnerat ense,*
> *qua collo est confine caput, saxoque cruentum*
> *deicit et maculat praeruptam sanguine rupem.*)

(I. 713-19)

It is a moment of great suspense, immediately prior to the murder. As noted by Hermann Fränkel, "The sudden transition from lulling echoes to stern action gives a good dramatic effect"[99]—an intuition shared by both Rubens and Velázquez.

The darkness of the scene, the lack of landscape, the very ordinary "mortal" representations of Mercury and Argus serve to increase the tension of the moment in its naked simplicity. In comparing it to Rubens's painting with its lush background, Tolnay comments that

Su composición no está animada por corrientes dinámicas, casi no tiene paisaje y se concentra en su simplicidad, tan sólo en el drama humano. Velázquez acierta en la evocación de la dramática tensión del momento y del inminente cumplimiento del destino. Debe observarse también que en Velázquez faltan los rasgos burlescos que Rubens da a la caracterización de Argos. A pesar del realismo prevalece la noble belleza.[100]

The moment is one of dramatic significance in the narration; it is also, however, the focal point of the moral interpretations of the commentators. Sigler's allegory (appended to the Bustamante edition) explains that

Es dado el hombre en guarda a Argos, que es la razon que vee con muchos ojos, la qual adormida por Mercurio, que es el deleyte de los objectos propinquos viene a ser muerta del, y sus ojos se ponen en la cola del pauon de Juno, que es el inchado desseo de las riquezas, y honras y de las baxas e imperfectas bellezas. (p. 229v)

Sánchez de Viana y Pérez de Moya concentrate on the astrological meanings, but Pérez de Moya does include a passage to the effect that

Matar Mercurio a Argos y tomarle a Io, Mercurio significa la mala agudeza de la carne y a los halagüeños carnales deleites, los cuales engañan a la razón. Mercurio engañó a Argos cantando, porque la razón, viendo delante los carnales deleites que al hombre halagan, como a las orejas es dulce canto, adormécese, no apartándose de aquello que le es ocasión de mal, y entonces durmiendo muere.[101]

If the tradition of emblematic mythology is indeed relevant to the mythological paintings in the Hall of Mirrors, Velázquez's *Mercury and Argus* can be interpreted as "The Sleep of Reason" (or Prudence).

At a time when the strictures of the Council of Trent had caused mythological painting to become increasingly an erudite exercise in allegorical interpretation, Rubens is credited with revitalizing the genre by saving it from its affliction of uninspired intellectualization. According to Seznec:

At precisely the moment when, in Italian art, mythology is being relegated to the stage machinery of opera, Flanders, with Rubens, recalls it to primitive realities, to brute and elemental force. Sated with wine, gorged with meats and fruits, the gods are nourished to a point where their majesty, it is true, may be lost, but their animal vigor reappears. The naturalism of the North once more lends them its own flesh and blood, while the intoxicating effects of pantheism free them from all restraint.[102]

Velázquez, too, must be considered an innovator. The mysteries surrounding his mythological paintings remain. Whatever his sources of inspiration may have been, the artist reveals a profound appreciation of both the humor and the tragedy of Ovid's gods and goddesses, whose very "humanity" makes them both sublime and ridiculous. Knowledgable about the Christian moralizations of the myths, a much more active tradition in the art than in the fiction of the period, Velázquez added a far greater depth of understanding and appreciation of the complexities and contradictions of the Ovidian text, where love and lust, harmony and violence, charity and revenge coexist. If his gods seem to be caricatures, it is because Ovid's gods, too, are caricatures. Velázquez painted the gods accordingly—as mere mortals, playing out their tales of lust and violence, but also graced with inordinate beauty.

Notes

1 Discussed by Neumeister, *Mythos und Repräsentation*, pp. 283-92, who stresses that this is not a "revolutionary" painting in any social sense, but that it does indicate a concept of art different from that of Calderón, for whom God, not man, is the "creator" in any true sense (pp. 289-90): "Dies ist keine Revolution, und der Maler bleibt wie alle auf dem Bilde sichtbaren Personen zweifelsfrei dem Herrscher unterstellt, der den Auftrag für das Bild erteilt hat. Immerhin: Nicht König und Königin werden gezeigt, sonder ihre Abhängigkeit vom Tätigwerden des Malers" (p. 289).

2 Summarized by Jonathan Brown, "On the Meaning of *Las Meninas*," in *Images and Ideas in Seventeenth-Century Spanish Painting* (Princeton: Princeton University Press, 1978), p. 88, from Francisco J. Sánchez Cantón, *"Las Meninas" y sus personajes* (Barcelona, 1943).

3 Julián Gállego, *Visión y símbolos en la pintura española del Siglo de Oro*, trans. from French (Madrid: Aguilar, 1972), pp. 267-68, as quoted from P. Andrés Mendo, S. J., *Príncipe perfecto y Ministros adjustados*, Documentos políticos y morales (Salamanca, 1657), document VIII (also quoted in Neumeister, p. 286). The mirror appears frequently in Carreño's portraits of Charles II.

4 George Kubler, "Three Remarks on the *Meninas*," *The Art Bulletin*, 48 (1966), p. 214, as quoted from the unpublished Portuguese text, *Antiquity of Painting*, fol. 102 (Yale University Library).

5 "On the Meaning of *Las Meninas*," p. 109. This interpretation had been broached, but not developed, by Charles de Tolnay, "Velázquez' *Las Hilanderas* and *Las Meninas* (An Interpretation)," *Gazette des Beaux Arts*, 35 (1949), 21-38 and Kubler, "Three Remarks on the *Meninas*." Madlyn M. Kahr (after Brown) also supports this interpretation in "Velázquez and *Las Meninas*," *The Art Bulletin*, 57 (1975), 225-46 and in the final chapter of her book *Velázquez: The Art of Painting* (New York: Harper and Row, 1976), suggesting as a precedent the genre of the Flemish (mainly Antwerp) "Gallery Pictures" (*Cabinets d'amateurs*), in which the painter is often present and in which the dignity of the art of painting is affirmed.

6 See Brown, "Theory and Art in the Academy of Francisco Pacheco," in *Images and Ideas*, pp. 21-83.

7 The 154 volumes are itemized in F. J. Sánchez Cantón, "La librería de Velázquez," in *Homenaje a Menéndez Pidal* (Madrid: Hernando, 1925), III, pp. 379-406. See also his "Los libros españoles que poseyó Velázquez," in *Varia Velazqueña*, I (Madrid: Publicaciones de la Dirección General de Bellas Artes, 1960), pp. 640-48.

8 José López-Rey, *Velázquez. The Artist as a Maker, with a Catalogue Raisonné of His Extant Works* (Lausanne-Paris: Bibliothèque des Arts, 1979), pp. 160-61, n.78, is uncertain about this attribution. If he did actually portray Quevedo, it could have been done in 1622, between 1623 and 1629, or between 1631 and 1639 (at which time Quevedo was imprisoned). Versions of the portrait are included in López-Rey's earlier *Velázquez: A Catalogue Raisonné of His Oeuvre* (London: Faber and Faber, 1963), perhaps copies of a lost original.

9 See Shirley B. Whitaker, "The First Performance of Calderón's *El sitio de Bredá*," *RenQ*, 31 (Winter 1978), 515-31; Everett W. Hesse, "Calderón and Velázquez," *Hispania*, 35 (1952), 74-82. For an interesting study of the reverse

direction of influence between poet and painter see Frederick A. de Armas, "Lope and Titian," *CL*, 30 (Fall 1978), 338-52, who shows that three paintings of Titian entered into the composition of Lope's *La santa liga* (the subject of which is the battle of Lepanto).

10 Pt. III, *Crisi* XII, p. 998 in the *Obras completas*.

11 *Primor* VII, pp. 17-18 in the *Obras completas*. Arturo del Hoyo (pp. 17-18, n.1) notes the opinion of the critic Angel Vegue y Goldoni, "Un lugar común en la historia del arte español: El cambio de estilo en Ticiano, Navarrete, El Greco y Velázquez," *Archivo Español de Arte y Arqueología*, no. 10 (Jan.-April 1928), pp. 57-59, that the reference is not to Velázquez but to Navarrete el Mudo.

12 As quoted (p. 231) from *Las Tres Musas últimas castellanas. . .* (Madrid: Imprenta Real, 1670) in the study of Luisa López Grigera, "La silva 'El pincel' de Quevedo," in *Homenaje al Instituto de Filología y Literaturas Hispánicas "Dr. Amado Alonso" en su Cincuentenario, 1923-1973* (Buenos Aires: Instituto de Filología, 1975), pp. 221-42, who considers this version a late variant of the poem. J. M. Blecua (I, #205, pp. 400-06) does not include these verses in his edition.

13 Cossío, *Fábulas mitológicas*, p. 685; Gállego, *Visión y símbolos*, pp. 64-65.

14 José Camón Aznar, *Velázquez* (Madrid: Espasa-Calpe, 1964), II, p. 945, and Gállego, *Visión y símbolos*, p. 29. Critics also stress that, because the collection was inherited, at least in part, from his father-in-law Pacheco, it may not faithfully reflect his own taste.

15 Noted by Diego Angulo Iñiguez, *La mitología en el arte español del Renacimiento* (Madrid: Editorial Maestre, 1952), p. 13; F. J. Sánchez Cantón, *Velázquez y "Lo Clásico"* (Madrid: Taurus, 1961), pp. 13-14; Gállego, *Visión y símbolos*, p. 49; Brown, *Images and Ideas*, pp. 71-72.

16 Rosa López Torrijos, *La mitología en la pintura española del siglo XVII* (Ph.D. diss., Universidad Complutense de Madrid, 1982), p. 164. I thank Prof. Jonathan Brown for making the text available to me. On the special relationship of Titian with the earlier Hapsburgs, Charles V and Philip II (for both of whom he was the official portrait painter) see de Armas, "Lope and Titian" and Erwin Panofsky's "Titian and Ovid," in *Problems in Titian* (New York: New York University Press, 1969), pp. 139-71.

17 Angulo Iñiguez, *La mitología*, pp. 13-15; Gállego, *Visión y símbolos*, pp. 71-73; Brown, *Images and Ideas*, pp. 71-73; López Torrijos, *La mitología*, pp. 10-20. According to Frederick A. de Armas, "Lope de Vega and Michelangelo," *Hispania*, 65 (May 1982), 172-79, similar moral concerns of the Counter-Reformation account for Lope de Vega's sometimes negative evaluations of Michelangelo, to whom he was also opposed because of the painter's anti-Medici, pro-republican political stance.

18 In vol. I of F. J. Sánchez Cantón's edition of the original manuscript (Madrid: Editorial Maestre, 1956), lib. 2°, cap. VII, p. 412.

19 Ibid., p. 413.

20 *Images and Ideas*, p. 72.

21 Ibid., pp. 72-81. Angulo Iñiguez, *La mitología*, pp. 139-46 also includes a description and interpretation, which is further developed and refined by Brown.

22 Angulo Iñiguez, *La mitología*, dedicates a substantial portion of his volume to the representations of Hercules in Spain (pp. 65-134); the iconographi-

cal alliance established between the Hapsburgs and Hercules is discussed on pp. 70-74. See also Brown and Elliott, *A Palace Fit for a King*, pp. 156-61 and López Torrijos, *La mitología*, pp. 274-463. On the general resurgence of the allegorization of the myth following the Council of Trent, see Seznec, *The Survival of the Pagan Gods*, pp. 264-78.

23 For example, Kahr, *Velázquez*, p. 92, stresses the amorous rather than heroic connotations of the Mars figure, suggesting a satirical intent; José López-Rey, *Velázquez. The Artist as a Maker*, states of *Los Borrachos* that "The picture is, of course, a baroque, double-edged parody of the world of the fable and of sinful human ways" (p. 43) and of *Mars* that "It is a masterful scaling down of a god to a human shape – and a worthless one at that – achieved by a pictorial play on his very attributes, without detracting from the plastic integrity of the nude" (pp. 82-83). Enriqueta Harris, *Velázquez* (Oxford: Phaidon Press, 1982), p. 133, denies these "negative" interpretations; Diego Angulo Iñiguez, "La fábula de Vulcano, Venus y Marte y *La Fragua* de Velázquez," *AEA*, 33 (1960), 149-81, denies any parodic intent or even any irony in Velázquez's treatment of these myths, which he considers "dentro de la noble tradición clásica renacentista y creo que es ajena a la actitud burlesca de los poetas españoles contemporáneos e inmediatamente posteriores" (p. 175). López Torrijos, *La mitología*, denies any burlesque intent in the paintings (pp. 22-23), an interpretation with which Sánchez Cantón, *Velázquez y "Lo Clásico,"* does not agree, stressing, however, that "ha de advertirse que a la elegancia espiritual de Velázquez repugnaba extremar la caricatura y hasta la chocarrería que los poetas españoles de su tiempo empleaban para ridiculizar el paganismo todavía cantado en serio por muchos entonces" (p. 17).

24 "Introducción a Velázquez (1943)" in the *Obras completas*, VIII (Madrid: Revista de Occidente, 1962), pp. 481-82.

25 Brown, *Images and Ideas*, p. 82.

26 Ibid.

27 López-Rey, pp. 41-42; Harris, pp. 70, 73. Poets as well commemorate Rubens's presence in Spain, as is attested to by Lope's poem "Al Quadro y retrato de su Majestad que hizo Pedro Pablo de Rubens, Pintor excelentíssimo," written in praise of Rubens's portrait of Philip IV (see de Armas, "Lope and Titian," and Simon A. Vosters, "Lope de Vega y Rubens," in *Lope de Vega y los orígenes del teatro español*, ed. Manuel Criado de Val, pp. 733-44 [Madrid: Edi-6, 1981]).

28 Svetlana Alpers, *The Decoration of the Torre de la Parada* (London: Phaidon Press, 1971), p. 78.

29 Ibid., pp. 78-100.

30 Ibid., p. 110.

31 Ibid., p. 107.

32 Ibid., p. 155. Alpers follows the interpretation of Ovid in Brooks Otis, *Ovid as an Epic Poet*.

33 Ibid., pp. 156-57; 160-65.

34 In "La librería de Velázquez," pp. 405-06, item no. 150 and "Los libros españoles que poseyó Velázquez," p. 642, n.9. Angulo Iñiguez, *"Las Hilanderas,"* *AEA* 21 (1948), p. 4 also suggests the Bustamante edition, a supposition with which M. S. Soria agrees, in *"La fragua de Vulcano, de Velázquez," AEA*, 28 (1955), p. 142, n.4.

The date of the *princeps* edition is uncertain, but according to Beardsley,

Hispano-Classical Translations (p. 36, n.42), the date of 1543 is "usually postulated"; Menéndez Pelayo knew the 1551 edition but assumed the existence of an earlier edition; López Torrijos, *La mitología* (p. 57), lists the date as 1545.

35 Soria, "*La fragua de Vulcano*, de Velázquez," notes that one edition is based on Gabriel Giolito's Venetian edition of 1553 (1558, 1568(?), 1676, 1688); another, based on Domenico Farri's ("Fatti" in Soria) Venetian edition of 1570, using some woodcuts from a 1561 edition, as well as fifty copied from the first Italian edition of 1497. It is not known which edition Velázquez possessed, the 1553 or 1570 (pp. 142-43). (I have consulted is the 1570 edition.) See also López Torrijos, *La mitología*, p. 62.

36 This is the edition referred to throughout: *Las transformaciones de Ovidio en lengva española* (Anvers, Pedro Bellero, 1595), courtesy of The Hispanic Society of America. The initials of the illustrator, Virgilio Solís, are found on some of the prints (see López Torrijos, *La mitología*, pp. 60-61). The Salomon edition consulted at The Hispanic Society is the Lyon, Ian de Tovrnes, 1564 one; Anguillara's *Le metamorfosi* is available at The Hispanic Society in the Venice, Oratio de Gobbi, 1581 [1580] edition.

37 B. W. Ife, *Dos versiones de Píramo y Tisbe: Jorge de Montemayor y Pedro Sánchez de Viana*, p. VIII, considers Bustamante's and Mey's translations "traducciones 'chuleta.'" Antonio Pérez Sigler's version *Los quinze libros de los metamorphoseos* (Salamanca, Iuan Perier, 1580) and *Metamorphoseos* (Burgos, Juan Baptista Varesio [for] Pedro de Osete, 1609) and Pedro Sánchez de Viana's *Las transformaciones*, with *Anotaciones* (Valladolid, Diego Fernández de Cordoua, 1589) are certainly more "faithful" to the original text, though also less "colorful."

38 For dates I have followed López-Rey's *Catalogue Raisonné* in his *Velázquez*.

39 "Fábulas mitológicas de Velázquez," *Goya*, nos. 37-38 (1960), p. 106.

40 Kahr, *Velázquez* (p. 57) suggests Titian's Bacchic scenes, known to Velázquez in the Royal Collections, as particularly relevant. Harris also notes the influence of Venetian Bacchanals (p. 73).

41 Delphine F. Darby, "In the Train of a Vagrant Silenus," *Art in America*, 31 (July 1943), p. 145. Brown, *Images and Ideas*, adds that "A copy of the Greco-Roman relief that inspired Ribera was in the collection of the Duke of Alcalá and thus almost certainly was known to Velázquez" (p. 81, n.45). On Ribera's *Teoxenia*, severely damaged by fire, see López Torrijos, *La mitología*, pp. 987-93.

42 Harris, *Velázquez*, p. 74, plate 66. The engraving (inspired by a copy of Michelangelo's statue of *Bacchus*) was identified by M. S. Soria in his discussion of this painting "La *Venus, Los Borrachos* y la *Coronación*, de Velázquez," *AEA* 26 (1953), pp. 278-83 and further discussed as a "fiesta de vendimia" by Charles de Tolnay, "Las pinturas mitológicas de Velázquez," *AEA*, 34 (1961), p. 32.

43 Sigler's "alegoría" (p. 231 in the Bustamante edition) praises the "castidad figurada por Alcitoe, quan enemigos le sean el vino y el ocio, procura despreciando el fragil gusto de la demasiada beuida, y con el continuo exercicio defender y conseruarse en el vigor de su propia virtud." Sánchez de Viana notes of Bacchus that "Pintaronle moço, porque la borrachez nunca es sesuda, y tambien desnudo, porque los borrachos dizen desnudamente los secretos q̄ saben," and the result of imbibing is "parleria, temeridad, perdicion de la hazienda,

desuerguenças, enemistades y otras cosas desta manera" (p. 77v in the "Anotaciones").

44 *Philosophia secreta*, I, p. 264.

45 Ibid., p. 265.

46 Paul Barolsky, *Infinite Jest. Wit and Humor in Italian Renaissance Art* (Columbia and London: University of Missouri Press, 1978), p. 52.

47 Pérez de Moya, I, p. 266.

48 Angulo Iñiguez, "La fábula de Vulcano, Venus y Marte y *La Fragua* de Velázquez," pp. 179-80, reviews the suggestions of deceit (Justi), Christian significance of Apollo in keeping with the interpretation of *Joseph's Blood-Stained Coat* as a prefiguration of the death of Christ (Harris) and his own suggestion of envy (on the part of Apollo and of Joseph's brothers).

49 Soria, "*La fragua de Vulcano*, de Velázquez," pp. 142-45, suggests the Salomon illustration of Thetis visiting the forge of Vulcan to request arms for Achilles as a possible source; Angulo Iñiguez, "La fábula de Vulcano, Venus y Marte," notes that the Antonio Tempesta engravings of the *Metamorphoses* include a scene of Apollo visiting the forge in which a Cyclopes is present (p. 172); Tolnay, "Las pinturas mitológicas de Velázquez," mentions that Tintoretto's painting, *The Forge of Vulcan*, includes the Cyclopes (p. 33). Harris, *Velázquez*, pp. 84-85, suggests the influence of antique marble reliefs in Rome, in particular *Vulcan and the Cyclopes Forging the Shield of Achilles* of the Hadrianic period.

50 *Velázquez*, p. 80, plate 71.

51 This attitudinal difference is stressed by Angulo Iñiguez, "La fábula de Vulcano, Venus y Marte," p. 174, and López Torrijos, *La mitología*, pp. 782-85.

52 See above, n.48.

53 "Las pinturas mitológicas de Velázquez": "la pintura podría más bien describirse como la visita de Apolo, representante de las nobles artes, al taller del artesano, llevando a las tinieblas la luz de las *artes maiores*" (p. 33).

54 "Anotaciones" in *Las transformaciones*, pp. 81r and v. On astrological interpretations in general see Seznec, *The Survival of the Pagan Gods*, bk. I, chap. II, "The Physical Tradition," pp. 37-83; on Venus and Mars in particular see Wind, *Pagan Mysteries in the Renaissance*, chap. V, "Virtue Reconciled with Pleasure," pp. 78-88.

55 *Philosophia secreta*, I, p. 176.

56 Ibid., p. 168.

57 Ibid., pp. 174-75. Angulo Iñiguez, "La fábula de Vulcano, Venus y Marte," p. 170, mentions that Juan de la Cueva in his poem, "Los amores de Marte y Venus" (1604), identifies four Cyclopes—Brontes, Pyracmon, Steropes, Aemonides—while Pérez de Moya and Vitoria only list the first three names.

58 Angulo Iñiguez, "La fábula de Vulcano, Venus y Marte," p. 179, notes that "Y digo esto porque ya Justi protestó de que Stirling y otros reprochasen a Velázquez que encontrándose a la sombra del Vaticano y de Rafael pintase un Apolo tan innoble, y de que otros le tachasen de falta de fantasía y de fuerza ideal." Soria, "*La fragua de Vulcano*, de Velázquez," comments that this figure, whom he incorrectly identifies as Mercury, "parece un tanto femenina" (p. 143).

59 *Philosophia secreta*, I, p. 205.

60 López-Rey, *Catalogue Raisonné* in *Velázquez*, p. 419 (italics in original).

61 Carl Justi, *Diego Velázquez and His Times*, trans. A. H. Keane (London: H. Grevel Co., 1889) in his discussion of *Mars*, pp. 458-61; Tolnay, "Las pin-

turas mitológicas de Velázquez," p. 35; Angulo Iñiguez, *Velázquez; cómo compuso sus principales cuadros* (Sevilla: Laboratorio de Arte de la Universidad de Sevilla, 1947), pp. 90-93.

62 Tolnay, "Las pinturas mitológicas de Velázquez," p. 36.

63 Angulo Iñiguez, "Fábulas mitológicas de Velázquez," p. 117.

64 Kahr, *Velázquez*, p. 92.

65 *The Decoration of the Torre de la Parada*, p. 136.

66 Ibid., p. 105. Alpers specifies Xenophon, *Cynegeticus* (I.18) as the *locus classicus* of the hunt as a peaceful school of war (p. 102, n.220).

67 *Don Quijote de la Mancha*, II, ch. XVII, p. 655, in the edition of Martín de Riquer (Barcelona: Editorial Juventud, 1971).

68 Barolsky discusses Botticelli's painting, pp. 37-44, and Tintoretto's painting, p. 176. Also see Wind, pp. 78-88.

69 Sánchez Cantón, "*La Venus del espejo*," *AEA*, 33 (1960), pp. 141-44, "La historia de *La Venus del espejo*"; López-Rey, *Catalogue Raisonné* of *Velázquez*, p. 451. Kahr, *Velázquez*, p. 103, n. 75, points out that Velázquez may indeed have painted other female nudes, judging from the titles of his lost works, *Venus and Adonis* and *Cupid and Psyche*; López Torrijos, *La mitología*, pp. 918-19, mentions allusions to a "*Venus tendida* de Velázquez de dos baras," as well as "una *mujer desnuda* de mano de Velázquez."

70 Tolnay, "Las pinturas mitológicas de Velázquez," pp. 37-38, who also mentions Michelangelo's nude figure in the Sistine Chapel. In addition, Soria, "La *Venus, Los Borrachos* y la *Coronación*, de Velázquez," pp. 271-78, suggests as a source a print of *Venus and Adonis* by Antonio van Blocklandt (Bloeklandt), noting significant changes; Sánchez Cantón, "*La Venus del espejo*," pp. 146-48, calls attention to three prints, in particular one by Agostino Veneziano.

71 Sánchez Cantón, "*La Venus del espejo*," p. 141, discounts this supposition.

72 Gállego, *Visión y símbolos*, p. 267. He mentions a painting by Georges de la Tour of the Magdalene, in which a mirror reflects a skeleton; also Soria, "La *Venus, Los Borrachos* y la *Coronación*, de Velázquez," pp. 276-78. It is important to emphasize that Ripa's *Iconologia* is catalogued in Velázquez's library (no. 146, p. 405 in Sánchez Cantón's "La librería de Velázquez").

73 Gállego, p. 324.

74 Sánchez Cantón, "La librería de Velázquez," p. 397, no. 77.

75 The English citations are from Sir Thomas Hoby's 1561 translation of *The Book of the Courtier*, Everyman's Library (London and Toronto: J. M. Dent & Sons; New York: E. P. Dutton & Co., 1948). The Italian citations refer to the following edition: *Il Cortegiano*, ed. Vittorio Cian (Florence: G. C. Sansoni, 1916).

76 See Otto Brendel, "The Interpretation of the Holkham *Venus*," *The Art Bulletin*, 28 (June 1946), 65-75, for a discussion of the Neoplatonic intentions of Titian's paintings, *Venus and the Luteplayer* and *Venus and the Organplayer*, two versions of which are in Madrid.

77 Barolsky, *Infinite Jest*, "corrects" Brendel's interpretation as an "over-Neoplatonic" reading that ignores the satirical overtones and playful sensuality of the paintings (pp. 165-71). Velázquez's Venus is a very chaste figure compared to Titian's versions.

78 *Catalogue Raisonné* of *Velázquez*, p. 452.

79 *Philosophia secreta*, II, pp. 36-39.

80 The earlier date is listed in López-Rey, *Catalogue Raisonné* of *Velázquez*; the later date appears in Kahr, *Velázquez* (after 1657), p. 204; Harris, *Velázquez* (about 1656-58) p. 160; López Torrijos lists about 1657 (p. 805). There is also a seated portrait of Arachne (1644-48).

81 López-Rey, p. 455 (italics in original).

82 "*Las Hilanderas,*" *AEA*, 21 (1948), 1-19; see also López Torrijos, *La mitología*, pp. 805-14.

83 This interpretation is suggested by Angulo Iñiguez, "*Las Hilanderas,*" p. 15.

84 The illustrations of the "illustrated Ovids" are discussed by Angulo Iñiguez, "*Las Hilanderas*: Sobre la iconografía de Aracne," *AEA*, 25 (1952), 67-84.

85 "*Las Hilanderas,*" p. 15.

86 Ibid., pp. 9-14.

87 "Velázquez' *Las Hilanderas* and *Las Meninas* (An Interpretation)," pp. 21-38. López-Rey, pp. 106-07, interprets the figure of the seated Arachne as the personification of Painting.

88 Tolnay, p. 32.

89 *Philosophia secreta,* II, p. 50.

90 Otis, *Ovid as an Epic Poet,* p. 148.

91 *Las transformaciones,* p. 121v.

92 *Philosophia secreta,* II, p. 59.

93 *Velázquez,* p. 210.

94 Guy de Tervarent, *Attributs et symboles dans l'art profane 1450-1600* (Geneva: Droz, 1958), I, pp. 151-52.

95 From Sebastián de Covarrubias Orozco, *Emblemas morales,* II (1610) in *Emblemata. Handbuch zur Sinnbildkunst des XVI. und XVII. Jahrhunderts,* ed. Arthur Henkel and Albrecht Schöne (Stuttgart: J. B. Metzler, 1967), p. 1298.

96 *Emblemata,* p. 1416, from Georgia Montanea, *Monumenta Emblematum Christianorum virtutum* (MDCXIX).

97 Ibid., p. 1656, from Alciatus, *Emblemata* (1550) as *Superbia.* Also in Horozco y Covarrubias, *Emblemas morales,* III (1589).

98 The iconographical plan for the ceiling of the Hall of Mirrors, depicting the fable of Pandora, was designed by Velázquez and executed by Carreño, Rizi, and Colonna. See López Torrijos, *La mitología,* pp. 1110-20, who comments:

> Pero aún hay una noticia más chocante en lo que se refiere a estas pinturas y es que la serie de Pandora termina con el final feliz de las bodas de Epimeteo y Pandora sin hacer alusión alguna a los males que escaparon de su vaso y que quedaron para siempre entre los hombres. No cabe duda pues, que dentro del programa proyectado por Velázquez hubo una intención aún difícil de comprender. El hecho de no incluir el aspecto negativo de la historia y el que se dedicase el espacio principal a la dotación de los dioses a Pandora hace pensar en una interpretación de ésta como "Don de todos" según las palabras de Panofsky. [The author refers to the study of Dora and Erwin Panofsky, *Pandora's Box: The Changing Aspects of a Mythical Symbol* (New York: Pantheon Books, 1956).] (p. 1120).

Of the pair "Venus and Adonis" and "Cupid and Psyche" López Torrijos writes:

> Sería fácil atribuir a estos dos cuadros de Velázquez, pensados para lugares opuestos dentro del mismo salón, una significación alegórica también contrapuesta, dentro del contexto que estamos viendo para la fábula de Psique y que podía ser una alegoría del Amor Divino (Cupido y Psique) con un final feliz de la historia como corresponde a la de los

hechos, frente a una alegoría del Amor Humano (Venus y Adonis), con un triste final, consecuencia de los "peligros que suceden a los que usan de los ojos corporales para sus deseos" en palabras de Mallara (Mal Lara). (p. 1037)

99 *Ovid: A Poet Between Two Worlds*, p. 85.

100 "Las pinturas mitológicas de Velázquez," p. 41. He also relates the poses of the figures in the painting to a Michelangelo *ignudo* and to an antique statue, *Galo moribundo* (pp. 41-42).

101 *Philosophia secreta*, II, p. 78. López Torrijos, *La mitología*, p. 837, notes that in the *Emblemas morales* of Horozco y Covarrubias (XIII) the story of Mercury and Argus is used as a warning against the charm of flattery: "En que se nos muestra clara semejança de lo que puede el son apazible de la lisonja, pues el mas despierto engaña fácilmente con la blandura."

102 *The Survival of the Pagan Gods*, p. 322.

Conclusion

In the weaving of her beautiful tapestry, Arachne confronts Pallas Athena in a war of conflicting interpretations: to the goddess's majestic official version of a *deorum concilium* of "twelve heavenly gods on lofty thrones in awful majesty" (*bis sex caelestes medio Iove sedibus altis/ augusta gravitate sedent* [VI.72-73]) sitting in dreadful judgment of "upstarts" from the mortal world, Arachne responds with a comical version of the gods' lustful and deceitful transformations, beginning with Jupiter's rape of Europa in the guise of a bull. With her colorful threads, she brings to life these paradoxical "heavenly crimes" (*caelestia crimina* [v. 131]). Her tapestry is, in effect, a parody of Pallas Athena's; as she is "singing after the style of an original but with a difference," Arachne "discrowns" the mythological gods in an act of carnivalistic reversal.

Like Arachne, these artists of seventeenth-century Spain are engaged in a battle of signification, primarily with their own predecessors' interpretations of the erotic mythological tales (be they Boscán, the *romancistas*, the hackneyed bevy of *culterano* poets; in the case of Góngora, the artist himself is the target as he performs his own elaborate deconstruction in his 1618 *romance* on Pyramus and Thisbe, "La ciudad de Babilonia." The same may be true for Calderón's *Céfalo y Pocris*). The poets and playwrights "lay bare" the devices of construction of previous versions in order to discard them.

In their revisions they reject, as does Velázquez, the inflexible monolithism of the moral-allegorical readings, and they avoid the grandiose Ovid who charts in the *Metamorphoses* the course of history from the Creation to the Age of Augustus. Like Arachne they focus on the amatory fragments, exposing the frailties and foibles of these all-too-human gods. Paradoxically, as they dismantle previous misreadings, their decentered, indeed "eccentric" reading of the erotic tales often affords them insights into crucial implications in the original text. This is particularly apparent in Góngora's disarticulation of Boscán's "translation" of Musaeus's epyllion, *Hero and Leander*, or in Velázquez's penetration of Ovid's disturbing and fascinating ambiguity, lost in the iconographical tradition of painting. Other poets uncover the lust and violence, as well as the sensuality and wit in these tales. As Arachne opposed Pallas Athena's "official" reading of pagan theology, so too do these artists subvert the "authoritative" versions of the past.

Arachne is considered arrogant in a social as well as an ethical sense. She is not only a mere mortal, she is in addition "low-born" (*de plebe* [v.10]), an "overreacher" who respects neither the authority of old age (she rebuffs the advice of the old woman, Pallas in disguise), nor the necessary superiority of a divinity. In her actions, as in her tapestry picture, she shows herself to be antiauthoritarian, antihierarchical, subversive of the established order and accustomed norms. When Pallas Athena removes her disguise and reveals herself, the other nymphs "worshipped her godhead" (*venerantur numina nymphae* [v.44]), while "Arachne alone remained unafraid" (*sola est non territa virgo* [v.45]).

A similar hint of *superbia* is evidenced by these artists as they engage in their polemic with previous texts: they are recalcitrant to imitation in any form, of classical or contemporary authors, preferring the surprises and incongruities of unexpected displacements. Discourse becomes increasingly self-conscious, and the artist intrudes in the text, straining the metalinguistic functions of language, adopting metacritical stances with frequency. The writers invade the space of the text as obviously as Velázquez trespasses the boundaries of the picture frame, an interloper in the space of the painting. In their assertion of the centrality of creativity and of themselves as creators, they declare the previously essential systems, consecrated by time and custom, as marginalia.

Arachne suffered a hideous fate. Having provoked the wrath of the goddess, she attempts to hang herself; Pallas Athena allows her to live but condemns her to continue her weaving in the form of spinning – as a spider. What made Pallas Athena so angry? Ovid attributes her ire to envy: "The golden-haired goddess was indignant at her success, and rent the embroidered web with its heavenly crimes" (*doluit successu flava virago/et rupit pictas, caelestia crimina, vestes* [vv.130-31]). Bustamante, in his translation and interpretation, stresses another aspect:

Palas quãdo vio que tãbiẽ auia texido, vuo dello grã pesar, no porque le parescio mal, ni vuo embidia de la tela, mas porque vio los dioses en ella pintados y descubiertos sus vicios cõ tã grãdes deshonrras. (p. 83r)

Is this a misunderstanding, or a profound understanding of the Ovidian tale? Bustamante perceived that Arachne's laughter at the gods constitutes a radical decentering of the ideological world: this, rather than her artistry, proved to be an unbearable threat to the goddess.

Plato in his *Republic* had censured the laughter of the gods; more recently, Jorge da Burgos in Umberto Eco's *Il nome della rosa* fears (literally to death) the liberating effects of laughter. Laughter is subversive and critical of all hierarchical order. We recall that *Céfalo y Pocris* was presented during Carnival, an exceptional period when reversals and blasphemy are sanctioned, and therefore "safe" – at least in part.

What we do not know, and cannot know, is if "Sus Reales Majestades" laughed, and if so, how comfortably or uncomfortably? These parodic transformations and unorthodox accents, some frivolous and some profound, are more than secondary and supplemental exercises. They bear testament to a revolution in people's perception of the world and of their place in the world. So it appeared, it seems, to Pallas Athena, and her revenge was swift and certain.

Bibliography of Works Cited

Alarcos García, Emilio. "Quevedo y la parodia idiomática." *Archivum*, 5, no. 1 (1955), 3-38.

Alatorre, Antonio. "Fortuna varia de un chiste gongorino." *NRFH*, 15 (1961), 483-504.

——. "Los romances de Hero y Leandro." *Libro jubilar de Alfonso Reyes*, pp. 1-41. México: Dirección General de Difusión Cultural, 1956.

Alcázar, Baltasar del. *Poesías*. Ed. Francisco Rodríguez Marín. 2 vols. Madrid: Librería de los Sucesores de Hernando, 1910.

Allen, Don Cameron. *Mysteriously Meant*. Baltimore and London: Johns Hopkins University Press, 1970.

Alonso, Dámaso. *Góngora y el "Polifemo."* 3 vols. 6th ed. Madrid: Gredos, 1974.

——. *La lengua poética de Góngora*. Parte primera. 3d ed. *RFE*, anejo XX. Madrid: C.S.I.C., 1961.

Alpers, Paul. *The Singer of the "Eclogues."* Berkeley and Los Angeles: University of California Press, 1979.

Alpers, Svetlana. *The Decoration of the Torre de la Parada*. London: Phaidon Press, 1971.

Amezúa y Mayo, Agustín González de. *Opúsculos histórico-literarios*. 3 vols. Madrid: C.S.I.C., 1951-53.

Angulo Iñiguez, Diego. "La fábula de Vulcano, Venus y Marte y *La Fragua* de Velázquez." *AEA*, 33 (1960), 149-81.

——. "Fábulas mitológicas de Velázquez." *Goya*, nos. 37-38 (1960), 104-19.

——. "*Las Hilanderas*," *AEA*, 21 (1948), 1-19.

——. "*Las Hilanderas*: sobre la iconografía de Aracne," *AEA*, 25 (1952), 67-84.

——. *La mitología en el arte español del Renacimiento*. Madrid: Editorial Maestre, 1952.

——. *Velázquez; cómo compuso sus principales cuadros*. Sevilla: Laboratorio de Arte de la Universidad de Sevilla, 1947.

Araya, Guillermo. "Shakespeare y Góngora parodian la fábula de Píramo y Tisbe." *Estudios Filológicos*, no. 1: *En homenaje a Eleazar Huerta*, pp. 19-40. Valdivia: Facultad de Filosofía y Letras de la Universidad Austral de Chile, 1965.

Aubrun, Charles V. "*Eco y Narciso*." *Homenaje a William Fichter*. Ed. A. David Kossoff and José Amor y Vázquez, pp. 47-58. Madrid: Castalia, 1971.

Bakhtin, Mikhail. *Problems of Dostoevsky's Poetics* (1929). Trans. R. W. Rotsel. Ann Arbor, Michigan: Ardis, 1973.

——. *Rabelais and His World* (1965). Trans. Hélène Iswolsky. Rpt. Cambridge: M.I.T. Press, 1968.

Ball, Robert. "Góngora's Parodies of Literary Convention." 2 vols. Ph.D. diss., Yale University, 1976.

Barnard, Mary E. "Myth in Quevedo: The Serious and the Burlesque in the Apollo and Daphne Poems," *HR*, 52 (1984), 499-522.

Barolsky, Paul. *Infinite Jest. Wit and Humor in Italian Renaissance Art*. Columbia and London: University of Missouri Press, 1978.

Barrera y Leirado, Cayetano Alberto de la. *Catálogo bibliográfico y biográfico del teatro antiguo español, desde sus orígenes hasta mediados del siglo XVIII* (1860). London: Tamesis, 1968.

Baudelaire, Charles. *Curiosités esthétiques*. Ed. M. Jacques Crépet. Paris: Louis Conard, 1923.

Beardsley, Jr., Theodore S. *Hispano-Classical Translations Printed Between 1482 and 1699*. Duquesne Studies Philological Series, no. 12. Pittsburg: Duquesne University Press, 1970.

Benveniste, Emile. *Problems of General Linguistics*. Trans. Mary Elizabeth Meek. Miami Linguistic Series, no. 8. Coral Gables, Florida: University of Miami Press, 1971.

Bergman, Hannah E. "A Court Entertainment of 1638." *HR*, 42 (Winter 1974), 67-81.

Beverley, John R. *Aspects of Góngora's "Soledades."* Purdue University Monographs in Romance Languages, vol. 1. Amsterdam: John Benjamins B. V., 1980.

Booth, Wayne C. *A Rhetoric of Irony*. Chicago and London: University of Chicago Press, 1974.

Born, Lester K. "Ovid and Allegory." *Speculum*, 9 (1934), 362-79.

Boscán, Juan. *Las obras de Juan Boscán*. Ed. William I. Knapp. Madrid: M. Murillo, 1875.

Brendel, Otto. "The Interpretation of the Holkham *Venus*." *Art Bulletin*, 28 (June 1946), 65-75.

Brown, Jonathan. *Images and Ideas in Seventeenth-Century Spanish Painting*. Princeton: Princeton University Press, 1978.

—— and J. H. Elliott. *A Palace Fit for a King*. New Haven: Yale University Press, 1980.

Bush, Douglas. *Mythology and the Renaissance Tradition in English Poetry*. Minneapolis: University of Minnesota Press, 1932.

Cabañas, Pablo. *El mito de Orfeo en la literatura española*. Madrid: C.S.I.C., 1948.

Calderón de la Barca, Pedro. *Comedias*, a facsimile edition. Vol. VIII of *Tercera parte*, 1664. Ed. D. W. Cruickshank and J. E. Varey. London: Gregg Int. Publishers Ltd. and Tamesis, 1973.

——. *Comedias*. Ed. D. Juan Eugenio Hartzenbusch. 4 vols. *BAE*, vols. 7, 9, 12, 14. Madrid: Rivadeneyra, 1849-51.

——. *Obras completas*. Ed. Angel Valbuena Briones (1 and 2), Angel Valbuena Prat (3). 3 vols. Madrid: Aguilar, 1952-66.

——. *Céfalo y Pocris*. Ed. Alberto Navarro González. Salamanca: Almar, 1979.

——. *Celos aun del aire matan*. Ed. Matthew D. Stroud. San Antonio: Trinity University Press, 1981.

——. *Eco y Narciso*. Ed. Charles V. Aubrun. Flers: Imprimerie Folloppe, 1961.

——. *El verdadero Dios Pan*. Ed. José M. de Osma. University of Kansas Humanistic Studies, no. 28. Lawrence: University of Kansas Press, 1949.

Camón Aznar, José. *Velázquez*. 2 vols. Madrid: Espasa-Calpe, 1964.

Carew, Thomas. *The Poems of Thomas Carew*. Ed. Rhodes Dunlap. Oxford: Clarendon Press, 1949.

Caro Baroja, Julio. *El Carnaval*. Madrid: Taurus, 1965.

Carvalho (Carballo), Luis Alfonso de. *Cisne de Apolo* (1602). Ed. Alberto Porqueras Mayo. 2 vols. in 1. Madrid: C.S.I.C., 1958.

Castiglione, Baldassare. *The Book of the Courtier*. Trans. Sir Thomas Hoby (1561). Everyman's Library. London and Toronto: J. M. Dent & Sons; New York: E. P. Dutton & Co., 1948.

———. *Il Cortegiano*. Ed. Vittorio Cian. Florence: G. C. Sansoni, 1916.

Castillejo, Cristóbal de. *Obras*. Ed J. Domínguez Bordona. 4 vols. Madrid: Ediciones de "La Lectura," 1926-28.

Castillo Solórzano, Alonso de. *Donayres del Parnaso*. Pt. 1. Madrid, Diego Flamenco, 1624. *The Hispanic Society of America*.

Castro, Francisco de. *Metamorphoses a lo moderno y otras poesías*. Ed. Kenneth R. Scholberg. México: Colegio de México, 1958.

Catullus. *Catullus*. Trans. F. W. Cornish. Loeb Classical Library. 1913; rpt. Cambridge: Harvard University Press; London: William Heinemann Ltd., 1976.

———. *Catullus*. Trans. Reney Myers and Robert J. Ormsby. London: George Allen and Unwin Ltd., 1972.

———. *Odi et Amo. The Complete Poems of Catullus*. Trans. Roy Arthur Swanson. Indianapolis: Bobbs-Merrill, 1959.

Cervantes, Miguel de. *Don Quijote de la Mancha*. Ed. Martín de Riquer. 2 vols. Barcelona: Editorial Juventud, 1971.

———. *Novelas ejemplares*. Ed. Francisco Rodríguez Marín. Clásicos castellanos, 2 vols. Madrid: Espasa-Calpe, 1943.

Chapman, W. G. "Las comedias mitológicas de Calderón," *RL*, 5 (1954), 35-67.

Cirot, G. "Góngora et Musée," *BH*, 33 (1931), 328-31.

Close, Anthony. *The Romantic Approach to "Don Quixote."* Cambridge: Cambridge University Press, 1978.

Coleman, Robert. *Vergil: Eclogues*. Cambridge: Cambridge University Press, 1977.

Collard, Andrée. *Nueva poesía: conceptismo, culteranismo en la literatura española*. Madrid: Castalia, 1967.

Cossío, José María de. *Fábulas mitológicas en España*. Madrid: Espasa-Calpe, 1952.

Cotarelo y Mori, D. Emilio. *Colección de entremeses, loas, bailes, jácaras y mojigangas*. 2 vols. *NBAE*, vols. 17 and 18. Madrid: Bailly y Bailliére, 1911.

Crespo Matellán, Salvador. *La parodia dramática en la literatura española*. Acta Salmanticensia, Filosofía y Letras, no. 107. Salamanca: Ediciones Universidad de Salamanca, 1979.

Croll, Morris W. *Style, Rhetoric, and Rhythm; Essays*. Ed. J. Max Patrick *et al*. Princeton: Princeton University Press, 1966.

Culler, Jonathan. *Structuralist Poetics*. Ithaca, New York: Cornell University Press, 1975.

Darby, Delphine F. "In the Train of a Vagrant Silenus." *Art in America*, 31 (July 1943), 140-48.

Darst, David H. *Juan Boscán*. Boston: Twayne Publishers, 1978.

De Armas, Frederick A. "Lope de Vega and Michelangelo." *Hispania*, 65 (May 1982), 172-79.

———. "Lope de Vega and Titian." *CL*, 30 (Fall 1978), 338-52.

Díaz Rengifo, Juan. *Arte poética española* (1592). Barcelona: Imprenta de María Martí, viuda, ded. 1703.

Díez Borque, José María. *Sociología de la comedia española del Siglo XVII*. Madrid: Cátedra, c. 1976.

Dixon, Victor. "Juan Pérez de Montalbán's *Segundo Tomo de las Comedias*." *HR*, 29 (April 1961), 91-109.

Dunn, Peter N. *Castillo Solórzano and the Decline of the Spanish Novel*. Oxford:

Blackwell, 1952.

Eichenbaum, Boris. "The Theory of the 'Formal Method.'" *Russian Formalist Criticism: Four Essays*. Ed. Lee T. Lemon and Marion J. Reis, pp. 99-139. Lincoln and London: University of Nebraska Press, 1965.

Ettinghausen, Henry. *Francisco de Quevedo and the Neostoic Movement*. Oxford: Oxford University Press, 1972.

Forster, Leonard. *The Icy Fire. Five Studies in European Petrarchism*. Cambridge: Cambridge University Press, 1969.

Fränkel, Hermann. *Ovid: A Poet Between Two Worlds*. 1945; rpt. Berkeley and Los Angeles: University of California Press, 1969.

Freud, Sigmund. *Wit and Its Relation to the Unconscious*. Trans. A. A. Brill. 1916; rpt. London: Kegan Paul, Trench, Trubner & Co. [1922].

Gállego, Julián. *Visión y símbolos en la pintura española del Siglo de Oro*. Trans. from French. Madrid: Aguilar, 1972.

Gallego Morell, Antonio. *Garcilaso de la Vega y sus comentaristas*. Granada: Urania, 1966.

García Lorca, Federico. *Obras completas*. Ed. Arturo del Hoyo, 13th ed. Madrid: Aguilar, 1967.

Garcilaso de la Vega. *Poesías castellanas completas*. Ed. Elias L. Rivers. Madrid: Castalia, 1969.

Gates, Eunice Joiner. "New Light on the *Antídoto* Against Góngora's 'Pestilent' *Soledades*." *PMLA*, 66 (September 1951), 746-64.

Gendreau, Michèle. *Héritage et création: recherches sur l'humanisme de Quevedo*. Lille: Université de Lille, 1977.

Góngora y Argote, Luis de. *Documentos gongorinos*. Ed. Eunice Joiner Gates. México: Colegio de México, 1960.

——. *Obras completas*. Ed. Juan e Isabel Millé y Giménez. 6th ed. Madrid: Aguilar, 1972.

——. *"Píramo y Tisbe," con los comentarios de Salazar Mardones y Pellicer*. Ed. A. Rumeau. Paris: Ediciones Hispano-Americanas, 1961.

——. *Poems of Góngora*. Ed. R. O. Jones. Cambridge: Cambridge University Press, 1966.

——. *Romances*. Ed. Antonio Carreño. Madrid: Cátedra, 1982.

——. *Romances, Letrillas, Sonetos y Canciones. Fragmento de la Soledad Primera*. Ed. Alicia Galaz Vivar. Santiago de Chile: Editorial Universitaria, 1961.

Gracián, Baltasar. *Obras completas*. Ed. Arturo del Hoyo. 3d ed. Madrid: Aguilar, 1967.

Green, Otis H. *The Literary Mind of Medieval and Renaissance Spain*. Lexington: The University Press of Kentucky, 1970.

——. "On Juan Ruiz's Parody of the Canonical Hours." *HR*, 26 (January 1958), 12-34.

——. Review of Amédée Mas, *La caricature de la femme, du mariage, et de l'amour dans l'oeuvre de Quevedo. HR*, 28 (January 1960), 72-76.

Guyler, Samuel L. "Góngora's *Polifemo*: The Humor of Imitation." *RHM*, 37, no. 4 (1972-73), 237-52.

Harris, Enriqueta. *Velázquez*. Oxford: Phaidon Press, 1982.

Henkel, Arthur and Albrecht Schöne. *Emblemata. Handbuch zur Sinnbildkunst des XVI. und XVII. Jahrhunderts*. Stuttgart: J. B. Metzler, 1967.

Herrero, Miguel. "Génesis de la figura del donaire." *RFE*, 30 (1941), 46-78.

Hesse, Everett W. "Calderón and Velázquez." *Hispania*, 35 (1952), 74-82.

Hidalgo, Gaspar Lucas de. *Diálogos de apacible entretenimiento que contienen unas Carnestolendas de Castilla. BAE*, vol. 36, pp. 278-316. Madrid: Rivadeneyra, 1855.

Highet, Gilbert. "The Philosophy of Juvenal." *TAPA*, 80 (1949), 254-70.

Hilborn, Harry Warren. *A Chronology of the Plays of D. Pedro Calderón de la Barca*. Toronto: The University of Toronto Press, 1938.

Householder, Fred W. "ΠΑΡΩΙΔΙΑ." *Classical Philology*, 39 (January 1944), 1-9.

Hulse, Clark. *Metamorphic Verse: The Elizabethan Minor Epic*. Princeton: Princeton University Press, 1981.

Hurtado de Mendoza, Diego. *Obras poéticas*. Ed. William I. Knapp. Libros españoles raros ó curiosos, vol. 11. Madrid: Miguel Ginesta, 1877.

Ife, B. W. *Dos versiones de "Píramo y Tisbe": Jorge de Montemayor y Pedro Sánchez de Viana (Fuentes para el estudio del romance "La ciudad de Babilonia" de Góngora)*. Exeter Hispanic Texts, 9. Exeter: University of Exeter, 1974.

Iffland, James. *Quevedo and the Grotesque*. 2 vols. London: Tamesis, vol. I, 1978; vol. II, 1982.

Jammes, Robert. *Etudes sur l'oeuvre poétique de Don Luis de Góngora y Argote*. Bibliothèque de l'Ecole des hautes études hispaniques, fasc. 40. Bordeaux: Féret et Fils, 1967.

——. "Notes sur *La fábula de Píramo y Tisbe* de Góngora." *Les Langues Néo-Latines*, no. 156 (1961), 1-47.

Jáuregui, Juan de. *Orfeo*. Ed. Pablo Cabañas. Madrid: C.S.I.C., 1948.

Johnson, Ragnar. "Two Realms and a Joke: Bisociation Theories of Joking." *Semiotica*, 16, no. 3 (1976), 195-221.

Joplin, Patricia Klindienst. "The Voice of the Shuttle is Ours." *Stanford Literature Review*, 1 (Spring 1984), 25-53.

Jordán de Urríes y Azara, José. *Biografía y estudio crítico de Jáuregui*. Madrid: Sucesores de Rivadeneyra, 1899.

Justi, Carl. *Diego Velázquez and His Times*. Trans. A. H. Keane. London: H. Grevel Co., 1889.

Juvenal. *Fourteen Satires of Juvenal*. Ed. J. D. Duff. 1898; rpt. Cambridge: Cambridge University Press, 1940.

——. *The Satires of Juvenal*. Trans. Rolfe Humphries. Bloomington and London: Indiana University Press, 1958.

Kahr, Madlyn M. "Velázquez and *Las Meninas*." *The Art Bulletin*, 57 (1975), 225-46.

——. *Velázquez: The Art of Painting*. New York: Harper and Row, 1976.

Keach, William. *Elizabethan Erotic Narratives*. New Brunswick, New Jersey: Rutgers University Press, 1977.

Keeble, T. W. "Some Mythological Figures in Golden Age Satire and Burlesque." *BSS*, 25 (October 1948), 238-46.

Kellenberger, Jakob. *Calderón de la Barca und das Komische*. Bern: Herbert Lang; Frankfurt/M: Peter Lang, 1975.

Kernan, Alvin. *The Cankered Muse. Satire of the English Renaissance*. New Haven and London: Yale University Press, 1959.

Kiremidjian, G. D. "The Aesthetics of Parody." *JAAC*, 28 (1969), 231-42.

Kristeva, Julia. *Desire in Language*. Ed. Leon S. Roudiez. Trans. Thomas Gora, Alice Jardine, Leon S. Roudiez. New York: Columbia University Press, 1980.

Kubler, George. "Three Remarks on the *Meninas*." *The Art Bulletin*, 48 (1966),

212-14.

Lapesa, Rafael. *La trayectoria poética de Garcilaso*. 2d ed. 1948; rpt. Madrid: Revista de Occidente, 1968.

Lázaro Carreter, Fernando. "Dificultades en la *Fábula de Píramo y Tisbe*." *Estilo barroco y personalidad creadora*, pp. 97-108. Salamanca: Anaya, 1966. Originally published in *Romanica et Occidentalia*, Etudes dédiées à la mémoire de Hiram Peri (Pflaum) (Jerusalem 1963), pp. 121-27.

———. "Situación de la *Fábula de Píramo y Tisbe*." *NRFH*, 15 (1961), 463-82. Also included in *Estilo barroco y personalidad creadora*, pp. 61-96.

Lelièvre, F. J. "The Basis of Ancient Parody." *Greece and Rome*, second series, 1 (June 1954), 66-81.

Lerner, Lía Schwartz. "Martial and Quevedo: Re-creation of Satirical Patterns." *Antike und Abendland*, 23 (1977), 122-42.

———. *Metáfora y sátira en la obra de Quevedo*. Madrid: Taurus, 1983.

Ley, Charles David. *El gracioso en el teatro de la Península (Siglos XVI-XVII)*. Madrid: Revista de Occidente, 1954.

López Grigera, Luisa. "La silva 'El pincel' de Quevedo." *Homenaje al Instituto de Filología y Literaturas Hispánicas "Dr. Amado Alonso" en su Cincuentenario, 1923-1973*, pp. 221-42. Buenos Aires: Instituto de Filología, 1975.

López Pinciano, Alonso. *Philosophia antigua poética*. Ed. A. Carballo Picazo. 3 vols. Madrid, C.S.I.C., 1953.

López-Rey, José. *Velázquez. The Artist as a Maker*, with *Catalogue Raisonné of His Extant Works*. Lausanne-Paris: Bibliothèque des Arts, 1979.

———. *Velázquez. A Catalogue Raisonné of His Oeuvre*. London: Faber and Faber, 1963.

López Torrijos, Rosa. "La mitología en la pintura española del Siglo XVII." 2 vols. Ph.D. diss., Universidad Complutense de Madrid, 1982.

MacCurdy, Raymond R. "Parodies of the Judgement of Paris in Spanish Poetry and Drama of the Golden Age." *PQ*, 51 (January 1972), 135-44.

Martin, H. M. "Notes on the Cephalus-Procris Myth as Dramatized by Lope de Vega and Calderón." *MLN*, 66 (April 1951), 238-41.

Martial. *Epigrams*. Trans. Walter C. A. Ker. Loeb Classical Library. 2 vols. 1920; rpt. New York: G. P. Putnam's Sons, London: William Heinemann Ltd., 1927.

Mas, Amédée. *La caricature de la femme, du mariage et de l'amour dans l'oeuvre de Quevedo*. Paris: Ediciones Hispano-Americanas, 1957.

Mason, H. A. "Is Juvenal a Classic? An Introductory Essay." *Arion*, 1 (Spring 1962), 8-44, and *Arion*, 1 (Summer 1962), 39-79.

Medvedev, P. N. and M. M. Bakhtin. *The Formal Method in Literary Scholarship. A Critical Introduction to Sociological Poetics* (1928). Trans. Albert J. Wehrle. Baltimore and London: Johns Hopkins University Press, 1978.

Menéndez Pelayo, Marcelino. *Antología de poetas líricos castellanos*, IX and X (Parte 3ª: Boscán). *Obras completas de Menéndez Pelayo*, vols. 25 and 26. Santander: Aldus, 1945.

———. *Estudios sobre el teatro de Lope de Vega*, II. *Obras completas de Menéndez Pelayo*, vol. 30. Ed. Enrique Sánchez Reyes. Santander: Aldus, 1949.

Miller, Nancy K. "Arachnologies: The Text, the Woman, and the Critic." *Poetics of Gender*. Forthcoming.

Milner, G. B. "Homo Ridens: Towards a Semiotic Theory of Humour and Laughter." *Semiotica*, 5 (1972), 1-30.

Monte, Alberto del. *Itinerario de la novela picaresca española*. Trans. Enrique Sordo. Barcelona: Editorial Lumen, 1971.

Montemayor, Jorge de. *Los siete libros de la Diana*. Ed. Francisco López Estrada. 3d ed. Madrid: Espasa-Calpe, 1962.

Montesinos, José F. "La figura del donaire en el teatro de Lope de Vega." *Homenaje a Menéndez Pidal*. Madrid: Hernando, 1925. I, pp. 469-504.

Moya del Baño, F. *El tema de Hero y Leandro en la literatura española*. Murcia: Universidad de Murcia, 1966.

Musaeus. *Hero and Leander* (with "Fragments" of Callimachus). Ed. T. Gelzer. Trans. C. Whitman. Loeb Classical Library. Cambridge: Harvard University Press; London: William Heinemann Ltd., 1975.

Neumeister, Sebastian. *Mythos und Repräsentation: Die mythologischen Festspiele Calderóns*. Munich: Fink, 1978.

O'Connor, Thomas A. "The Mythological World of Augustín de Salazar y Torres: Is *El amor más desgraciado, Céfalo y Pocris* a Tragedy?" *RomN*, 18, no. 2 (1977), 1-9.

Orozco Díaz, Emilio. *Lope y Góngora frente a frente*. Madrid: Gredos, 1973.

Ortega y Gasset, José. "Introducción a Velázquez (1943)." *Obras completas*. Madrid: Revista de Occidente, 1962. VIII, pp. 457-87.

Otis, Brooks. *Ovid as an Epic Poet*. 2d ed. Cambridge: Cambridge University Press, 1970.

Ovid. *The Art of Love and Other Poems*. Trans. J. H. Mozley. Loeb Classical Library, 1929; rev. and rpt. Cambridge: Harvard University Press; London: William Heinemann Ltd., 1962.

——. *Heroides* and *Amores*. Trans. Grant Showerman. Loeb Classical Library. 1914; rpt. Cambridge: Harvard University Press; London: William Heinemann Ltd., 1963.

——. *Metamorphoses*. Trans. Frank Justus Miller. Loeb Classical Library. 2 vols. 3d ed. 1916; rpt. Cambridge: Harvard University Press; London: William Heinemann Ltd., 1977.

——. *Metamorphoses*. Venice, Georgius de Rusconibus, 1517. Bound with *Tristia* and *Fasti*. *Rare Book and Manuscript Library, Columbia University*.

——. *La métamorphose d'Ovide figurée*. French trans. unknown. Engravings by Bernard Salomon. Lyon, Ian de Tovrnes, 1564. *The Hispanic Society of America*.

——. *Le trasformationi*. Italian trans. Lodovico Dolce. Venetia, Domenico Farri, 1570. *Rare Book and Manuscript Library, Columbia University*.

——. *Los quinze libros de los Metamorphoseos*. Spanish trans. Antonio Pérez Sigler. Salamanca, Iuan Perier, 1580. *The Hispanic Society of America*.

——. *Le metamorfosi di Ovidio*. Italian trans. Giouanni Andrea dell'Anguillara (con l'annotationi de M. Gioseppe Horologgi). Venetia, Alessandro Griffio, 1584. *Rare Book and Manuscript Library, Columbia University*.

——. *Las transformaciones* with *Anotaciones*. Spanish trans. Pedro Sánchez de Viana. Valladolid, Diego Fernandez de Cordoua, 1589. *The Hispanic Society of America*.

——. *Las transformaciones de Ovidio en lengua española*. Spanish trans. Jorge de Bustamante. Anvers, Pedro Bellero, 1595. *The Hispanic Society of America*.

——. *Metamorphoseos*. Spanish trans. Antonio Pérez Sigler. Burgos, Iuan Baptista Varesio, for Pedro de Osete, 1609. *The Hispanic Society of America*.

Ovide Moralisé en prose (Text du quinzième siècle). Ed. C. De Boer. Amsterdam:

North Holland Publishing Co., 1954.

Pacheco, Francisco. *Arte de la pintura*. Ed. F. J. Sánchez Cantón of original manuscript (24 January 1638). 2 vols. Madrid: Editorial Maestre, 1956.

Pailler, Claire. "El gracioso y los «guiños» de Calderón: apuntes sobre «autoburla» e ironía crítica." *Risa y sociedad en el teatro español del Siglo de Oro*, pp. 33-48. Actes du 3ᵉ colloque du Groupe d'Etudes Sur le Théâtre Espagnol, Toulouse 31 janvier - 2 février 1980. Paris: Editions du C.N.R.S., 1980.

Panofsky, Erwin. *Problems in Titian*. New York: New York University Press, 1969.

Parker, A. A. *The Allegorical Drama of Calderón*. Oxford: Dolphin Book Co., 1968.

Parker, Jack H. *Juan Pérez de Montalván*. Boston: Twayne Publishers, 1975.

Pérez de Montalván, Juan. *Orfeo en lengua castellana*. Ed. Pablo Cabañas. Madrid: C.S.I.C., 1948.

Pérez de Moya, Juan. *Philosophia secreta*. Ed. Eduardo Gómez de Baquero. 2 vols. Los clásicos olvidados, vols. 6 and 7. Madrid: Blass, 1928.

Pitollet, Camille. "A Propos d'un 'Romance' de Quevedo." *BH*, 6 (1904), 332-46.

Poetas líricos de los siglos XVI y XVII. Vol. II. Ed. Adolfo de Castro. *BAE*, vol. 42. Madrid: Rivadeneyra, 1875.

Poggioli, Renato. *The Oaten Flute*. Cambridge: Harvard University Press, 1975.

Polo de Medina, Salvador Jacinto. *Obras escogidas*. Ed. José María de Cossío. Los clásicos olvidados, vol. 10. Madrid: Compañía General de Artes Gráficas, 1931.

Previtera, Carmelo. *La poesia giocosa e l'umorismo*. Storia dei generi letterari italiani, vol. 16. 2 vols in 1. Milan: Francesco Vallardi, 1939 (vol. I); 1942, 2d ed., 1953 (vol. II).

Quevedo, Francisco de. *Obra poética*. Ed. José Manuel Blecua. 4 vols. Madrid: Castalia, 1969-81.

———. *Obras completas*. Ed. Luis Astrana Marín. 2 vols. (vol. I, *O.C. en verso*; vol. II, *O.C. en prosa*). Madrid: Aguilar, 1943 (vol. I); 1945 (vol. II).

Rand, Edward K. *Ovid and His Influence*. New York: Cooper Square Publishers, 1963.

Reichenberger, Arnold G. "Boscán and the Classics." *CL*, 3 (Spring 1951), 97-118.

———. "Boscán and Ovid." *MLN*, 65 (June 1950), 379-83.

———. "An Emendation of the Text of Boscán's *Historia de Leandro y Hero*." *MLN*, 65 (November 1950), 493.

Riffaterre, Michael. *Semiotics of Poetry*. Bloomington and London: Indiana University Press, 1978.

Risco, Vicente. "Notas sobre las fiestas del Carnaval en Galicia." *Revista de Dialectología y Tradiciones Populares*, 4 (1948), 163-96, 339-64.

Rodríguez, Evangelina and Antonio Tordera. *Calderón y la obra corta dramática del Siglo XVII*. London: Tamesis, 1983.

Rodríguez de la Cámara (o del Padrón), Juan. *Obras*. Ed. Antonio Paz y Melia. La sociedad de bibliófilos españoles, no. 22. Madrid: M. Ginesta, 1884.

Rothe, A. *Quevedo und Seneca: Untersuchungen zu den Frühschriften Quevedos*. Geneva: Droz, 1965.

Ruggerio, Michael. *The Evolution of the Go-Between in Spanish Literature Through the Sixteenth Century*. University of California Publications in

Modern Philology, vol. 78. Berkeley and Los Angeles: University of California Press, 1966.

Russell, P. E. *"Don Quixote* as a Funny Book." *MLR*, 64 (April 1969), 312-26.

Sage, Jack. "Nouvelles lumières sur la genèse de l'opéra et la zarzuela en Espagne." *Baroque*, 5 (1972), 107-14.

Sánchez Alonso, B. "Los satíricos latinos y la sátira de Quevedo." *RFE*, 11 (1924), 33-62 and 113-53.

Sánchez Cantón, F. J. "La librería de Velázquez." *Homenaje a Menéndez Pidal.* Madrid: Hernando, 1925. III, pp. 379-406.

———. "Los libros españoles que poseyó Velázquez." *Varia Velazqueña.* Madrid: Publicaciones de la Dirección General de Bellas Artes, 1960. I, pp. 640-48.

———. *Velázquez y "Lo Clásico."* Madrid: Taurus, 1961.

———. *"La Venus del espejo."* *AEA*, 33 (1960), 137-48.

Scarron, Paul. *Virgile travesti.* Ed. Victor Fournel. Paris: Garnier Frères, 1875.

Schalk, F. "Zur Rolle der Mythologie in der Literatur des Siglo de Oro." *Classical Influences on European Culture, A.D. 1500-1700.* Ed. R. R. Bolgar, pp. 259-70. Cambridge: Cambridge University Press, 1976.

Schevill, Rudolph. *Ovid and the Renascence in Spain.* University of California Publications in Modern Philology, vol. 4, no. 1. Berkeley: University of California Press, 1913.

Segal, Charles Paul. *Landscape in Ovid's "Metamorphoses": A Study in the Transformations of a Literary Symbol.* Wiesbaden: Franz Steiner Verlag, 1969.

Segal, Erich. "Hero and Leander: Góngora and Marlowe." *CL*, 15 (1963), 338-56.

Serralta, Frédéric. "La comedia burlesca: datos y orientaciones." *Risa y sociedad en el teatro español del Siglo de Oro*, pp. 99-125. Actes du 3ᵉ colloque du Groupe d'Etudes Sur le Théâtre Espagnol, Toulouse 31 janvier - 2 février 1980. Paris: Editions du C.N.R.S., 1980.

Seznec, Jean. *The Survival of the Pagan Gods. The Mythological Tradition and Its Place in Renaissance Humanism and Art.* Trans. Barbara E. Sessions. Bollingen Series, no. 38. 1953; rpt. Princeton: Princeton University Press, 1972.

Shakespeare, William. *As You Like It.* Ed. S. C. Burchell. The Yale Shakespeare, rev. ed., vol. 10. 1954; rpt. New Haven and London: Yale University Press, 1965.

Shergold, N. D. and J. E. Varey. *Representaciones palaciegas: 1603-1699. Estudio y documentos.* Fuentes para la historia del teatro en España, vol. 1. Madrid: Tamesis, 1982.

———. *Teatros y comedias en Madrid: 1651-1665. Estudio y documentos.* Fuentes para la historia del teatro en España, vol. 4. London: Tamesis, 1973.

———. *Teatros y comedias en Madrid: 1666-1687. Estudio y documentos.* Fuentes para la historia del teatro en España, vol. 5. London: Tamesis, 1974.

Shklovsky, Victor. "Art as Technique," "Sterne's *Tristram Shandy*: Stylistic Commentary." *Russian Formalist Criticism: Four Essays.* Ed. Lee T. Lemon and Marion J. Reis, pp. 3-24, 25-57 respectively. Lincoln and London: University of Nebraska Press, 1965.

Solalinde, Antonio G. "La fecha del *Ovide Moralisé."* *RFE*, 8 (1921), 285-88.

Solís y Rivadeneyra, Antonio. *Comedias.* Madrid: Melchor Alvarez, 1681.

———. *Varias poesías sagradas y profanas.* Ed. Manuela Sánchez Regueira. Clásicos hispánicos, serie II, vol. 16. Madrid: C.S.I.C., 1968.

Soons, Alan. *Alonso de Castillo Solórzano*. Boston: Twayne Publishers, 1978.

Soria, M. S. *"La fragua de Vulcano*, de Velázquez." *AEA*, 28 (1955), 142-45.

——. "La *Venus, Los Borrachos* y la *Coronación*, de Velázquez." *AEA*, 26 (1953), 269-84.

Stewart, Susan. *Nonsense: Aspects of Intertextuality in Folklore and Literature*. Baltimore and London: Johns Hopkins University Press, 1978.

Stroud, Matthew D. "Stylistic Considerations of Calderón's Opera Librettos." *Crítica Hispánica*, 4, no. 1 (1982), 75-82.

Subirá, José. *"Celos aun del aire matan,"* ópera *del Siglo XVII (texto de Calderón y música de Juan Hidalgo)*. Publicacions del Departament de Musica, vol. 11. Barcelona: Institut d'Estudis Catalans, Biblioteca de Catalunya, 1933.

——. *La participación musical en el antiguo teatro español*. Publicaciones del Instituto del Teatro Nacional, no. 6. Barcelona: Diputación provincial, 1930.

Tejada, Amelia. *Untersuchungen zum Humor in den Comedias Calderóns: unter Ausschluss der "Gracioso"–Gestalten*. Berlin and New York: Walter de Gruyter, 1974.

Terry, Arthur. "An Interpretation of Góngora's *Fábula de Píramo y Tisbe.*" *BHS*, 33 (1956), 202-17.

Tervarent, Guy de. *Attributs et symboles dans l'art profane 1450-1600*. 2 vols. Geneva: Droz, 1958-59.

Testa, Daniel P. "The Pyramus and Thisbe Theme in Sixteenth and Seventeenth Century Spanish Poetry." Ph.D. diss., University of Michigan, 1963.

Tolnay, Charles de. "Las pinturas mitológicas de Velázquez." *AEA*, 34 (1961), 31-45.

——. "Velázquez' *Las Hilanderas* and *Las Meninas* (An Interpretation)." *Gazette des Beaux-Arts*, 35 (1949), 21-38.

Truman, R. W. "Lázaro de Tormes and the 'Homo Novus' Tradition." *MLR*, 64 (January 1969), 62-67.

——. "Parody and Irony in the Self-Portrayal of Lázaro de Tormes." *MLR*, 63 (July 1968), 600-05.

Valbuena Briones, Angel. *Perspectiva crítica de los dramas de Calderón*. Madrid: Rialp, 1965.

Van Ghent, Dorothy. *The English Novel: Form and Function*. New York: Rinehart & Co., 1953.

Varey, J. E. "La creación deliberada de la confusión: estudio de una diversión de Carnestolendas de 1623." *Homenaje a William L. Fichter*. Ed. A. David Kossoff and José Amor y Vázquez, pp. 745-54. Madrid: Castalia, 1971.

Vega, Lope de. *Obras de Lope de Vega*. Vol. XIV. Ed. Marcelino Menéndez Pelayo. *BAE*, vol. 190. Madrid: Atlas, 1966.

——. *Obras escogidas*. Vol. II. Ed. Federico Carlos Sainz de Robles. Madrid: Aguilar, 1946.

Vélez de Guevara, Juan. *Los celos hacen estrellas*. Ed. J. E. Varey and N. D. Shergold, with ed. of music by Jack Sage. London: Tamesis, 1970.

Vilanova, Antonio. *Las fuentes y los temas del "Polifemo" de Góngora*. 2 vols. Madrid: C.S.I.C., 1957.

Villegas, Antonio de. "Historia de Píramo y Tisbe." *Inventario*. Vol. II. Ed. Francisco López Estrada. Madrid: La Gelindense, 1956 (Vol. I, 1955).

Vitoria, Baltasar de. *Theatro de los dioses de la getilidad*. Part 1. Salamanca, Antonio Ramírez, 1620. *The Hispanic Society of America*.

Vosters, Simon A. "Lope de Vega y Rubens." *Lope de Vega y los orígenes del tea-*

tro español. Actas del I Congreso Internacional sobre Lope de Vega. Ed. Manuel Criado de Val, pp. 733-44. Madrid: Edi-6, 1981.

Waley, Pamela. "Enfoque y medios humorísticos de la *Fábula de Píramo y Tisbe.*" *RFE*, 44 (1961), 385-98.

Whitaker, Shirley B. "The First Performance of Calderón's *El sitio de Bredá.*" *RenQ*, 31 (Winter 1978), 515-31.

Wilkinson, L. P. *Ovid Recalled*. Cambridge: Cambridge University Press, 1955.

Wind, Edgar. *Pagan Mysteries in the Renaissance*. New Haven: Yale University Press, 1958.

Index